WITHNAIL
AND US

D1565881

Cinema and Society series
GENERAL EDITOR: JEFFREY RICHARDS

WITHNAIL AND US

Cult Films and Film Cults in British Cinema

Justin Smith

I.B. TAURIS
LONDON · NEW YORK

INDIANA UNIVERSITY
LIBRARIES
BLOOMINGTON

Published in 2010 by I.B.Tauris & Co Ltd
6 Salem Road, London W2 4BU
175 Fifth Avenue, New York NY 10010
www.ibtauris.com

Distributed in the United States and Canada Exclusively by Palgrave Macmillan
175 Fifth Avenue, New York NY 10010

Copyright © 2010 Justin Smith

The right of Justin Smith to be identified as the author of this work has been asserted
by him in accordance with the Copyright, Designs and Patents Act 1988.

All rights reserved. Except for brief quotations in a review, this book, or any part
thereof, may not be reproduced, stored in or introduced into a retrieval system, or
transmitted, in any form or by any means, electronic, mechanical, photocopying,
recording or otherwise, without the prior written permission of the publisher.

ISBN: 978 1 84885 092 7

A full CIP record for this book is available from the British Library
A full CIP record is available from the Library of Congress

Library of Congress Catalog Card Number: available

Printed and bound in India by Replika Press Pvt. Ltd.
from camera-ready copy edited and supplied by the author

The devil's in the man that he cannot understand;
He cannot have a harbouring here.

'Go From My Window'
Trad. 17th-century English

For Shaz

Whoever you are

CONTENTS

ILLUSTRATIONS

ACKNOWLEDGEMENTS

I should like to thank, first and foremost, Sue Harper. I am deeply indebted to her on three counts. Firstly, for the intellectual instinct which understood the potential of this project before I did. Secondly, for the enthusiasm which drove and shaped it. And thirdly, for her tireless policing of my sometimes wayward pen.

For their generous assistance and attention to detail I am grateful to the staff at the library of the British Film Institute, and to Ian Bonar and Greta Friggens at Portsmouth's fine University library.

I wish to pay tribute to fellow film historians at the Institute for Historical Research seminars under the auspices of Mark Glancy, for their ongoing encouragement, especially James Chapman and Tony Aldgate. Thanks are due in particular to Vincent Porter, for the treasures of his extensive library and sage advice.

I am the fortunate beneficiary of the continued support of Tony Chafer, Director of the Centre for European and International Studies Research at the University of Portsmouth, and Esther Sonnet and colleagues in the School of Creative Arts, Film and Media. They have been doubly tolerant: in allowing me the freedom and space to dedicate to this work; and in trusting me to test its efficacy in the classroom. Special thanks should go to my colleagues involved in the AHRC-funded research project on British cinema in the 1970s, and particularly to Dave Allen for allowing me to quote from his unpublished conference paper on *Quadrophenia* and to Sian Barber for the BBFC correspondence relating to *The Wicker Man*.

At the University of Sussex I should like to thank Dorothy Sheridan and staff at the Mass-Observation archive.

At I.B.Tauris thanks to the invaluable advice and encouragement of series editor Jeffrey Richards and commissioning editor Philippa Brewster in bringing this book to fruition, and to Jayne Ansell for preparing the manuscript, also the page design and typesetting at Initial Typesetting Services by Carolann Martin. For assiduous editing, proofreading and indexing, thanks are due to Maria Fritsche, Merlin Cox and Wendy Baskett.

Finally, I am grateful to my cousins, Rosemary and Robert Edgar of Castle Douglas, Kirkcudbrightshire for their hospitality, and to my mother and friends on the Isle of Wight for their patience, loyalty and good humour. Last but not least, thanks to Katherine Mortimer, Trish Campbell and Christina Vince. I owe each of them a debt I could never adequately repay: their love.

GENERAL EDITOR'S INTRODUCTION

As Justin Smith observes at the start of this important and thought-providing study, 'cult' is a much-used, perhaps overused, word in the lexicon of writers about film. He sets out to define the term, explain its rise to critical prominence and analyse what makes a cult film. In so doing, he draws on the work of sociologists, anthropologists and psychoanalysts as well as exponents of cinema and cultural studies. He identifies the period 1968–1996 as the age of the cult film. It is this period which, he suggests, saw the development of 'niche taste' communities and the rise of the youth-orientated counter-culture. No doubt everyone has their own idea of what constitutes a cult film. But few would probably quarrel with Justin Smith's choice of examples. They include *The Rocky Horror Picture Show* with its legion of fans who turn up to showings in character costumes and chant along with the dialogue; *Performance* with its psychedelic mix of gangland violence and rock star hedonism; *A Clockwork Orange* with its stylised and futuristic celebration of teenage gang aggression; *The Wicker Man*, the so-called '*Citizen Kane* of horror movies' with its joyous evocation of paganism in the Scottish islands; *Tommy*, The Who's rock opera transferred to the screen by Ken Russell, living embodiment of the 'cult director'; *The Man Who Fell to Earth* examining the plight of David Bowie's extra-terrestrial stranded on Earth and *Withnail and I*, featuring the comic misadventures of two unemployed actors in the demi-monde. In discussing each film, Justin Smith examines the production, distribution, exhibition, exploitation and reception of his chosen examples and considers narrative, genre, performance, music and visual style for evidence of the hallmarks of cult appeal. What appears to bind all the films together is the fact that their protagonists – criminals, pagans, aliens, dropouts – are invariably outsiders and that they all deal in one way or another with transgression, excess and hybridity. These characteristics make a direct and potent appeal to that section of the youthful audience seeking an outlet for their nonconformity.

JEFFREY RICHARDS

INTRODUCTION

Beginnings

What is a *cult* film? What does the adjective mean? Are we talking here about a peculiar kind of film text? Or is the noun itself more important: the film cult? And what might it have in common with other kinds of cult? Does this concern certain unusual cultural practices? This book will venture to consider all these questions. But before approaching definitions it is important to address the purpose.

One reason for mounting this investigation has been the proliferation of the term cult across popular discourses in recent years. Indeed, the word might be said to have been reinvented for and by a secular, consumption-based culture. For scholars of film or historians of culture, it is necessary to pay attention to such phenomena. The other reason is, perhaps, more idiosyncratic.

In July 2003 I was touring the coast of Dumfries and Galloway seeking out the real locations of *The Wicker Man* (1973).[1] St Ninian's Cave which was featured in the film's climax is little more than a slit in the cliff-face on the Isle of Whithorn. Ninian, the fifth-century saint who is credited with bringing Christianity to Scotland, is commemorated by a shrine in the village of Whithorn; but this cave, whether he actually visited it or not, is also recognised as a place of memorial and retreat. Early pilgrims (from the eighth century) left carvings in the rock and rough-hewn standing stones. Lately, crosses have been fashioned from withy twigs and driftwood, and epitaphs scrawled in graffiti on the walls and surrounding boulders. And, since the cult of the film has developed, the Christian symbolism is augmented with a secular, if not Pagan, spirit. Amidst the genuine tributes to loved ones who had died too young, one rock stood out with the profanity of its recent claim: 'SHAZ WAZ ERE B4U, 28/5/03'. Despite the fact that subsequent damage (deliberate or accidental) had partly obliterated the artist's name, the message remained clear. We each want to declare our part in historical processes, no matter how vague the legend or crude our claim. And though we are but the latest, there is a swagger in the self-assurance that we are not the last. In certain places, monuments, objects and texts, there is a quality which, though obscure, is both accessible and compelling. That is where we leave our mark. Here is where history is present(ed) and made personal. I left nothing of mine on that beach. But when I returned, I embarked upon this work.

Figure 1: 'Shaz waz ere B4u'
[AUTHOR'S OWN IMAGE]

Rationale

As Julian Petley remarks, the word 'cult' is overused and often misused.[2] This is the *raison d'être* for my study: firstly, to address the currency of the cult, and secondly, to define it more precisely than hitherto. By 'define'

I mean to address certain key questions. Who has used the term and in what contexts? What meanings has it accrued? What kind of texts has it been applied to and why? What kind of fan responses does it describe?

But before I come to consider who uses the term, where and how, we must address broader issues of definition and set out the parameters of this work. Cult is a critical label applied across a wide range of popular media: cult films, cult TV, cult books, cult fashion, cult music, cult bands, cult personalities and so on. Indeed, within the world of film alone its applications are various and particular. As Karl and Philip French note in the Introduction to one of many similar popular surveys which line the shelves of high-street book stores in seemingly ever greater numbers: 'There are cult movies, cult directors, cult actors, and even cult film composers . . . There are also cult posters and cult stills'.[3]

Some words, it might be argued, have deep cultural roots and almost perennial significance: Classicism, Romanticism, Modernity. Others flourish at a given moment and then fade: Ruralism, Dada, Vorticism, Psychedelia. In both cases, the condition of the cultural ground is crucial in bringing them forth at particular times. For the purposes of this book, I want to propose within the period 1968–1996 two overlapping time frames: the age of the cult film and the age of the film cult. Put another way, I want to explore the relationship between certain film texts and new critical responses to those texts in the contexts of the culture from which both emerged.

As my subtitle implies, the relationship between the text and its reception is central. I am interested in the textual qualities that engender cult responses, and the determinants on those texts. At the outset, however, a note of caution must be sounded. It is important to ensure that our procedure avoids inductive methods. I shall first explore what qualities may set cult films apart, and second, try to trace their origins in the historical contexts of their production. But the initial impetus behind the choice of texts themselves is their critical reception across a range of fields: personal, fannish, popular, journalistic and academic. Each of the films covered in this book is already considered to be cult. In this sense I am not claiming anything new. My questions – the ones which have yet to be properly addressed – are why, and what does this mean?

What of my particular focus then? Across existing critical discourses many different kinds of films are considered cult: from American independent and underground cinema to European horror, Hong Kong martial arts and even, in some quarters, 'Bollywood'. No attempt has been made in this book to address cult film as an international phenomenon, or to venture comparisons between different categories of cult film. Such enterprises are fraught with difficulty (as some recent efforts show), and may ultimately be pointless. I have also chosen largely to ignore US cult films (on which early critical interventions in the field concentrated), though certain well-known examples are mentioned in passing. What I do acknowledge, however, is the critical heritage in American film culture which nurtured the idea of cult, and I consider the American reception of several of the British films I have included in this work. My choice has depended upon certain conditions. Pragmatically, the selection has been determined by the availability of audience material and the rise of critical awareness. Personally, British television outings and university film society screenings from the early 1980s have brought these texts to prominence. Moreover, historically, these can be identified as specific artefacts in a culturally grounded account of British cinema from the late 1960s onwards. It seems to me that it is fruitful to speculate about a number of distinctive films which flourished around the same period, and the reasons why they have subsequently become cult.

Dealing with Definitions

The *Oxford English Dictionary's* etymology of the word 'cult' yields three important variations upon a notional theme: 'formed from *colere* inhabit, cultivate, protect, honour with worship'.

> Worship – 1683.
>
> A particular form of religious worship; esp. in reference to its external rites and ceremonies 1679.
>
> transf. Devotion to a particular person or thing, now esp. as paid by a body of professed adherents 1711.[4]

Additionally, the *Oxford English Dictionary On-line* offers the following significant 'Draft Additions of September 2004':

> **cult**, *n.* and *a.*[2]
>
> Designating cultural phenomena with a strong, often enduring appeal to a relatively small audience; (also) designating this appeal

or audience, or any resultant success; fringe, non-mainstream. Hence: possessing a fashionable or exclusive cachet; *spec.* (of artistic figures or works) having a reputation or influence disproportionate to their limited public exposure or commercial success. Freq. in *cult figure*, *status*.

A relatively small group of people having religious beliefs or practices regarded by others as strange or sinister. [5]

Several useful inferences may be drawn from these two sets of derivations and in particular the additions of 2004. The first is that the word's origins are adverbial rather than adjectival: cult describes an *act* and not a thing. Secondly, 'devotion' and 'worship' are defining attitudinal expressions. Thirdly, there is the implication of an idol or iconic object which is *worked upon* – note the particularly active associations of 'inhabit, cultivate, protect' and 'honour'. Hence the cult object is defined and sustained by and through the activity of cult worship. Finally, cult allegiance is a corporate and declared activity, implying a collective and enunciative discourse.

Particularly instructive here is the third dimension which shows that the cult of admiration to a particular person or thing can be traced back as far as the early eighteenth century, though perhaps it acquired a more widespread significance in the Victorian nostalgia for Romanticism. The draft additions of 2004 establish the more recent cultural orthodoxy of the term with two more contemporary associations. There is the rather pejorative description of new religious movements, regarded as 'strange or sinister'. But, more germane to our purposes, we have a small, perhaps subcultural, but devoted audience which accords a 'disproportionate' enthusiasm for neglected or marginalised works or producers. The key word here – which links the fan cult to the cult object – is *disproportionate*. It may well be that issues of proportion, both in terms of cult texts themselves and the manner of their reception, will be crucial to this debate.

Surveying the Field

Of course, as these definitions make clear, the cult has a history altogether independent of recent popular culture. So, it is first worth considering what may be gleaned from other discourses in which cult has figured. In this regard I shall touch briefly on religious connotations, anthropological accounts, and cultural theory.

Sociological accounts of religious practice have dealt both with histories of nonconformist religious sects and occult practices associated with witchcraft, as well as the range of post-1960s new religious movements (NRMs). Key to Durkheim's description of primitive religion is its establishment of rituals and symbols which express community values and which outlaw taboo or antisocial ideas: 'magic' and 'witchcraft'.[6] Essentially, organised religions policed the boundaries of the sacred and profane through the rigorous pursuit of separation. At times Durkheim's insistence upon a shared psychology of belief seems to anticipate Jung's quasi-religious theory of the collective unconscious.[7] But it also parallels the Althusserian conception of ideology as the expression of shared belief which is a *misrecognition* of its socio-economic determinants.[8]

Anthropologists have pursued the complexities of difference with regard to belief systems in a now copious body of literature on witchcraft – a topic upon which many attributes of the cult converge. Mary Douglas's *Purity and Danger* is doubly useful as a starting point.[9] She firstly contrasts Durkheim's sociology of religion with a measured critique of Sir James Frazer's monumentally apocryphal *The Golden Bough*, which at once captures its breadth, endurance and influence, and diagnoses its evolutionary hokum.[10] Secondly, Douglas elaborates ideas about the relationship between hygiene, pollution and the taboo, which remain extremely apposite in the case of secular cults (see especially my chapters two, six and seven). Elsewhere, she is the editor of a definitive collection of essays on the subject of witchcraft.[11] Significantly for this study, the generic tropes of horror cinema found new impetus in the resurfacing of interest in the occult during the 1960s, and aspects of magic and witchcraft are touched upon in my chapters on *Performance* (chapter two) and *The Wicker Man* (chapter four).

Beyond this, work focusing on NRMs since the 1960s has explored various aspects of the cultural circumstances and specific natures of modern charismatic cults.[12] It is possible that some of the specific (and unusual) social relations found within such cults find echoes in the relations between cult fans and their objects in what are unusual consumption practices. But for the time being, this must remain a matter of speculation. Indeed, apropos this recent work, it seems important that we draw a distinction between the nature of these sects and the cult in popular cultural discourse, while acknowledging the profit to be made from superficial similarities. One important historical consideration may be their shared roots in the counter-culture of the late 1960s. Yet while common elements such as affective belief, obsessive behaviour, group identification, ritual practices, and extreme devotion might appear to characterise both, it must be remembered that my work concerns film texts and their fans. My approach will therefore be informed by some sociological and anthropological studies on belief in general and cults in particular, but only in so far as these explanatory models may illuminate the central relationships between cultural production, texts and their audiences. It is therefore to Cultural Studies that I turn next.

The so-called 'cultural turn', as one of its British pioneers Stuart Hall makes clear, has been a critical reaction to social changes.[13] The substantive change has been the steady rise to prominence of cultural texts and practices and their widespread commodification in the context of the media-rich western industrial nations. This change has involved a number of significant aspects. Firstly we must note the post-war growth in the diversity and number of cultural texts available to consumers. Secondly, the 1960s witnessed the hegemonic blurring of erstwhile class-based divisions between high and popular categories of art and consumption practice. And thirdly, the relative increase in consumers' leisure time and disposable income has resulted in cultural consumption becoming located firmly in the domestic arena via privately owned technology.

These broad changes signalled the need to re-examine the social function of popular culture and specifically to reconsider the relationship between the economic base and ideological superstructure in late capitalist western society. It has been necessary also to re-evaluate the operation of hegemony across this diverse, fragmented cultural field. If consensus remains wherein does it lie? What are the most influential factors in maintaining social cohesion? How are distinctions between notions of mainstream and alternative or oppositional culture expressed? Where are the fault-lines to be found? Finally, and most importantly, how useful are such terms in accounting for the relationship between cultural texts and historical processes? It is self-evidently beyond the scope and remit of this book to answer such large questions. But it is also inevitable that in the course of addressing issues germane to my local topic, I shall adopt attitudes towards those overarching themes, and draw inspiration from writers who have engaged with them directly.

I am minded also at the outset to contemplate the end of theory, or at least its limits. Mary Douglas reminds us sagely that 'any structure of ideas is vulnerable at its margins'.[14] At the margins of cultural theory is the spectre of subjectivity. Subjects are produced in and occupy psychological and physical spaces. Proper cognisance therefore needs to be taken, where appropriate, of psychoanalysis, psychology, and behaviourist studies. These necessary points of reference have much to offer, either directly or indirectly, concerning the nature of film as text and cinema as cultural process. For example, aspects of psychoanalytical theory have been usefully employed to explore issues of film spectatorship, while screen representation relies upon shared understandings of the dominant signifying practices of the body in space. Yet such theoretical approaches will always tend to universalise their subject, removing it from cultural and historical circumstance and, if not from gender, frequently from ethnicity and class. And the anthropological entreaty towards ethnographic immersion in the field of study presents methodological problems of its own.

Empiricist history, on the other hand, teaches invaluable lessons about the grounding of interpretation in material evidence. For example, it is possible to account persuasively for the fragmentation of the post-war mass audience for cinema in terms of the industry's economic decline vis-à-vis competing cultural commodities and leisure interests. And in this regard, the archives can be a rich source of information about the circumstances of production and critical reception of specific film texts, if handled judiciously. But the archives can't tell us the whole story. Key evidence may be partial or missing, and sometimes fragments of broken 'fact' resist piecing together. We cannot assume that empirical work, be it ever so thorough, can yield a definitive account, though often it offers the best one available.

Aside from the useful overviews of Alexander Walker and John Walker, the history of British cinema in the 1970s specifically remains thinly drawn, although forthcoming work suggests that this may be about to change.[15] Leon Hunt's media survey, British Low Culture: From Safari Suits to Sexploitation adumbrates some important themes, as does Andrew Higson's brief film chapter in Bart Moore-Gilbert's anthology The Arts in the 1970s: cultural closure?[16] Lately, popular cultural re-evaluations such as Howard Sounes's Seventies: The Sights, Sounds and Ideas of a Brilliant Decade, Dave Haslam's Not Abba: The Real Story of the 1970s,

Alwyn W. Turner's *Crisis? What Crisis? Britain in the 1970s* and Jonathan Coe's fictional memoir *The Rotters' Club*, along with television drama (*Life on Mars*) and reality show retrospectives, promise that thoroughgoing reappraisal is nigh.[17] But much work remains to be done.

The Seventies is the central decade in this study, though this book is not an attempt to plug that gap. Rather, it represents an effort to trace the evolution of a key critical term, as applied in particular discourses, to particular films of a particular period, and certain kinds of fan response to those films. In so doing, it may represent a small contribution to that patchy history in so far as it proposes that certain cultural ideas have specific lifespans and that their roots, growth, fruition and decay are historically determined. And I would hope that it might offer a new perspective on the relationship of certain texts to their historical contexts, and the peculiar nature of a distinctive kind of audience response.

In attempting to explain why some people inscribe their names in rocks on a remote Scottish beach, I cannot promise to leave no stone unturned, but I can subscribe to that restless desire to explain the strange sense of consolation which such obscure affiliation provides. In both senses of the phrase, what makes a film cult? I shall begin by examining the case of a film that might, without much dissent, appear on everyone's cult list. And I shall ask again: why?

1

THE ROCKY HORROR PICTURE SHOW (1975)

Introduction

This chapter aims to achieve three related goals. Firstly, to present a template for an approach to exploring cult films. Secondly, to raise a set of central research questions. And thirdly, to outline a vocabulary of key words relevant to this study.

'That the *Rocky Horror* cult has now lasted about 15 years continues to amaze me,' remarked the film critic Jonathan Rosenbaum in discussion with J. Hoberman in 1991.[1] J. P. Telotte describes the film as 'clearly the prototype midnight movie'.[2] 'It's no wonder *The Rocky Horror Picture Show* spawned the movie cult to end all cults', according to David Chute.[3] Gaylin Studlar agrees that it is 'perhaps the most famous of all cult films'.[4]

Amidst such a scholarly, not to mention popular, consensus, the difficulties of explaining the cult film phenomenon can easily be overlooked. So much so, that it might invoke the old adage about 'great art': I can't describe it, but I know it when I see it. And indeed that sense of aesthetic, if not divine, mystery only contributes to the aura surrounding the object itself and its rarefied place on the margins of popular culture. That there is 'something' there, that we are indubitably not gazing upon the Emperor's New Clothes, seems transparently obvious. True, new critical categories have a modishness about them, but fashions arise (and return) for particular reasons. Not for nothing do new forms and new

FIGURE 2: Tim Curry camping it up in *Rocky Horror's* cinematic pastiche
[20TH CENTURY FOX/THE KOBAL COLLECTION]

critical responses to those forms become visible at particular moments, and contribute to the colours and contours of the cultural map of the period. It is vital that we ask: why have they taken on these specific forms, and why now, and why here?

In order to address these 'big questions' – questions that could and should be asked of any substantial and distinctive artefacts about their relationship with the culture from which they emerge – I propose to employ *The Rocky Horror Picture Show* (1975), the avouched archetypal cult film, as an exemplar. To begin with, it will be necessary to establish that we are indeed dealing with a distinctive and different conception of cinema when talking about cult films – that the classification itself holds water. But further, defining the boundaries and qualities of the cult film may depend as much upon an awareness of contextual issues as upon careful textual analysis.

Firstly, perhaps, we ought to consider whether visible textual qualities which make such films distinctive can be traced back to the circumstances of their origins, specifically to the dispersal of creative agencies at work during the production. How do certain ideas get into film and how are they realised there? What creative struggles, power relations, grand designs or fortuitous accidents produced the text as it is? Secondly, attention to the distribution and exhibition histories, and to censorship and changing media technologies, may be instructive in part in determining how the text came to be viewed as distinctive.

This leads us on, thirdly, to reception. For Mark Jancovich et al., '"cult" is largely a matter of the ways in which films are classified in consumption'.[5] Certainly any thoroughgoing account of the cult film cannot ignore the cult that has grown up around the film itself. But fan practices alone may only be part of this reception culture. For surely it also depends upon fans' relationships with, participation in and representation through academic, journalistic and marketing discourses. It is only through such mediation (including fan performance and self-representation, technologies and merchandise) that fandom may be brought to the surface, enmeshed in discourse. This may be but the public face of what are largely private obsessions, but cultural visibility, expression and placement may be significant factors too. Indeed, the complex relationship between the public and private contexts could well be central to the cult phenomenon itself. But let us return for now to the text.

What Is a Cult Film?

It is perhaps best to approach the cult text firstly from the standpoint of familiar film terminology: at the levels of plot, genre and narrative.

(i) *Plot*
Key to the fanciful scenario of *The Rocky Horror Picture Show* is the blurred line it treads (or dances) between fantasy and credibility. It eschews the particularity and ordinary verisimilitude of realism in pursuit of that more vivid fidelity: the dreamscape. Yet, as in the most potent dreams, it is anchored within the realm of possibility, within the scope of the imagination. This critical poise, perhaps central to the experience of cult films, is constituted in a number of ways.

First, we might highlight the essential ingredients present here. We have the square all-American college couple, Brad and Janet, naive, conventional and repressed, taking the traditional route toward matrimonial union. Their clichéd misadventure (broken down car, stormy night, spooky mansion) invites our identification and sympathy. They are our narrative initiation, our familiar point of entry to an unfamiliar world of fantasy and permission.

Then we discover the alien convention is peopled by curiously benevolent, or at least charismatically persuasive eccentrics. Sexual ambiguity, seduction and the exercise of power are the key themes in this hierarchical community.

Finally, as the corrective to the potentially uncontrolled hedonism of Frank's sexual experiments, punishment and dissolution result. Indeed, there is something of the psychological and emotional play associated with the ritual practices of sado-masochism here. And of course, the whole fantasy is executed with a camp spontaneity and kitsch humour, with tongue firmly in cheek (if not elsewhere!).

(ii) *Genre*
One of the ways in which this world of fantastic possibility is rendered is through its apparently random and gratuitous ransacking of generic motifs. *The Rocky Horror Picture Show* is firstly a camp pop musical (derived from Richard O'Brien's successful London stage show) which draws upon and extends the conventional fantasy/reality boundary that the classic film musical pursues. In fact, it appears to exploit this tradition to ingenious

effect. It reverses the familiar device by which the audience willingly accepts that song and dance act as extensions of and displacements for the psychic and emotional lives of the characters (as established through the diegetic narrative). Here, it is rather the case that the diegetic world is an extension of the fantasy world of the pop song and that it pastiches the musical tradition itself, culminating in 'a Busby Berkeley parody on a set duplicating the old RKO Radio Pictures logo'.[6] Characters act in the emotional register of figures in rock 'n' roll mythology ('Toucha Toucha Me' for example) – a device which recurs in *Tommy* (also 1975) and is later pursued in retro-musicals such as *Grease* (1978). Parody and pastiche, of course, invoke the spirit of play that pervades the whole film. Where, in the classical musical, this was frequently framed in a controlled way by use of the 'backstage' performance device (for example, nostalgically in *Singin' in the Rain* [1952] and *The Band Wagon* [1953]), here pastiche is rampant. And its range of inspirational sources extends beyond the world of the classic musical.

Rocky Horror also parodies a wide range of 'B'-horror, sci-fi and monster movies and TV series of the 1950s, and seminal horrors from the 1930s such as *Frankenstein* (1931) and *King Kong* (1933). Specifically, Alexander Stuart locates the device of the Criminologist/Narrator (played by a wonderfully voyeuristic Charles Gray) in the Edgar Lustgarten thrillers of the late Fifties and early Sixties: 'spouting a self-righteous commentary to the action in a series of "cutaways" filmed in a suitably shadowy, box-file-lined study'.[7] Not only is this subtle parody, it works as a framing device which structures the narrative as a spurious psychological case study. The implication here seems to be a critique of the then fashionable psychological investigations of delinquency and deviance. The work of Skinner and of Laing, for example, is also implicated ironically in the 'cases' of *A Clockwork Orange* (1971) and *Tommy*, not to mention the medical examination of the alien in *The Man Who Fell to Earth* (1976).[8]

But what can the evidence of such wide-ranging and sensitive pastiche reveal? Rosenbaum and Hoberman refer to Eco's work on *Casablanca* when considering the matter of intertextuality:

> He [Eco] also says that *Casablanca* became a cult movie because it is not one movie – it is 'the movies'. The major thing that *The Rocky Horror Picture Show* has in common with *Casablanca* is that it's not one movie but every movie.[9]

So to some extent, the perspective of distanciation which intertextuality entails points us towards a distinctive mode of spectatorship which relies in part upon a nostalgic celebration of cinema itself. However, genre hybridity and parody may be important aspects of the cult film for reasons beyond the nostalgic celebration of popular cinema itself.

Although other cult films draw on pre-existing popular genres (such as science fiction, horror and the musical), they are often, it seems, generic hybrids (*The Wicker Man*), or adopt an ironic or playful attitude to generic conventions (*Rocky Horror*), or use generic elements in a highly selective manner (*Performance*). This suggests that they promise recognisable codes and conventions within incomplete, random, mixed or ironic frames of reference.

One of the hallmarks of genre films is the sealed, impermeable nature of the worlds they create, realised through the consistent deployment of familiar codes and motifs. For the most part, they are highly structured, regularised forms, even in examples (such as Hammer Horror) which threaten on occasion to destabilise the emotional coherence of their hermeneutic worlds. Indeed, it would be interesting to speculate whether periods when conventional generic types were particularly dominant were also times of relative social cohesion, such is the strength of order within genre films. Conversely, genre parody (which really begins in Hollywood and later in Britain after the Second World War and reaches its climax from the late 1960s through the 1970s) suggests a self-reflexive concern with form itself, and a some-times playful, sometimes nostalgic, sometimes satirical regard for past certainties.

The adoption of generic elements in a pick 'n' mix fashion (as in *Rocky Horror*) surely goes beyond cinematic homage though. It appears that certain generic ingredients, when extracted from their balanced and controlled original environment, take on an extra potency, an iconic resonance, a *hypersignification*. What they might signify seems less important than the fact of them being cast off, floating free in a weightless semiotic space devoid of the gravity and anchorage that generic convention provides. Their poignancy is palpable, if their precise meaning remains indistinct. This unorthodox attitude towards generic resources may have important implications for the narrative texture of cult films too.

(iii) *Narrative*

One of the keywords most often associated with cult films in the burgeon-
ing critical literature on this subject is 'excess'. Some scholars have gone as
far as to propose this as a common denominator which underpins disparate
kinds of text (as in Sconce's use of the category of exploitation cinema).[10]
There is some truth in this and it is a useful term up to a point, but not in
the manner in which it is most frequently deployed: excesses of nudity/sex/
violence/blood/gore and other taboo-breaking ingredients. Too often, this
interpretation of excess is used in a crude way to classify films as beyond
the boundaries of acceptable norms as far as censorship and matters of
taste are concerned, and therefore indicative of a radical, subcultural (often
masculinised) kind of rebellion at work in such low-budget, independent
films and their fans. But this oppositional agenda is limited.

To begin with, cult attribution is usually retrospective. Sometimes,
indeed, appropriation amounts to a rediscovery (*Rocky Horror, The Wicker
Man*) or an against-the-grain rereading (from *The Wizard of Oz* [1939] to
The Sound of Music [1965]) of a residual, popular text. In the case of films
of 'excess', the 'excess' in question has frequently lost its notoriety or edge;
its original power to shock has become diluted. Indeed, it is celebrated for
once having been shocking. This opens up an interesting paradox about
some cult films (for example *The Exorcist* [1973] and *A Clockwork Orange*):
their radicalism is largely redundant, spent; far from breaking taboos, they
are now safe, viewed from the comforting vantage of nostalgia. They offer
vicarious thrills at a safe, predictable distance. Once ground-breaking, they
are now icons of familiarity. In this sense, they are works of pure kitsch. It
is clear from this that it will be difficult to explain the distinctiveness of cult
films without taking into account the viewing context.

But to remain for now at the textual level, even here the idea of 'excess'
deserves thinking through more carefully. For 'excess' not only means
'taken to extremes', but more simply, a 'surfeit' of certain elements. And
such gratuitousness may exist not just at the level of content, but at the
level of style and form. It may be worth considering that cult films reveal
a surfeit of certain ingredients within the mise-en-scène *in excess of* their
narrative function. This is the true meaning of 'camp'.[11] Let's apply this
proposal to our case study.

Excess within *Rocky Horror* resides not merely within the hedonistic
permission of Frank N. Furter's transsexual regime. Indeed, as noted
above, in this respect the film is far from explicit, in fact quite tame. No,

it is gratuitous, but in a very different way: at the level of style, design and performance. Beyond the elements of genre cliché, the treatment of which is frequently heavy-handed, the film is designed visually in a garish, crude sequence of rather slapdash quotations which meld neon-lit, low-budget, retro sci-fi with sets from children's television and steals from pop art and glam rock. Indeed the whole is a studied exercise in bad taste, and a celebratory one at that.

It is perhaps useful to consider the structures of feeling in play here. Take, for example, costume. The black and red corsetry worn initially by Frank and his followers and later (as a uniform of initiation) by Janet too is quite specific in its terms of reference. It is neither indicative exactly of the heterosexual eroticism of pornography, nor yet of the grotesque, exaggerated parody of the drag artist. To that end, it is exquisitely ambiguous, resolutely transsexual. It is both flamboyant and ostentatious. It is indeed high camp, potent in its iconic charge; but it is also a piece of kitsch, an empty gesture, a triumph of presentation over content: it is *costume*. And it is precisely because it frees itself of diegetic determination, and offers itself as a plaything, an item of wardrobe, that it is available to appropriation, to extra-filmic use.

Performance is similarly doubly encoded, and ambivalently so. On the one hand there is the cartoon caricature of the emotional register: O'Brien's sinister hunchback, Brad's nerdish retention, Janet's sexual transformation, and of course Curry's deliciously provocative queen. Yet, at the same time, these 'actions and gestures of exaggerated emphasis', of stylised refinement, ultimately also betray themselves as *performances*.[12] The self-effacement of realism is gone. We have a glimpse of the mechanism at work, we know it is fake. Such glimpses behind the scenes, through the performances, constitute a disrupted, incoherent viewing experience, what Umberto Eco has called the 'glorious ricketiness' of cult narratives.[13] Conventional narratives, on the other hand, tend to be characterised by balance in the orchestration of elements within the mise-en-scène. We are used to an economy of style, a familiar repertoire of generic tropes, character types, a harmonious rendition of mise-en-scène and covert narrative operation.

(iv) *Keywords*
Certain keywords have emerged from this textual overview of *The Rocky Horror Picture Show* which may be useful to carry forward as tentative

contributions to the definition of the cult film. First, we have noted certain themes: sexual permission and transgression, rites-of-passage initiation, charismatic authority, partial resolution, and psychological investigation. Secondly, we have considered the role of pastiche and parody in redeploying familiar generic features in ways which are sometimes challenging, sometimes reassuring, often nostalgic for cinema itself. And it has been suggested that iconic elements derived from familiar genres can take on a supra-diegetic force, which renders them potent, if ambiguous signifying marks. Finally, the issue of narrative unevenness has been broached. Here, we might conjecture that codes of excess exist in matters of performance style, art design and narrative form. The camp and the kitsch are characteristics which may distinguish cult narratives from conventional cinema. But how do such films as *Rocky Horror* come to look and feel different? Is it possible to trace these distinguishing features back to their origins? Were such designs deliberate or the products of chance? It is to the production history we must look next in order to find answers to these questions.

Production History

Adaptation (whether from literary works, theatrical plays, musical shows, comic books or television series) has been the lifeblood of the cinema throughout its history and, as such, there is nothing unusual about the source material of cult films. What is often instructive, however, besides the source itself, is the nature of the transformative process: the gap or leap between page or stage and screen. The effects of this are quite evident in the case of *The Rocky Horror Picture Show* and can be identified at several levels, each contributing to the film's subsequent cult status.

Actor Richard O'Brien was uninspired by the London stage scene of the early 1970s, which included 'a few quasi-religious shows like *Godspell* and *Jesus Christ Superstar*'.[14] He was cast as a replacement Herod in a Robert Stigwood production of the Tim Rice/Andrew Lloyd Webber musical, directed by Australian Jim Sharman. However, 'Stigwood didn't like the way I played it, so I was paid off as I had signed a contract. I lived off these proceeds while I wrote the [*Rocky Horror*] show', originally entitled *They Came From Denton High*.[15] Sharman became interested in O'Brien's musical revue and, when 'The Royal Court asked Sharman to do a play at the Theatre Downstairs . . . he said yes, only if he could have a bit of fun in the Theatre Upstairs first.'[16]

The show, produced by Michael White, opened in June 1973 to rave reviews in the London press. Typical of many, Jack Tinker in the *Daily Mail* wrote: 'O'Brien's spangled piece of erotic fantasy is so fast, so sexy and so unexpectedly well-realized that one is in danger of merely applauding it without assessing it'.[17] It is telling that this particular theatre critic recognised the show's visceral kind of power and immediacy. Jonathan Rosenbaum has since reflected on this factor in the work's immediate appeal:

> During the first year or so of the play's run, it was quite apparent that it had personal and political importance for many of my English friends who were roughly the same age (early thirties), women in particular. It was as if some of the more liberating aspects of the counter-culture and 'swinging London', rock and cinephilia, had become attached to a specific dream of sexual liberation – a dream rather than a more explicit invitation to action, because the overall emotional tone of the play, despite the overt violence and kinkiness, exuded tenderness, shyness and innocence of a specifically English variety.[18]

Some of the issues highlighted by Rosenbaum (the work's appeal to women, its dreamlike attraction to a certain kind of middle-class Englishness, the discourses of liberation, its cosy reworking of recognisable pop culture clichés, the invitations to audience participation) I shall return to in due course.

For now, it is worth noting the location of its origin (The Royal Court's studio Theatre Upstairs) as synonymous with radical artistic innovation (rather than popular success). And also the particular theatrical climate sketched by O'Brien (above) which, for all his general disapproval, was characterised by a flourishing of young, innovative theatrical and musical talent behind which, very often, stood the entrepreneurial vision of Australian record producer Robert Stigwood (who also produced Ken Russell's film of The Who's rock opera *Tommy*). Similarly, O'Brien himself had been involved in *Hair*, as had the 28-year-old Tim Curry who was cast as Frank. N. Furter and had previously auditioned for *Jesus Christ Superstar*, and the show's director, Jim Sharman. *Rocky Horror*, therefore, not only drew on familiar cinematic and musical iconography, it also positioned itself shrewdly in London's contemporary performance scene between radical theatre, Soho sex revue and pop musical, and emanated from a definite theatrical coterie. The cultural conditions whereby such boundary-crossing became possible are a matter I shall return to at the end of this chapter.

However, as Jones notes, by the end of June 1973 it was obvious that 'just playing to 60 people per night [at the Theatre Upstairs] was not enough',[19] and the show moved not by coincidence to premises which were both converted former cinemas: firstly the Classic Chelsea (where it was staged in front of a blank cinema screen), and later the Kings Road Theatre (opening 29 October 1974).[20] That this was a homage, in no small measure, to a cinema now in decline was quite explicit. It won the *Evening Standard*'s 'Best Musical of 1973' award. But fashionably bohemian Chelsea remained its particular milieu until it moved to the West End's Comedy Theatre where it played until 1980.[21] At this point in its production history, however, the show went through two transformative changes which may account to some extent for its subsequent cult potential.

The American rock executive and theatrical impresario Lou Adler saw the London show and agreed a deal with Michael White for the American rights. Adler opened it first in 'a Los Angeles rock club, The Roxy on the Sunset Strip with Paul Jabara who had left *Jesus Christ Superstar*'.[22] It ran there successfully for ten months in 1974 during which time Adler invited Gordon Stulberg, then head of Twentieth Century Fox, to a performance. 'Stulberg witnessed the enthusiastic reaction of the theatre audience and was impressed enough to invest one million dollars of Fox's money in the project'.[23]

Filming began at Hammer's now forlorn Bray Studios near Windsor, in October 1974. Again, structural parallels between the show's horror pastiche content and its production context were more than coincidence. Jim Sharman, who already had one picture to his name (*Shirley Thomson versus the Aliens*, Australia, 1972), logically transferred his direction of the stage show to the screen version. And casting continuity was maintained as much as possible. Sharman told *Photoplay* during the shoot about the concern with consistency:

> What we are trying to do with this is to keep the core of the thing. We have kept both the original designers and the Frankenstein family who originated the roles. Although we are approaching the movie differently, we are still operating from the same premise as in the

theatre. For example, Frank N. Furter's idea of everything was rather grand, but in reality, it was rather tatty. We have tried not to lose that image of grit and grime . . . And we are not trying to integrate the songs into the action, they just develop from it.[24]

Production conditions sustained this ambition rather well, as it turned out. Patricia Quinn, who played the Usherette in the stage show but was recast as Magenta in the film version, recalls that the old mansion studio was in a parlous state of disrepair. 'We were a bit uncomfortable because this house was sort of leaking; it was pretty cold hanging about that place in your underwear! And the laboratory scenes were quite agonising because they took rather a long time – even though it was only a nine week shoot'. However, such hardships were clearly ameliorated by the sense of camaraderie on set. 'The great thing was that most of us had done it together on the stage so it created this fantastic family and also makes a much better film because all the relationships developed'.[25] One wonders whether such creative intimacy does not lend a special quality to films produced under otherwise quite ramshackle conditions. There are earlier examples of such production arrangements producing distinctive visual results in British cinema: for example, Hammer films and Gainsborough melodramas. Perhaps this is also the case here.

Important as this sense of unity in the face of adversity might be to the success of the finished film, as significant surely was the casting, at the insistence of Fox, of two then relatively unknown American actors in the roles of Brad and Janet; for Barry Bostwick and Susan Sarandon were certainly outsiders. Sarandon, a friend of Tim Curry, had been cast almost by accident following a social call to the film's production offices.[26] Although she admits 'Everyone thought I was crazy to do it' because 'I did it for no money and it didn't catch on for quite a while', she has fond memories of the experience and Quinn found her 'very nice' and 'superlative as Janet'.[27] Barry Bostwick, on the other hand, 'was moody' according to Quinn's memory. He admits on reflection that

I was a sort of fish out of water, it was my first time in England and everyone had a tendency to see me as the character. They were treating me like I was Brad Majors and, because of my style of work, I tend to take on some of the elements of my character, so maybe I had a certain stand-offishness or criticalness, and people weren't responding well to me. I always sort of felt they were kind of wilder or more complicated, maybe even more mature than me. Beyond Tim and Susan, I was scared of them all so I didn't extend myself to being friends with them.[28]

This commentary is revealing indeed, confirming both the sense of Bostwick's own outsider status and the emotional identification between himself and his role as Brad. And it is really the repressed Brad's 'sacrifice' at the hands of Frank, which provides the central sexual dynamic of the film, particularly when compared with the willing corruptibility of Sarandon's Janet. Bostwick reveals more about this central dichotomy in interview:

> I think everybody in the piece would like to be Frank N Furter; to be *that* flamboyant; that's a side of our personalities which we don't tap into enough. You know, just tap into your dreams, don't be afraid, dress the way you want to dress; act the way you want to act; be what you want to be; don't play the role, be the role; don't dream it, be it. That's the attitude we all wish we could pursue more in our lives, and he [Frank/Curry] was the symbol of that, so that's why I would have liked to have experienced that role. I think it would be not only fun but personality altering.[29]

It is rather easy to read into Bostwick's confessional reflection here the tone of an innocent, rather straight Brad Majors. Arguably, it was the fidelity of this dynamic which produced such compelling central screen performances.

However, this must also be set against another distinction in the shooting experience. For while Christopher Biggins and his fellow Transylvanians 'were stoned every single day we were making the film', Richard O'Brien was less comfortable with the experience and the result: 'The more you've got to do with it – I was the author and acting in it – the more you feel you've got to lose and therefore your nervousness comes into that kind of area . . . The film was very much Jim's kind of vision rather than mine, but I was happy to see it turn out the way it did'.[30] Biggins, by contrast, remembers the anticlimax of the film's premiere in September 1975: 'It was so depressing and everyone felt that this was the biggest flop ever. It certainly wasn't well received'.[31]

In fact, reviews were rather mixed, but most agreed that the screen adaptation was a poor rendition of the stage show's power and wit. Most positive was Alexander Stuart in *Films and Filming*, who thought

'Richard O'Brien and Jim Sharman seem to have got away with it rather successfully'.[32] He notes the film's topical costume and design references to the pop scene's 'glamrock' era, and Tim Curry's inclusion of 'performance elements of everyone from Mick Jagger and David Bowie to the Queen', while 'the rest of the cast all survive through sheer indulgence, each trying to out-camp the others'.[33]

Variety lamented that 'Where the campy hijinks was acceptable and even moderately fresh on stage, it only seems laboured in celluloid blowup . . . Overall . . . most of the jokes that might have seemed jolly fun on stage now appear obvious and even flat. The sparkle's gone'.[34] The Hollywood Reporter, while praising individual performances, agreed that 'Sharman has not been able to re-create the excitement and theatricality of the original, and what was once camp and glitter has now become almost grotesque and perverse'.[35] Tony Rayns, writing in the Monthly Film Bulletin, condemns Sharman and O'Brien's 'pointless and completely expendable attempts to "open out" the play'. The whole is at best 'self-consciously slick' and at worst 'damagingly misconceived'.[36]

Critical consensus seems to rest upon the precise problems of transforming highly camp theatrical material to the screen. Curry remarked that after two years on stage, Frank N. Furter had become 'a sort of mad giant inside me' and explained the requirement 'to bring him right down for the movie' – a feat, most agreed, he seemed to have accomplished successfully.[37] But this 'mental adjustment' to the correct pitch of the histrionic display, as Rayns notes, is also demanded of an audience. This proved too much for many and the film was a commercial failure on release.

It opened in London at the Rialto on 14 August 1975 with a poor promotional campaign, which included a poster trumpeting 'Lotsa larfs and sex', 'gorgeous girls' and 'thrills and chills' in the manner of a (then modish) Confessions of . . . romp.[38] Jones suggests pragmatically that the studio 'had just got burned over Brian de Palma's Phantom of the Paradise [1974] which had cost them a million dollars for the distribution rights and had died at the box office, and they didn't want to promote a film that to them seemed in a similar vein'.[39]

The American experience was even worse. Lou Adler had transferred the stage show from LA to Broadway in spring 1975, where a specially renovated Biltmore Theatre created a cabaret setting. Fox bulk-purchased tickets for a press preview but the show bombed, playing for only 45

FIGURE 3: When Rocky met Janet – Peter Hinwood and Susan Sarandon
get up close and personal [20TH CENTURY FOX/THE KOBAL COLLECTION]

performances. Adler confessed 'Everything I did was wrong . . . It was
all a matter of mistakes. I kept it running for three or four weeks, though
based on the reviews and ticket sales it should have closed after opening
night'.[40] Adler's explanation was that it was 'too LA' for Broadway tastes.[41]
Others have considered that by mid-1975 its moment had passed and

New Yorkers found it too passé. O'Brien disagrees, for him it was still topical: 'The timing of the show was extremely lucky. It hit at exactly the time of the glam-rock/bi-sexuality trend that was happening'. He explains the Broadway debacle in terms of Adler's poor staging: 'We wanted it handled exactly the way it had been handled here [in London], by leasing an old cinema, but unfortunately it was his ego at stake and he was proved wrong'.[42]

The impact of this Broadway flop on the American film release was immediate and devastating. It was 'only half-heartedly promoted' and, according to some sources, 'was a secret release. 20th [Century Fox] kept the film secret by sending out only seven prints . . . It's no wonder there weren't many reviews'.[43] Whatever the case, its autumn 1975 Los Angeles opening was curtailed and the first run came to an abrupt and unsuccessful end. Essentially, the film was buried.

The Birth of a Cult

That a film is quirky, uneven, even poorly finished; that it is unpopular, forgotten, marginalised, cannot *guarantee* cult status, but both conditions must be attendant at its rebirth. What kind of catalyst is required to then breathe life back into such a work? It needs to find its audience and to speak to it. It requires the circumstances for that mirror moment, that mutual recognition.

Only a few months following its aborted American first run, according to Rosenbaum, 'two publicists – Bill Quigley and Tom Deegan – persuaded Fox to open [*Rocky Horror*] as a midnight movie in New York, specifically at the Waverly Theatre in Greenwich Village, in April 1976'.[44] Contrary to popular mythology, *Rocky Horror* did not invent the midnight movie – this particular exhibition strategy was already well established in a range of independent cinemas across urban America. Indeed, in some ways, the midnight movie became, from the late Sixties, what the drive-in movie had been to the generation before: a youth-oriented social event which, while celebrating cinema itself, was as much about the space of the 'auditorium' as it was about the particular film on screen.

As with the social circumstances which gave rise to the success of the *Rocky Horror Show* on stage, the midnight movie phenomenon grew from a combination of cultural factors attendant upon the rise of the late-

Sixties counter-culture in the USA and the decline of mainstream, popular cinema-going. As has been well documented by Douglas Gomery, the steady closure of cinemas during the post-war period forced studios, distributors and exhibitors to look for new ways of marketing film to new, niche audiences, and particularly to the growing youth market.[45] At the same time, as critics such as Andrew Sarris and Greg Taylor have established, from the late 1950s film had begun to be considered by a wider middle-class and expanding youth audience, either as an object of nostalgia and/or a potentially radical art form.[46] Midnight movies, which drew inspiration from underground, avant-garde and independent film-making during the Sixties, positioned their nostalgic and/or challenging fare in cinemas which might otherwise close, at a time and in locations of appeal to a youth audience.[47] Thus, films from *Night of the Living Dead* (1968) to *Pink Flamingos* (1972) found their niche market with product that was both subversive and celebrated cinema itself. The conditions for cult film to appear were established.

In the first year of its midnight run at the Waverly in Greenwich Village, the *Rocky Horror Picture Show* made $3 million. And its popularity on this specialist circuit soon spread. Certainly, perceptive business acumen was at work here, but there was something else also.[48] This film culture was fulfilling a certain kind of social need. By 1982, *Screen International* reported that the film had been showing at The Tiffany in Los Angeles for five years:

> The film has become a cult fad, with youngsters going to the show dozens and dozens of times, dressing in costumes similar to those seen on screen, singing along with the cast, and even going up on stage to perform numbers from the movie.[49]

Critics have since ventured a range of explanations for what J. P. Telotte describes as the 'audience's ritualistic "performance" of the film'.[50] Robert Wood argues that it is the film's uneasy combination of cinema and theatre which inspires these copycat charades.[51] Bruce Kawin suggests the film offers an example of the 'rhetoric of direct address', its performance style is so compelling that it 'says "you" when it means "us"'. In that sense it is a narrative not only directed out towards its imagined audience, but for Kawin it is an illustration of 'how a film might literally construct an audience after its own likeness', though he stops short of explaining how this actually works.[52]

I have suggested (above) that the answers to this question may lie in three specific areas. Firstly, there is the hypersignification of certain iconic and transferable signifiers which the fragmented nature of the narrative structure allows to become detached from the text itself, and used by an audience. Secondly, we observed the charismatic performance style which combines camp excesses with kitsch sensibility and ironic self-consciousness inviting both identification and exploitation. And thirdly, the themes of sexual transgression and rites-of-passage initiation would appear to offer both stimulus and reassurance in equal measure. Let us now look more closely at the nature of audience responses to this film in the light of these proposals.

Rosenbaum has interviewed a number of the 'pioneers' of the original Waverly group, who claim credit for initiating certain features which have become ritualised in the *Rocky Horror* performance routine. Sal Piro, who allegedly had seen the film about 300 times, was apparently 'one of the first to dress up like one of the film's characters and then reproduce all his or her gestures precisely beneath the screen, under flashlight beams'.[53] Louis Farese Jr. 'began the practice of shouting out "appropriate" lines during pauses in the film in order to supplement (respond to, anticipate, mock or echo) its dialogue'.[54] Rosenbaum comments:

> Collectively, these lines represent a text that is perpetually changing, a complex of layers at any given performance, consisting of both a traditional catechism and a series of fresher contributions, each of which earns a different reputation and life-span existentially, like a jazz solo, at the moment of delivery (and 'democratically', in competition with all the others) . . . Presumably the use of props and more general audience participation (the flurries of rice thrown in the opening wedding sequence, and the water pistols and umbrellas brandished to accompany the rainstorm) were embellishments that came later.[55]

The religious connotations of 'catechism' are as significant here as the link with jazz, in the sense that every rehearsal, every act of worship is an improvisation based upon and departing from a known musical score, or a common litany. The three elements of performance: costume, props and dialogue, make this a piece of total theatre. Yet Rosenbaum goes further in suggesting also that 'it can be viewed as an unconscious yet authentic act of film criticism . . . A specifically Barthesian act of criticism and commentary on a Text'.[56] The reference to Barthes is telling because this confirms my own observation that the film offers its unfinished, detachable signifying practices to just such manipulation. In a very real sense a performance of *Rocky Horror* is a total combination of everything that takes place in a particular cinema on a given night, which constitutes an open text that may involve contributions from the exhibitors and cinema staff in addition to the interaction of the audience with the film itself. So much for its structural dynamics. What does this experience offer to an audience?

Barry Bostwick has his own ideas:

> Nothing has the raw energy and rudeness of *The Rocky Horror Show* and eventually it became a big party: a place to see your friends and enter some rivalry. It's also something you had to reach a certain age to see . . . It was a coming-of-age experience for many people.[57]

If Bostwick highlights the rites-of-passage function of the film for generations of youth audiences, David Chute agrees that the cult of midnight movies generally 'appealed primarily to feelings of awkwardness and alienation, to people who themselves felt "different" or anathematized – teens, gays, college kids'.[58] But he goes on to elaborate usefully on this thesis in respect of *Rocky Horror* in particular:

> It stands for the failure of nerve that saw an initially anti-orthodox movement transformed into a rigid new "alternate" orthodoxy, a mass-participation ritual. At precisely the right moment, *Zeitgeist*-wise, *Rocky Horror* opted not for the bitter vengefulness and romanticized self-pity of earlier midnight films, but for a clarion call to pride – in the soothing context of conformity.[59]

Whilst it is always risky to speculate upon the Zeitgeist, interesting here is the oxymoronic notion of alternative orthodoxy, the sense of pride and the comfort of conformity. Chute explains this in terms of an ironic attitude at the heart of the midnight movie's cultural capital:

> The Midnight Movies filled a transitional need for their followers, while authentic exploitation fare was just a tad too earnest in its efforts to offend. It lacked the snooty edge of irony that seems a prerequisite of success with the hipper-than-thou late-night crowd.[60]

Yet if irony is at the heart of this subcultural distinction, this is perhaps the playful and 'snooty' side to a ritual devotion which is every bit as 'earnest' as gross-out or splatter films are in their 'efforts to offend'. As J. P. Telotte proposes:

> In effect, a body of ritual, of the sort that marks both the religious and theatrical experiences, attends the cult film experience and, in the process, gives it, almost in spite of itself, a clearly social dimension. It effectively constructs a culture in small, and thus an island of meaning for an audience that senses an absence of meaningful social structures or coherence in the life outside the theatre.
>
> In essence, therefore, every cult constitutes a community, a group that "worships" similarly and regularly, and finds a strength in that shared experience.[61]

This description of a micro-culture and its palpable religious sense of observance accounts for an aspect clearly present in the example of *Rocky Horror*. And he too touches upon the sense (as from religion) of comfort and sustenance audiences derive from this ritual, as compensation for an absence in their own lives, a certain lack. But what is the nature of this lack, and this comfort, and to whom does it appeal?

Author Richard O'Brien suggests its appeal lies partly in the ordinariness which is the conventional backdrop or imaginary other to the film's camp masque:

> A lot of *Rocky*'s success has something to do with normal hetero-sexual society. It seems to titillate them as they seem to think it's rude and vaguely naughty whereas the truth of the matter is that it is very innocuous and innocent. That is its charm.[62]

Here, O'Brien expresses what is perhaps the greatest irony about *Rocky Horror*: for all its invitation to 'be it' rather than simply 'dream it', what it offers is a dream, an escape, a fantasy of transgression, of the kind Barry Bostwick dreamt of in his reflection quoted above. What it actually reinforces are the limits of that dream – the duration of a celluloid feature, the space of a movie theatre. In reality it offers reassurance to an audience both male and female, straight and gay, that it is possible to be different, to be other, or to be yourself, and also to conform, ultimately to belong. Perhaps this reassuring sense of belonging (to people who ordinarily feel that in some way they don't) is what the cult film offers above all else.

Similarly, Kinkade and Katovich couch the ironies of transgression and conformity thus: 'Cult filmgoers' paradoxical perspective holds "nothing is sacred" on the one hand, and "our film is sacred" on the other. The paradox is further enhanced as cult films are a type of social criticism, yet often validate and can be read as surface affirmations of society'.[63] This last point is a paradox the authors find at the heart of the *Rocky Horror Picture Show*, especially as embodied in the figures of Brad and Janet, and the charismatically ambiguous Frank N. Furter:

> Brad and Janet, apparent conservatives in Frankenfurter's [*sic*] horrific and radical world, are stripped, literally and figuratively, of their exterior middle American identity documents . . . [Yet ultimately] the destruction of Frankenfurter's world and Brad and Janet's escape from it (presumably to wed) reaffirm the necessity of a heterosexual procreating society. Thus, a conservative ideology contains Rocky Horror's outrageous appearances.[64]

Setting aside the rather prescriptive terms in which this essential paradox is expressed, this reading nevertheless confirms ultimate conformity. Nonetheless, it is a conformity that is achieved through a necessary (perhaps daunting) but really painless initiation. This rite of passage is one rehearsed symbolically by 'Rocky Virgins' at midnight screenings, according to Rosenbaum. Additionally, accounts of the *Rocky Horror* cult suggest these events are heavily rule-based and hierarchically structured rituals, with local 'senior performers' welcoming newcomers, introducing star performers from out of town, and explaining rules and guidelines for this particular performance. There exist competitive rivalries between different *Rocky* cults and star performers.[65]

Rosenbaum also notes how the constitution of the US *Rocky Horror* cult has changed both geographically and over time. Citing the ethnographic work of Margery Walker Pearce who 'followed the cult over a two-year period on the west coast, at the Strand Theatre in San Diego', the period 1976–8 saw the composition of the cult change from mainly homosexual males under 21 to a mainly heterosexual group of male and female college students. Local news reports then led to an influx of newcomers (including an older generation), while gays tended to drift away because of incidents of harassment outside the cinema. The early 1980s saw the influence of punk and new wave youth styles 'which placed more emphasis on the violence, leather and chains in the film (and less emphasis on the transvestism and transsexuality)'. But after about six weeks the territory was reclaimed by a mixed bunch of students.[66] It is possible of course that different factions within these changing audience groupings derive different specific pleasures from the *Rocky Horror* experience and there remains scope for further ethnographic work in this area, especially in Britain, where similar rituals (imported from the USA) developed in London and elsewhere during the 1980s.

If one clear appeal seems to be that 'cult films allow deviation and yet engender conformity', whereby 'viewers experience alienation as a source for feelings of belonging, and find resolve in a lack of resolution',[67] another seems to be the way in which *Rocky Horror* in particular 'evokes and weirdly resurrects, as if in a haunted house, a form of cinema as community that once flourished . . .'.[68]

As John Patterson noted in his *Guardian* column, the age of the midnight movie has largely faded in the wake of new technologies – firstly video, latterly DVD – which have altered the consumption culture of marginal film tastes. Meanwhile the *Rocky Horror* experience continues as a kind of kitsch cultural heritage event both in the USA and Britain. On this point it was instructive to note in a recent local newspaper clipping that The Station Theatre, Hayling Island, Hampshire is screening *The Rocky Horror Picture Show* ('a cult comedy musical') in its future programme. One can only wonder whether this is a sign that depravity has finally reached the sleepy hollows of the English south coast (beyond Brighton), or that the film has lost some of its power to shock.

Whilst not in direct competition with the public cult event, personal technologies allow easier domestic access to objects of cult adoration and facilitate the personal privacy of much cult fandom. With them and their collectors' edition products, the cult has become commercially absorbed, recuperated and popularised in a manner which to some extent must affect its marginality and sanctity. Similarly, print fanzines like *The Transylvanian* and *Flash* have been subsumed within the broader and more interactive fan culture of the internet, where *Rocky* fans create their own interactive websites and communicate about forthcoming shows, memorabilia, the awfulness of the sequel, *Shock Treatment* (Sharman, 1981) and their personal fandom.[69]

That personal investment in this film and its performance rituals is a significant element in its fan culture can be illustrated by brief reference to one specific, though not untypical, example, recorded in the 1999 Spring Directive of the Mass-Observation Archive at the University of Sussex. This 25-year-old, female 'Senior Support Worker in a supported housing project for adults with learning disabilities and mental health needs' lives alone in London, but has 'a Dutch boyfriend who lives in Holland'.[70] While as a rule she goes to the cinema 'infrequently', when she does go she enjoys her 'personal space' and would ideally 'prefer to be in an almost empty cinema':

> Having said the above, if the *Rocky Horror Picture Show* was showing at the cinema, I would prefer a full audience, and would go at the weekend. This is because I love the audience participation involved in the *Rocky Horror* and always go dressed up and completely take part in the audience participation. In the last few years, however, more and more people appear to be turning up to *Rocky Horror* nights at the cinema in normal clothes and appear to expect to sit quietly and watch the film.[71]

Throughout her testimony there is a visible tension between preference for privacy and anonymity in public spaces, contrasted with enthusiasm for 'taking part' in *Rocky Horror* nights and irritation with 'others' who don't 'take part'. She relates one particular experience 'when I last went to see the *Rocky Horror Picture Show* at the cinema':

> I had been looking forward to it for months . . . one of my favourite films was going to be on at my local cinema. I encouraged a few friends to join me and we met up in the pub for a few drinks.
>
> The film was a late night showing, starting at 11.30pm. At around 9pm, myself and my friend went to the ladies toilet in the pub to get changed into our Rocky gear. This involved fishnet stockings, stiletto heels, basques, white faces and outrageous make up. We then returned to the bar, where my friend's boyfriend was also dressed up as a character from the film, in white shirt, black jacket and half-bald wig [Riff Raff presumably]. Another friend arrived, a man, in full drag, wearing mini skirt, stilettos, make up and a long blonde wig. Dressed like this, we continue drinking in the bar until it was time to go to the cinema, where we were met by two friends who were dressed in black with backcombed hair.[72]

At the cinema, 'there were only two other people who were dressed up, the rest of the audience was in normal clothes'. When the film began and they started 'the usual shouts of audience participation' the manager came and asked them to be quiet. Despite protests that 'the *Rocky*

Horror is meant to be watched like this', he 'came back twice, eventually threatening to throw me out'.[73] A friend then poses as a representative from a company conducting research into cinema management. The friends continue the normal ritual and are not thrown out.

Three aspects emerge from this brief, single example. Firstly, the ritual itself is crucial, as is the sense that other people understand and respect its essential difference. Secondly, note the refusal to conform when challenged, despite feeling victimised by the 'ignorant' cinema manager. Thirdly, there is the distinction between this writer's usual desire for privacy and solitude and the social expectations of a *Rocky Horror* night and the permission to be 'outrageous' that it affords. As suggested at the outset, the complex relations between the public and the private in the attainment of social subjectivity would appear to be at the core of this investigation.

Summary

In this chapter I have employed *The Rocky Horror Picture Show* as an exemplar to raise some key questions about the cult film phenomenon. I have firstly proposed that the matter of defining cult as a critical category depends upon exploring textual and contextual issues. What has been uncovered textually? Genre hybridity, narrative incoherence, performance and visual style seem to be important. Alongside these, how significant are cinematic nostalgia, irony and excess, the taboo, the camp and the kitsch?

What more can we learn about the cult text from its production history? How have the arrangements of capital and creativity resulted in a product which is a 'one-off' and therefore has equal potential for valorisation and damnation? Distribution, exhibition and critical reception can often ensure, at least initially, that damnation comes first. Such historical misfortunes (and subsequent faddish rediscovery and buffish championing) may serve to position a cult film in marginal cultural territory. However, this positioning may also be in part determined by economics too; the midnight movie circuit was a product of the decline in cinema-going from the 1960s onwards. Finally, I have touched upon some aspects of cult fandom in the reception of this film. Much more is still to be addressed on that theme. But an important historical question remains.

What is the timeframe of the cult phenomenon? A picture is coming into focus that suggests three phases in its growth. Firstly, film culture and the counter-culture of the late 1960s. Secondly, ad *hoc* production conditions in the fragmented cinema culture of the 1970s. Thirdly, independent cinemas, the emergence of home video, and television screenings of 'uncommercial' films, from the mid-1970s to the mid-1980s.

If this much holds good for the case of what we might agree is the archetypal cult film, we need to test these proposals against other films of the period which have been designated cult. But in pursuing a historical trajectory it will first be necessary to return to the 1960s.

2

PERFORMANCE (1970)

Introduction

I have proposed that the distinctiveness of 1970s British films which later have come to be considered cult may have something to do with their attitudes to aspects of the late 1960s. I am thinking most obviously here of the themes of transgression and permission in the breaking of sexual and social taboos, the emphasis on youth and identity, and their explicit deployment of popular cultural references. But I am equally concerned with their formal and stylistic unconventionality. It is the combination of both which may be the key to subsequent cult eligibility. Both these factors have their origins, I believe, in the complex relationship between social change and cultural production that pertained in Britain from the mid-1960s onwards.

This set of relationships can be viewed from two perspectives. One approach concerns itself with the ways in which certain topical ideas (both thematic and formal) find their way into films of the period and are transformed there. The other approach considers how the institution of cinema itself (in respect of production, distribution, exhibition and censorship) was subject to a cultural repositioning for socio-economic reasons in the 1960s. This second level of analysis is useful because, as I suggested earlier, the rise of the cult film may have as much to do with changes in the social meaning of cinema during the period as it has to do with the particularities of specific films. Strangely, this issue has been accorded little attention in previous studies of the 1960s.[1] In this chapter

I propose to adopt this dual-lensed approach in considering the case study of *Performance*.

British Film and the Counter-culture, 1966–70

Much has been written about the rise of the so-called counter-culture in Britain during the second half of the 1960s. Less attention has been paid to how these cultural shifts impacted upon British cinema of the period. In order to address this issue it will first be necessary to characterise the state of the film industry at this time. Here is a situation where the Marxian base/superstructure model may be particularly helpful in thinking through the relationship between film economics and culture.

Cinema-going in Britain continued to decline during the decade, annual admissions falling from 1,102 millions in 1956 to 192 millions by 1970, the average number of visits per capita per year dwindling from 22.11 to 3.79 and the number of screens being reduced from 4,194 to 1,529 over the same period.[2] Yet, British production facilities entered something of a boom period. This paradox is explained by the large proportion of overseas investment in British-based film production. Domestic audiences were lured away from the cinema (as they had been since the mid-1950s) by a combination of cultural factors including the growth in the ownership of televisions (and especially the impact of ITV from 1957) and the diversity of other new popular culture (and specifically popular music). Yet film generally, and 'British' films in particular, enjoyed an artificially high-profile image in the context of what *Time* magazine famously dubbed 'Swinging London'.[3] However, while this image was at least partially illusory, and certainly short-lived, it also served to reconceptualise the cultural position of cinema itself. Let us examine how this came about.

First of all, the 1960s witnessed a further shrinkage of what might be termed the 'centre ground' in terms of British film production. During the 1950s, as has been admirably demonstrated by Sue Harper and Vincent Porter, power ebbed away steadily from film *producers* in Britain to the distributors and exhibitors.[4] This strengthening of the exhibitors' hand (concentrated in the duopoly of ABPC and Rank) had a paradoxically debilitating effect upon the domestic production sector as the market for films continued to contract. The Government's abolition of Entertainment Tax in 1960 did nothing to stem the tide of decline. A third, so-called 'National Circuit' was proposed but, with a shortage of films on release, distributors queued up to book their films into existing Gaumont, Odeon or ABC cinemas at the expense of the independent 'circuit'.[5] By 1963, any concerted hopes for this third circuit had been abandoned. In this year, out of a total number of 2,430 cinemas, Rank and ABPC together owned only 651 or 21 per cent, but this represented control of some 42 per cent of seats sold, by dint of their generally superior size, quality and location.[6] Additionally, the traditional restrictive practices of barring, and distribution agreements with the major Hollywood studios made for a system in which, as Alexander Walker put it, '"Circuit Power" was dominant – yet it was not competitive'.[7] Significantly, Murphy suggests that this situation prompted smaller circuits and independents 'to break away from the standard release pattern and programme their cinemas with popular classics, foreign sex and art films, and the "X" films which the circuits were reluctant to show'.[8] This marked the beginnings of a fragmentation of cinema at the exhibition level and the formation of niche markets in the general context of its continuing decline.

All this was extremely bad news for the already struggling independent distributor British Lion. Not only were Lion's debts and managerial squabbles a recurrent subject of Government scrutiny, but shifts in public taste prompted industry caution and made it extremely difficult to finance new projects or to obtain releases for films which did get made. The truth was that the system was insufficiently flexible to respond to market changes in consumer tastes.

A Monopolies Commission enquiry into the restrictive practices of Rank and ABPC conducted in 1964 appeared to offer some glimmer of hope. Indeed, the report when it came in 1966 severely criticised the structure of the distribution and exhibition sector, observing that 'Competition is deficient, mainly because of the structure of the industry which results from the dominant position of ABC and Rank'.[9] But it fell short of recommending the breaking up of the circuits ('a drastic step the results of which would be uncertain') and concluded that it was incumbent upon those organisations themselves to curb their excesses – what amounted to an empty threat. But significantly it appealed to the duopoly to open their markets 'to films whose appeal to the public is in doubt'.[10] Here is another indication of the economic need to take risks and to address more diverse and marginal tastes.

In reality, little changed, because the circuit majors were able to maintain (and often exceed) the requirements of the quota (30 per cent) while giving priority to more popular and safe American imports. For instance, as Alexander Walker relates, 'In the first fifty weeks of 1963 . . . the Rank circuit showed 23 British first features and 27 foreign (mostly American-made) ones; in the same period the ABC circuit showed 26 British and 24 foreign films'. And by the end of that year 'enough films were stockpiling in the distributors' vaults, or had finished shooting, to meet the quota requirements without a single new British film needing to be shot throughout the whole of the next year . . .'.[11] And, by this time, very many of those 'British' films were largely being bankrolled by the American studios.

British distributors were forced through economic prudence to maintain the traditional practice of venturing only 70 per cent of a film's budget while the far less certain 'end money' was the responsibility of the film producer, with whatever assistance might be mustered from the National Film Finance Corporation (NFFC). American studios, by contrast, were prepared to finance up to 100 per cent.[12] The reasons behind Hollywood's willingness to fund British films during the Sixties are several. As Sarah Street explains, 'As long as the technicians and casts were predominantly British, films sponsored by American companies qualified as British quota films and were entitled to subsidies from the Eady Levy'.[13] In addition, British production facilities and technical expertise represented very good value for money at a time when the dollar was strong against European currencies. At the same time, the abolition of the major studios' vertical integration with exhibition networks and the high cost and restrictive union arrangements of Hollywood production curbed domestic output, but made overseas investment attractive.[14] In fact, because of dollar strength and studio might, the Americans were able to respond positively to virtually the same set of deleterious circumstances that British cinema was undergoing. What came to be known as 'Runaway Production' grew steadily in France and Italy as well as in Britain during the 1960s. Beginning as simply a cheaper way to make American films overseas, the major Hollywood studios quickly devised ways of exploiting loopholes in each European country's state subsidy system which were intended, of course, to aid domestic film industries. Thomas Guback's study of this period calculates 'that for every dollar-equivalent of subsidy paid in France to US firms, two are paid in Italy and probably four in the United Kingdom'.

> Moreover, probably little more than 10 percent of subsidy payments went to British production companies in the mid-1960s. In some

cases of co-production, American producers have been able to receive subsidies from three countries for a single film, covering as much as 80 per cent of its cost. It is not surprising, then, that through the 1960s, American films financed abroad rose from an estimated 35 per cent to 60 per cent of the total output of US producers.[15]

The Monopolies Commission, when it reported in 1966, was all too well aware of the American threat. In the first half of the decade the percentage of 'wholly British financed films' had fallen from 67 per cent in 1960 to 46 per cent in 1965.[16] In 1966 'American finance accounted for 75 per cent of "British" first features or co-features given a circuit release, and the figure was to rise to 90 per cent in 1967 . . .'.[17] In that same year, another report, this time by the Federation of Films Unions, claimed that '70 per cent of screen time in 1967 was occupied by foreign films'.[18] By 1968 American investment reached an all-time high of £31.3 million.[19] All the American majors had established production offices in London by the mid-Sixties. Reviewing the decade up to 1971, Guback found that 'US firms were involved financially in almost five times more British films than was the British government's chosen banking instrument, the National Film Finance Corporation'.[20]

Having set out the economics of the situation, cultural factors now need to be taken into account. Britain was favoured by US investors over France and Italy not only because of its comparatively lucrative Eady Levy. Common language is one issue, speculative enterprise was the other. In the first half of the decade United Artists ventured to back three innovative and internationally successful films, *Dr. No* (1962), *Tom Jones* (1963) and *A Hard Day's Night* (1964). This, as Robert Murphy puts it, 'was to have a revolutionary effect on the British film industry',[21] Certainly by mid-decade the media-fuelled phenomenon of 'Swinging London', based largely upon pop music exports such as The Beatles and the Rolling Stones, made Britain's capital a brief epicentre for cultural interest and investment. More so than in France and Italy, the Hollywood studios in Britain became aware of the lucrative potential of the youth market in popular culture. In 1967 Warner Bros. approached the highly bankable star of *Performance*, Mick Jagger (recently arrested in a high-profile police drugs raid) to act as their corporation's 'youth advisor', an offer which the singer declined.[22] Nonetheless, this bid symbolised the majors' considerable investment of financial trust in an unprecedented, volatile and largely unknown cultural force. This unknown cultural force found opportunities in mainstream cinema not only because of the studios' willingness to speculate, but because a fragmented film market allowed for (and even necessitated) diversity and experimentation. Cultural significance (and briefly power also) moved from the mainstream to the margins; or to put it another way, the counter-culture came, for a short while, to fill the vacuum at the centre.

A new fluidity and openness to the avant-garde in part persuaded Italian director Michelangelo Antonioni to set *Blow-up* (1966) in London. Roman Polanski found British backing for *Repulsion* (1965) and *Cul-de-sac* (1966). Truffaut's *Fahrenheit 451* (1966) is set in a sterile, British futurescape. Lindsay Anderson, polemicist of the Free Cinema movement of the 1950s, followed the gritty realism of *This Sporting Life* (1963) with the surreal experiment *If . . .* (1968). Even Jean-Luc Godard centred his latest manifesto, *One-Plus-One* (1968) on a Rolling Stones London recording session. Joseph Losey continued his clinical dissection of British social class with *Accident* (1967). Meanwhile, Stanley Kubrick, between *Dr. Strangelove* (1964) and *2001: A Space Odyssey* (1968), had become resident. The sheer number and concentration of highly respected overseas directors working in Britain must surely be without comparison in any other period. Yet these are but isolated examples of a more general, underlying shift in the taste constituency of British cinema.

The establishment of the National Film Theatre and the BFI's Regional Film Theatres reflected a genuine interest in film art and education, two relatively new and now much more conspicuous attitudes towards film as a medium and its public exhibition. Avant-garde and experimental film found a variety of temporary homes during the 1960s, including the vibrant Institute of Contemporary Arts. Independent cinemas like the Scala grew up in London and Brighton. Film journals such as *Films and Filming* and the BFI's *Sight and Sound* increased their circulations. Film became the passionate concern of the educationalist, the buffish enthusiast and the bohemian dilettante alike. Robert Watson captures the new and poignant moment of cinema in Britain in the Sixties:

> It was a period when Film was part of what it meant to be young and intellectually curious. Film was not an academic discipline, nor yet a forbidding zone where competing theoretical discourses were elaborated; it was, or appeared to be, part of a more generous and

FIGURE 4: The ultimate performance: Warner Bros. got more than
they bargained for when cashing in on Mick Jagger's star image
[WARNER BROS./THE KOBAL COLLECTION]

openly enthusiastic culture. Film was a vibrant source of energy, and it
exemplified what the phrase 'a living art' is supposed to mean.[23]

But there was another side also to this vibrant, youth-oriented film culture.
As Robert Murphy suggested above, struggling independent exhibitors
(operating outside the circuit duopoly) saw a lifeline in attracting marginal
audiences with more provocative fare. The progressive relaxation of
censorship during the decade afforded new scope to such opportunities.
Sometimes this was the work of European auteurs like Antonioni and Fellini
or Godard and Truffaut; often it was low-budget exploitation material
ranging from lurid horror to soft porn. Both in the British and American
independent markets 'continental' was a euphemism for sex as the pages
of the popular magazine *Continental Film* confirm, thus forging a unique
conceptual link between the avant-garde and permissive interests.

Into this curiously permeable film world of strange alliances, speculative
investments and creative innovation, other kinds of new entrepreneur
also entered, from backgrounds as varied as television and fine art, the

theatre and fashion, public relations and, of course, popular music. Needless to say, film is by its nature a collaborative medium that draws in any number of specialist creative and technical skills as well as venture capitalists. But the unique circumstances arose in Britain in the second half of the 1960s whereby generous Hollywood studios were willing to back loose associations of diverse (sometimes untried) talent *without* the overarching control of conventional production regimes. The results of such an enterprise culture are exemplified nowhere better than in the case history of *Performance*.

Performance: A Case History

Robert Hewison provides a useful overview of the complex circumstances which gave rise to the counter-culture during the second half of the 1960s, in which 1968 was a tumultuous climax. He distinguishes between 'the affluent and hedonistic Sixties of "Swinging London", and the oppositional culture of the underground'. However, he also observes that the two trends had 'important cross-relationships':

> They both depended upon a particular set of economic circumstances, they were both heralded by particular developments in the arts, and they both aimed at a kind of personal liberation. Yet the logic of the underground was ultimately opposed to the materialism which had created the opportunity for it to flourish. The materialist culture, for its part, could not sustain itself, and the climacteric of 1968 anticipates the social conflicts of the 1970s.[24]

Hewison's analysis rightly touches upon the essential contradiction at the heart of privileged bohemianism, and reinforces the fact that the rise of the counter-culture was in part a reaction against its own material hedonism.

The fascinating questions remain as to how the new affluence rooted in material consumption and leisure pursuits during what Arthur Marwick calls the 'High Sixties' (1964–69) also produced such a sustained and diverse flourishing of creativity (in a way in which, for example, the consumer boom of the mid-1980s signally failed to do). And furthermore, why did the counter-cultural reaction to the material indulgences of that affluence manifest itself when it did, in such a profound, widespread, and in many places violent, political force? These are questions beyond the scope of this book (and ones for which Hewison, Marwick and others have their own answers). However, they are pertinent in so far as they are at the heart of *Performance* itself. What we see dramatised here in both graphic and allusive form is the revolt of the world of ideas against the world of objects which 1968 so forcefully symbolised elsewhere.

Colin MacCabe's impeccable monograph on *Performance* traces carefully the diverse cultural origins of this extraordinary film in the figures of the persons involved. At its core is the mercurial figure of Donald Cammell, artist and dilettante turned screenwriter, who drew his inspiration for the project largely from personal acquaintances in the Chelsea set of the mid-1960s. The whole enterprise captures the unprecedented manner in which establishment figures of the day rubbed shoulders with London's criminal fraternity at parties thrown by artists, fashion designers and pop stars on budgets provided by television executives, advertising agents, record moguls and pornographers. This was, to be sure, a rarefied, select milieu, but one which at least temporarily forgot class boundaries. New money was the great leveller, hedonism the common cultural currency. But it was a vibrant, cocksure scene from which some ultimately dropped out.

Both Cammell and Jagger have since acknowledged the model of ill-fated Rolling Stone Brian Jones. The Courtfield Road flat which he shared with Anita Pallenberg was decorated by Christopher Gibbs, who became the design consultant on the film.[25] Jones and Pallenberg frequently held court here to a wide circle of friends and acquaintances including Cammell. But, as MacCabe notes, Cammell had quit the London scene of the late 1950s for Paris where he shared a flat with his girlfriend, the Texan model Deborah Dixon (who designed the costumes for *Performance*), so on his return he was very much an observer of events.[26] And while he was a frequent visitor to Courtfield Road and was evidently entranced by the coterie gathered there, it is clear that much of his inspiration for *Performance* came from French literature, and particularly from the work of Genet and Artaud.[27] MacCabe distils from his research Cammell's two predominant intellectual interests: sex and violent crime.[28] Following a couple of marketable, but ultimately run-of-the-mill scripts (*The Touchables* and *Duffy* [starring James Fox], both 1968), Cammell began work on a prototype of *Performance* called 'The Liars'. If the earlier projects had toyed unconvincingly with the ideas of a kidnapped rock star and a criminal heist respectively, 'The Liars' tries to combine these two spheres of interest. While MacCabe acknowledges that it 'tells a story which is both familiar and foreign, a tame ur-tale which has none of the power of its ferocious offspring', it secured the interests of those friends and associates who would be key to the final film: Anita Pallenberg, Mick Jagger, James Fox, Nicolas Roeg and a young American agent, Sanford Lieberson.[29]

Cammell's script 'The Liars' was proposed as a suitable vehicle for Brando and Jagger: a criminal on the run who holes up at the house of a reclusive rock star.[30] Unsurprisingly, 'Brando passed on this very early script and Cammell wrote a new version titled, "The Performers".'[31] At this point Lieberson approached his Hollywood friend Ken Hyman who had just been appointed head of production for Warner Bros. (now under the control of father Elliott Hyman's Seven Arts media corporation). Warners were very keen to back a project starring Mick Jagger, though he was untried as a screen performer.[32] But Lieberson had never produced a film either, any more than Cammell had directed one. Key to the project, therefore, was securing the experienced actor James Fox and the highly respected cinematographer Nic Roeg, though as MacCabe observes, 'In a pattern which repeats itself time and time again, it is probable that Roeg's most important qualification was that he knew Cammell socially'.[33] A budget of £400,000 was agreed for an eleven-week shoot, entirely on location, beginning in July 1968.

As it was, the project is remarkable in that such a scratch ensemble (at worst inexperienced, at best variously talented) were accorded such collaborative creative freedom. But, as with *The Rocky Horror Picture Show*, what is instructive here is how both industrial and cultural factors determine such unusual production conditions and how these mark the finished film itself. In the case of *Performance*, the conditions were reputedly more unusual than most.

The Production of the Text

Extremely thorough readings of the film have been provided by John Izod and by Scott Salwolke in their surveys of the work of Nicolas Roeg, in addition to the views offered by Colin MacCabe, Jon Savage and Peter Wollen.[34] Much has been made of the literary influences of Genet and Artaud, Borges, Burroughs and Hesse. Self-exploration, performance, (sexual) identity and image are clearly central preoccupations of the work. Such issues are elaborated in the studied deployment of costume and disguise and of mirrors and reflections. MacCabe concludes the film has as much to do with the magic of Aleister Crowley and the Kenneth Anger of *Scorpio Rising* (1964) as it does with personal liberation and the politics of '68.[35] And the underground's association with the occult is an interesting line of enquiry which will be pursued later.[36] But I want to concentrate here upon three aspects of the production which demonstrably had a decisive effect upon the look of the film as we know it. Firstly, the use of real locations, secondly, the employment of non-professional actors, and thirdly, the editing process. Each of these, I shall argue, contributes to a visual style and narrative structure which lend this film cult appeal.

Let us start, as MacCabe does, with the matter of genre. *Performance*'s deployment of the conventions of the gangster film (in the first half of the narrative) is highly unconventional, so much so that we might ask here, as with other cult films, whether attitudes to genre codes are not rather a point of departure, a creative springboard to launching something quite new. It may be, as I proposed earlier, that cult films, while never eschewing popular generic tropes entirely, adopt a more oblique attitude to their formulae. One could argue, indeed, that *Performance* owes as much to French New Wave treatments of the gangster film as it does to British crime precursors. And the reasons for this are bound up with the conspicuous documentary traits of *cinéma-vérité*: location shooting, the casting of non-professional actors and fast-paced editing. However, these techniques eschew the French legacy of American *film noir*; here they are applied to a very real and highly topical London underworld.

MacCabe documents this influence astutely. He recounts the 'high noon' of the celebrity Kray twins, and their infiltration of bohemian circles just prior to their arrest in 1968. Then there are the contributions to Cammell's script of the shady David Litvinoff, with whom the screenwriter shared a Chelsea flat on his return from Paris in 1967. Next, the rigorous 'method' training of the aristocratic James Fox in the Elephant and Castle pubs frequented by 'chaps' from 'the firm', and the casting of boxing trainer, print worker and friend of the mob Johnny Shannon as the film's gang boss Harry Flowers.[37] Additionally, David Cammell's thorough location scout yielded a brazen view of London, by turns run-down and tarted- or tooled-up, alighting at last upon the dilapidated former gambling club in Lowndes Square for Turner's Powis Square, Notting Hill retreat.

As MacCabe suggests:

> This authenticity is not however an end in itself but the raw material from which the film is then fashioned. If that raw material is produced from a studio in which actors and technicians take their *accustomed and easy physical and social places* then the material has not enough interest to warrant further work. It is the interaction of people and place on location which allows a spark of life to pass on to celluloid. [my italics][38]

This is useful. Firstly, it stresses that authenticity is the basis of authorship rather than merely the grounds for greater realism. Secondly, it contrasts such dynamic methods with the hidebound, workaday processes of studio filming which comprise the artifice of realism. But I would want to go further and suggest that the way in which these methods 'pass on to celluloid' also communicates a different kind of experience to the viewer, because it challenges the very notion of screen representation itself. For example, paradoxically, non-professional and therefore more naturalistic acting styles tend to militate against that psychological motivation which is the driving force of classical narrative realism.

An instance of this at work is the contrasting way in which facial close-ups of Fox's Chas in the first half of the film emphasise his poise and power in the steadiness of his gaze and eyeline matches when compared (ironically) with the amateur Johnny Shannon's Harry Flowers who 'talks the talk' but whose gaze patterns are distracted, thus dissipating his control. In the later, Powis Square interiors however, there are relatively few facial close-ups and those tend to be oblique and inscrutable. The power relations and visual organisation in the patterns of gaze within the mise-en-scène are key indicators of the relative stability of the fictional world, conveying to a viewer something of its ideological unity or, in this case, dissolution. Broader issues about representation, role-play and the veracity of the image are at the centre of *Performance*.

In a late interview Donald Cammell credited Anita Pallenberg with much of the inspiration for the second part of the film.[39] It was, in particular, her ability as an actor to totally be herself on screen (rather than playing a part called Pherber) and the effect this had on others (especially James Fox). Fox told Colin MacCabe that she taunted him on set for being too 'straight', a conflict which comes across clearly on screen.[40] And her experience of working in the experimental tradition of Artaud's Theatre of Cruelty clearly brought an emotional intensity to her performance.[41] James

Fox suffered incredibly from the experience of the film, leading him to withdraw from acting during the 1970s in pursuit of personal spirituality.[42]

Fox's 'professional' willingness to succumb to the experiment of *Performance* was, ironically, quite at odds with Jagger's 'amateur' reluctance to play the part of Turner, based as it so clearly was on the demise of Brian Jones. Cammell reflected in interview that Jagger

> was a little unenthusiastic about the essential part of that character. He was a little scared of it because it was about a guy who had gone over the top and taken a great fall. And Mick, you know, emotionally likes to take a very dominant view of things and it was a bit risky. I think the fact he did it made for it being a very good performance.[43]

Jagger's equivocation, between being himself and playing the part, between the personal charisma and iconic signification he brings (from his rock star image) to the performance, and the vulnerability and ordinariness visible through his untrained technique, is an interesting tension at the heart of this film. Of course it accounts perfectly for the nihilistic demise of the reclusive Turner which satisfies the narrative motivation, but it does more than this. It opens up the traditionally hermeneutic nature of screen stardom to a much more fluid, less deterministic, emotional register. Rather than star signification being reduced to a shorthand frame of reference, here it presents a diffuse, inscrutable range of meanings, and a more malleable structure of feeling. The result is a powerful, charismatic quality which engages the viewer on a new kind of emotional level. Trained screen actors develop a professional relationship with the camera which enables them to maintain a certain level of control, through experience, over how they present themselves. Amateurs don't have such control, even when they are performers used to being on stage and communicating through music with a large audience.

It is worth developing these ideas about the nature of representation and performance further. The testimonies of Cammell and Jagger are evidence enough that the second half of the film-making experience was more than just a shoot. It was a (largely unscripted) event or, in the parlance of the day, a 'happening' in its own right. As MacCabe suggests, 'It is not the sex and drugs which were the real scandal on the set of *Performance*; it was the fact that the performance of the actors ceased to be the representation of a text and became instead the acting out of their fundamental relationships'.[44]

Such circumstances demand both more and less than professional experience can supply. They demand a certainly level of intimacy, but above all absolute trust. What can result is a kind of unbridled charisma, a deeply human vulnerability which is gradually exposed from the intensity of the struggle for power. Here there is slippage or redundancy between the performed and the real, the intended and the unwitting, which brings the unconscious drives to the surface of the text. There is an excess of uncontrolled signification in both physical and oral utterance. At one level, indeed, the experience is an assault upon the 'professionalism' of Fox's Chas, a stripping away of his theatrical veneer. This is unaccommodated man, pared down to what Philip Auslander calls the body's irreducibly 'originary presence'.[45]

For the viewer this is unnerving, because it communicates in a different way. Firstly, it acknowledges itself as performance, which has the effect of making an audience self-conscious. Secondly, it invites emotional identification: the performances implicate us in their emotional display. It is because of the rawness of its improvised performance style that the characters communicate so directly, so accessibly to the viewer, despite the disorientation of the complex editing style. It is the complicated history of the film's post-production to which I shall turn attention next.

Warner Bros. refused to release the film as it was, insisting on a re-edit and shifting post-production to Los Angeles (as a way of burying it completely, presumably).[46] As MacCabe relates, the film's authorial team began to fragment: Roeg to shoot *Walkabout* on location in Australia and Lieberson to work on the abortive *Mary, Queen of Scots* with Alexander Mackendrick. They travelled briefly with Cammell to LA and 'agreed the principles of a new edit but Roeg and Lieberson then left for their new projects'.[47]

The first studio editor assigned to *Performance* was 'totally unsym-pathetic' but post-production supervisor Rudy Fehr then brought in Frank Mazzola, a hugely experienced editor who agreed to take on the project. He and Cammell then set about editing the material down, considerably shortening the first half so as to introduce Jagger more quickly into the equation and reduce the early sex and violence through a process of rigorous, sometimes dizzying montage. Finally, Jack Nitzsche's experimental soundtrack, with its showcase Jagger numbers and its unnerving electronic pulses, completed the new edit. However, Lieberson and Roeg were apparently unhappy with the results. Lieberson preferred the original London cut and Roeg had to be 'persuaded by Cammell not to take his name off the picture'.[48] By this time, autumn 1969, Warner-Seven Arts had been taken over by Kinney National Services and the new studio head, John Calley, agreed to release the Cammell/Mazzola cut, but not before 'Warner's president Ted Ashley saw the film and was so appalled that he ordered fresh cuts'. [49] This was the version finally released in the USA in August 1970.

It is worth pursuing these post-production shenanigans in all the detail afforded by the work of Walker and of MacCabe, because they illustrate not only the ongoing battle with the American financiers and the studio's role in shaping the film as we know it, but the way in which other creative interventions (specifically Mazzola's editing and Nitszche's soundtrack) added final but decisive dimensions to the project. Firstly, Warner Bros.' changes of ownership (following the retirement of Jack Warner in 1967) reflects a not uncommon diversification and corporatisation of American film interests from the late Sixties onwards amidst economic fluctuations and the ongoing decline in cinema attendance. *Variety* had called Seven Arts 'an "outsider" that had no glamorous traditions and was just a "conduit for material to the tiny screen"'.[50] But Kinney Services, Inc. who bought the company from Seven Arts for $400 million were a real estate and finance business, with interests 'primarily in car rental, parking lots, construction and funeral homes'.[51] By 1972, the corporation had been rebranded Warner Communications with the acquisition of a cable communications division.[52] Amusingly, 'merger' is a key word in the film itself. *Performance* was the unlikely, but fortunate, beneficiary of these corporate changes.

Secondly, Mazzola's signature is, perhaps ironically, the rapid intercutting and (seemingly) random analytical editing which is very much associated with the later narrative manner of Nicolas Roeg's own films. But the combination of Roeg's studied close-ups and Mazzola's acute positioning of those shots constitutes much of the film's distinctive visual style. This not only reinforces symbolic juxtapositions and parallels across the two phases of the film (the black Rolls-Royce at the beginning and the white one at the end is perhaps the most obvious of many examples), but creates that sense of dissonance and disorientation, a certain roughness in texture, which typifies the viewing experience of *Performance*. Jack Nitzsche's soundtrack echoes this visual dissonance perfectly, the innovatory use of synthesiser creating eerie electronic heartbeats and jarring discordances.

FIGURE 5: Anita Pallenberg, James Fox and Mick Jagger
in *Performance* – the *ménage à trois* becomes a game of charades
[WARNER BROS./THE KOBAL COLLECTION]

Semiotic theory provides a useful structural model for explaining this textual unevenness. The effects of this method might be seen as freeing objects from their purely symbolic place within the signifying system and according them a greater, if less definable, power. In chapter one I referred to this phenomenon as hypersignification. It may be that cult films manifest a different attitude to the world of physical objects and their arrangement, which enhances their fetishistic potency at the same time as it denies their secure position in the material world of concrete representation. Such an effect – in the manner of Dada, Surrealism and some pop art – is both stimulating and disturbing. It is liberating in that it allows us free psychic and emotional access to the world of representation which realism frequently restricts. It is disturbing because it brings to the surface currents of feeling that might otherwise remain in check and reveals to us, as it does to Chas, a self we might rather not acknowledge. I suggested earlier that the events of 1968 represented a revolt of the world of ideas against the world of objects; if *Performance* can be seen as a microcosmic rehearsal of those events then its process is to free objects from their ideologically determined signifying practices.

Cult Status

If historically *Performance* can be considered Janus-faced, so textually it is a turbulent watershed: a film of dissonance and discord, of an abrasive texture which is new in popular cinema at this time. Part of this is due, as I have suggested above, to the authenticity of locations and non-professional actors and especially to issues of performance. A 'performer', in the gangland parlance on which the film draws heavily, is a rough case. This certain roughness is also attributable to the film's remarkable camerawork and editing process. Moreover, it is also a feature associated with Romanticism both in texture and treatment. It might be contrasted usefully with the smooth finish, the patina of refined Classicism.

When we see inside Chas's underwear drawer after his opening S & M session with Dana (Ann Sidney), everything is ordered, folded neatly in its place. His apartment is a model of the latest clean lines and smooth surfaces. The glamour of the gangland world is about the clinical exercise of restraint and controlled force: from protection rackets, strip clubs and pornographic films to the 'rules' of sado-masochistic sex. Chas is first 'messed up' at the hands of (former lover?) Joey Maddocks (Anthony Valentine). From thereon, objects become displaced, and the Powis Square experience is a messy one of matter out of place. Turner's dark, semi-derelict mansion is the antithesis of Chas's modern flat. 'It's a right piss-hole, mate,' he says to his cousin Tony (Kenneth Colley) on the phone: 'Long hair, beatniks, druggers, free love, foreigners . . . you name it.' Chas's life (like his head) becomes literally messed up.

David Trotter is not the first to recognise that messes in works of fiction (as in life) can occupy psychologically ambivalent positions. Crucially, 'their meaning and value depends on other people's agreement not to clear them away':

> The untidy bedroom and the untidy office balance us between illusion and disillusionment: the objects we cram into them are made meaningful and valuable by the cramming, but not to the extent that they cannot be carelessly dumped and strewn.[53]

The signification of order in Chas's apartment is far less complex than the charged, allusive, totemic disorder of 81 Powis Square, in a film where objects stand both for what they are and their imaginative associations.[54] Yet, as William Ian Miller observes, 'Social and cognitive structures create dirt less by assigning something to play that role than as a consequence of categorisation itself'.[55] Thus, it is only because they are aware of order that their own chaos is made manifest. This is doubly true of Chas Devlin's descent: his readiness to embrace mess and disorder is as a freefall plummet from the particular standards of his own, pristine lifestyle.

The case of *Performance* exemplifies usefully a distinction between waste and mess which Trotter establishes. Waste is symptomatic, it implies a system; it is the by-product of what is useful, necessary. 'Waste-matter, unlike mess, is an effect which can be traced back to its cause. It bears the perceptible imprint of human agency, of human purpose, of system'. Mess, on the other hand, 'is waste which has not yet become, and may never become, either symptom or symbol'.[56] Here is the distinction between the governed world of Chas and the anarchic world of Turner. It is a distinction redolent of the revolt of Romanticism against the rational order. Another way of conceptualising the struggle between the world of objects and the world of ideas is in terms of the tension between Classicism and Romanticism. It may well be the case that such profound cultural antagonisms resurface at times of acute social and political crisis like 1968.

The film transforms one kind of heroism (Chas's violent, Nietzschean will-to-power) into another (Turner's Dionysian will-to-destruct). It transposes one Romantic hero (the glamorous, fast-living gangster who eclipses the slum degradation of his origins) into another (the iconic, hedonistic, burnt-out rock star). The trace themes of displacement, incongruity, disorder and the (im)possibility of escape are residual elements in *Performance*.

'The essence of a total performance,' in Cammell's words, 'is that the playing of a role becomes a transference of identity – a kind of "possession"'. The film's recurrent leitmotif for that transference is penetration.

> TURNER: I want to go in there, Chas. You see the blood of this
>   vegetable is boring a hole. This second hole is penetrating
>   the hole in your face. The skull of your bone. I just want
>   to get right in there. Do you know what I mean? . . . And
>   root around there like mandragora . . .[57]

CHAS: I said no. You're sick . . . You, you, you degenerate! You're perverted![58]

From the violent sex Chas metes out to Dana at the beginning of the film, through the shot he fires into Joey Maddocks, the narrative concludes with a single bullet (the ultimate penetration) which dissolves Chas's identity into that of Turner. Liberating sex is posited (*pace* Bataille) as a death of the self and a rebirth, redolent not only of the transcendent mantras of the counter-culture and the polemics of Herbert Marcuse but, moreover, rooted in the spirit of Romanticism.[59] Jon Savage sees the ending of *Performance* with the liberating fusion through death of Chas and Turner as 'satisfying and curiously hopeful'.[60] Yet the final denouement, in keeping with the moral ambiguity of the film, also posits a darker fate: the violent destruction of the radical but jaded dream that was the counter-culture. Harry's Rolls into which Chas/Turner climbs also symbolises the hegemonic ability of capitalism to absorb, repackage and neutralise dissent.

Politically 1968 was a watershed and *Performance* internalises within its own radical structure the twin potentialities of liberation and destruction, of radicalism and conformity. By the film's release in 1970, with the war in Vietnam more entrenched than ever, the darkness of *Performance* overshadowed its light. Perhaps its most celebrated line encapsulates the problematics of personal identity in the context of the political: 'The only performance that makes it, that really makes it, that makes it all the way, is the one that achieves madness. Right?'[61] Herein lies the Nietzschean fable in all its portentous glory.

Summary

Colin MacCabe wonders if *Performance* will remain 'a historical footnote, a cult film for *soixante-huitards*'.[62] I think not. I suggested in chapter one that nostalgia might also be one of the key words in the constitution of cultism. I suspect that for a generation who don't remember 1968 but who identify with its alternative portrait of radical transgression it has (alongside its US counterpart *Easy Rider* [1969] perhaps) become a touchstone. All of the contributors to the Yahoo *Performance* newsgroup who declared their ages appear to be firmly in the 18–30 range.[63] Today it could be considered postmodern in another, political sense – not in the vocabulary of Baudrillard or Lyotard, nor the attitudes of parody and camp, but as Fredric Jameson posits, as a textual ground for utopian political fantasies resurrected from the Romantic crisis it documents.[64] In this regard the following series of postings from the *Performance* internet newsgroup may be instructive:

> Greetings. I have just spent most of the past month with a nightly binge of "Performance," and feeling the need to communicate with any fellow fans of this awesome film who might be out there, I have joined this group. Hello.—
>
> * * *
>
> In *Performance_Movie1@yahoogroups.com, mygothicka@a* . . . wrote:
>   Wow, they have dubbed voices? I never knew that they dubbed
> Performance, unlike Barbarella·. . .
>
> * * *
>
> It's true, Harry Flowers, Moody and little Lorraine all have very thick cockney accents. The original american release dubbed them with weak voices not created by the actors.
>   I saw a european, X rated, cut of this film at an arthouse theater in boston back in 1976 that was the most complete version I have seen. I distinctly recall the following differences between that cut (rated X) and the current one (rated R);
>   (i) More intercuts of Chas being whipped in the opening of the film by Ann Sidney. The tables are then turned, and Ann Sidney is also shown being whipped in the intercuts. Also, most importantly, The song "Gone dead train" was from a different take in the X rated version of the movie, sounding closer to the take on the LP and now available on CD. The pulses of the song "Performance" then start;
>   Merry Clayton starts to wail and then fades out.
>   (ii) During the court scenes, flash cuts to a party for Harry Flowers with his "gang" in the nude singing and dancing except for Chas. More flash cuts

with Chas on his rounds, forcing someone out of frame, to say he is a "poof" under threat of knife (Joey Maddox or his father?).

(iii) More flash cuts of that "pervert" Harry Flowers in his bedroom with the "gang", when Joey Maddox is cleaning up his destroyed betting parlor and refers to him as above.

(iv) During Chas' violent beating there were flash cuts to him whipping Ann Sidney and to Ann Sidney whipping him. When remembering the past, and watching the current version on VHS tape this past weekend (my fourth time), there is also an aspect to the story line I have never noticed before . . . During the scene of Chas' beating, after he has shot Joey and the camera cuts to Chas who looks disoriented, it then cuts to Joey's hoodlum friend who had been kicked into the bathtub and knocked unconscious by Chas.

He has now been revived by the sound of the gun and by the water from the shower falling on him; he is standing in the corner of the shower and appears terrified as he looks at the mirror over the sink to see the half dressed man in the bathroom doorway holding a gun pointed at Joey who is stumbling at Chas' feet out in the room.

The camera then cuts to this hood's POV and we see the reflection of the back of a long haired man with his arms outstretched holding the gun, and one can clearly see, framed by the doorway and the man holding the gun, the overturned lamps on either side of the bed out in the room. This man is not Chas, but is in fact, Turner!!!!! This shot is then zoomed very quickly, before cutting back to Joey on his knees.

I always thought this was a "flash forward" to Turners bedroom, but on replaying the VHS it is clearly taking place in Chas' ruined bedroom !!!! At no other time does the film present another individuals POV of Chas looking like Mick Jagger other than at the end. Perhaps this is Cammel's

way of showing that Chas perceives his appearance
as that of James Fox, but in reality, physically
resembles Mick Jagger/Turner.

(v) The overall soundtrack in the X version was
much more crisp than the current R version and
the actors all have their original thick cockney
accents.

The current 105m version is a re-edited cut from
the X version that was 111 minutes long. Warner
edited the above scenes out for cable showings in
the early 80's, and had released 105m film versions
at this time. They also produced a heavily edited
version for HBO/cinemax in 1981 that ran only 98
minutes

***

Thanks for your reply – it's very interesting!
When I first saw it, in the early 70's on South St.
(where all the hippies meet!) in Philly, it had the
scene of Mick holding the gun in Chas apartment.
That, & the arm spray painting during Chas' hair
dye job. Not many people knew what scene I was
talking about!

I am surprised that there's no scenes added of
Anita, Mick & James, from the second half,which
is what I was always hoping for . . . but thanks
for the info! Btw, my friend, who is a professor
in the UK, is currently writing another book on
Performance, which should be interesting! Here's to
merry old England! Micki

***

Anita was so pretty in Performance. Wonder what
happened to the other girl. Michelle Breton. I
heard she died. Then I heard she was alive. I heard
she was an opium dealer in Pakistan. Crazy rumors!

***

I have heard all the same things, but I don't think
she is dead – I think Marianne Faithfull stated
that rumor somehere, maybe her book. But Michelle
was so traumatized, she never made a nother movie.

```
But she's still around . . . somewhere . . .
Micki
```

★★★

```
Let's just say, Mick was at his best between 68 &
75 - w/ the dark, long hair, make up - he was so
gorgeous! But, everybody ages. I think Steven Tyler
is holding out very well. And he's not much younger
than Mick, & they're both the same type. Maybe it
is the longer hair?
```

★★★

```
Yes, Mademoiselle Pallenberg - a new site which
ripped off Rollinggirl's Anita pix, & mine. The Per-
formance pix wre given to me by a friend writing
a book on Performance - he sent me those fotos and
an excerpt. A rival Anita group manager somehow got
hold of them, & created that French site using a net
translater. Anyway, it was spitefully done - I have
a private group. If anyone wants any fotos,for their
own use, all they have to do is ask me, but I made
it clear that those were "special", rare unpub-
lished fotos, & we were lucky to have them. . Also,
they could have atleast given due credit, so the
gentleman who sent them to me does not think I
profitted from them in any way. I'm mad because it
was done in a sneaky, nasty way ... I have to be
more careful - there's some real predatory jerks out
there ... just wanted to let you know ... luv, Micki
```

For cult fans everywhere, *Performance* keeps alive the Romantic vision of transcendent possibility. However, as we can observe from the examples above, that spirit of nostalgia is also tempered with critical exegeses which are fixated on detailed observation, and interpersonal wranglings between fans who are notably protective of their precious memorabilia. But above all *Performance* seems to afford, as perhaps all cult films do, the possibilities of transgression at a safe distance, through vicarious identification with its rough narrative world and its charismatic central performances. In this way, it is worth speculating that cult films in their excesses and incongruities allow us to confront and contest the borderlines between our own fears and desires at one remove. This is an argument that I shall consider in more detail in the next chapter.

CASE STUDY 1:

Get Carter (1971)

Two notable British gangster films were released within a few months of one another in 1971: *Get Carter* (Mike Hodges) and *Villain* (Michael Tuchner). One is a cult film, the other isn't. Why?

Steve Chibnall highlights the *Get Carter* Appreciation Society which 'marked the thirtieth anniversary of the film's location shooting by re-enacting various scenes in Newcastle and Gateshead on 28 July 2000'.[65] He also refers to several dedicated fan websites including those run by Mark Dear and Michael Brady.[66] The Owen Luder-designed multi-storey car park in Gateshead – which features in one of the film's most memorable scenes – made the national news when it was closed for demolition in 2008 after a 'stay of execution' attributable to its iconic part in the film.[67] As with *The Wicker Man*, *Get Carter* has its location tour, and also gained the dubious honour of a Hollywood remake starring Sylvester Stallone (Stephen Kay, 2000). To be sure, there is ample evidence of the film's cult status; but none of this explains why.

Get Carter is a revenge thriller based upon a mythic structure. In substituting Tyneside for the Humberside setting of Ted Lewis's hard-boiled source novel, *Jack's Return Home*, producer Michael Klinger and first-time director Hodges recognised that Newcastle provided the perfect backdrop: a cityscape where old-world values (and Victorian slum poverty) persisted cheek-by-jowl with 1960s urban planning, and where the boundaries between local enterprise and criminal activity could be conveniently blurred.

Chibnall claims that Michael Caine, as Carter, 'saw his performance as an ethnographic exploration of the moral beliefs and social mores that underlie the gangster's presentation of self'.[68] Yet Hodges was 'surprised and frightened' to discover that audiences 'actually liked him'. As a man 'incapable of forming relationships', he is a sympathetic anti-hero for the 'outsider' that is inside every cult fan.[69]

Music is frequently important in cult film texts, and here *Get Carter* is no exception. Roy Budd's jazz score employs the repeated motif with spine-chilling harpsichord and hypnotic bass riff to anchor what is arguably one of the most iconic thriller soundtracks since Bernard Herrmann's work on Hitchcock's *Psycho* (1960).

But perhaps the overriding quality which has gained *Get Carter* cult appeal is the self-effacing manner in which its apparently straightforward narrative, without sub-plots or flashbacks, yields deeper secrets on repeat viewing. Leavened by black humour (often relying on juxtaposition in montage, or incongruity in mise-en-scène), video release has enabled its complexities to be appreciated more fully. 'I have always been obsessed by the detail in pictures,' Hodges admits – an obsession every cult fan shares.[70]

Finally, *Get Carter's* journey from cult to classic has been lovingly documented in the pages of 1990s 'new lads' magazines (especially *Loaded* where it was serialised as a strip cartoon), reassuring their readers that it is permissible for the post-Tarantino generation, weaned on *Trainspotting* (1996) and *Lock, Stock and Two Smoking Barrels* (1998), to enjoy nostalgic rehearsals of unreconstructed machismo that cult films of the 1970s offer.

FIGURE 6: 'Is there a Mr Carter in the house?'
Michael Caine's Jack Carter returns home
[MGM/THE KOBAL COLLECTION]

3

A CLOCKWORK ORANGE (1971)

Introduction

So far I have adopted a pragmatic approach to a broadly Marxist base/superstructure analysis of British cult films in the context of their production histories. That is, I have tried to account for the rise of this distinctive kind of film text in material terms (drawing on observations about British society in the late 1960s and early 1970s as well as evidence about the state of the film industry at that time). But I have also suggested that such a materially grounded account cannot on its own explain the distinctive nature of these films nor their special appeal for subsequent generations of fans. And I have flagged up some diverse epistemologies (both academic and vernacular) which might help to illuminate the power of such films; more of those later. However, it is equally important not to lose sight of what can be offered by the conventional methodologies of film analysis. With this in mind, I have already considered the relevance of generic and narrative analyses, establishing how cult films seem to manifest aberrant attitudes in both cases. Additionally, some of the existing literature in the field (both academic and popular) stresses the significance of the figure of the cult auteur. For our purposes, at first sight at least, Stanley Kubrick might appear to fit the bill. However, following Timothy Corrigan's assertion that 'no film [. . .] is naturally a cult film; all cult films are adopted children', we need to think more carefully about the issue of authorship.[1] *A Clockwork Orange* provides a useful illustration.

To begin with, it is instructive to consider the contributions made to an internet site entitled 'Clockwork – A Fanlisting'.[2] Amongst the general veneration in which *A Clockwork Orange* is collectively held, it seems strange that relatively little regard is given to Stanley Kubrick; indeed, Anthony Burgess as the original author of Nadsat is more widely celebrated. Topics in order of importance (by number of references) are as follows:

```
The 'message' – 43 (f=24, m=19)
The language (Nadsat) – 42 (f=30, m=12)
The appeal of Alex – 24 (f=16, m=8)
Visual style (including art direction) – 16 (f=11, m=5)
Violence – 13 (f=10, m=3)
Music (especially Beethoven) – 6 (f=6)
```

Notable in this breakdown is the relatively high proportion of female contributors, many of whom mention having read the novel and for whom the appeal of Malcolm McDowell's eponymous hero Alex is especially strong. Typical among these tributes is the following: 'Alex's ability to distinguish right from wrong is just unorthodox. He is my role model'.

The first category is worth drawing attention to in passing. Not only does it represent statistically the closest relationship between male and female preferences, but it also covers a variety of different responses to both book and film. The film garners praise of the highest order from many quarters, such as:

> The imagery, the irony, the evilness, the contradictions, the entire mood and visuals represented in this entire film is something I tried to incorporate into my current website and life (LABYRINTH) – it's what inspires me, the eccentric, the strange . . . the utterly brilliant.

But equally there are several positive comments about the novel: 'The uniqueness and different setting of it. It's not just your daily book with the same plots and everything'. And again attention is drawn to: 'The rarity of a philosophical novel that was intended to be that way'.

This brief example of fan appreciation shows that factors beyond film authorship are often more important indicators of cult status, as is also true of a more recent example of cult literary adaptation, *Trainspotting*. I shall deal with a number of the topics raised by fans here in the course of my reading of *A Clockwork Orange*. But first and foremost, as before, we need to establish the diversity of the film's creative origins by charting its production history, thereafter considering more fully the matter of agency.

Production history

Controversy attended the publication of Burgess' futuristic, Orwellian satire long before a film adaptation was considered. 'My literary agent was even dubious about submitting it to a publisher, alleging that its pornography of violence would be certain to make it unacceptable', the author later remarked.[3] William Heinemann did however publish the book in London in 1962 in a version which Burgess considered definitive. Though the novel sold badly (only three thousand copies in the first year) it created a critical frisson. This was as much for its Joycean linguistic invention and aesthetic shape as for its subject matter. The first chapter was dramatised by the BBC alongside a Burgess interview on the *Tonight* programme. Later the same year W.W. Norton and Co. issued an American edition which, with only grudging consent from the impoverished author, cut the final chapter (in which Alex is reintegrated into society upon coming of age) and added what Burgess considered to be a totally superfluous glossary of Nadsat (the gang-speak in which the book is written). The book itself 'attained a certain cult popularity, especially among disaffected American youth, who were chiefly taken with the book's language'.[4] And 'in 1965, scenarist Ronald Tavel of Andy Warhol's "Factory" adapted Burgess's novella as the film *Vinyl*' which, according to critic J. Hoberman evoked 'only the bare bones of the book'.[5] Obscure and 'often indecipherable' as Warhol's version may have been, the American reception, treatment and underground positioning of the story laid the foundations of its future appeal.[6] By the mid-1960s the possibilities of a feature film treatment were also being considered in England.

In 1966, Terry Southern, Kubrick's screenwriter and collaborator on *Dr. Strangelove* (1964), sent the director a copy of Burgess's book. Kubrick, then preoccupied with work on *2001: A Space Odyssey* (1968), didn't have time to read it, but Southern remained keen. He bought a six-month option on the rights, roughed out a treatment and sent it to David Puttnam. Puttnam put the idea to the BBFC and approached Ken Russell to direct, but his submission to the Board was returned unopened and the project collapsed.[7] Meanwhile, Sandy Lieberson (who would go on to produce Cammell and Roeg's *Performance*) was attracted to the book by Michael Cooper, the photographer who had worked on Peter Blake's design for The Beatles' *Sergeant Pepper* (1967) album cover.[8] According to James Robertson, London International sent a screenplay written in the names of Terry Southern and Michael Cooper to the BBFC in May 1967. Audrey Field's report acknowledged that 'this script does of course contain a moral message' but that 'it presents an insuperable obstacle'.[9] Southern let his option drop and it was picked up cheaply by his lawyer Si Litvinoff and business partner Max Raab. Lieberson approached Litvinoff proposing Cooper as director, sketching out a Soho setting and envisaging his own clients Mick Jagger and the Rolling Stones as Alex and his droogs.[10] Litvinoff asked David Hemmings to star and John Schlesinger to direct and he also sounded out John Trevelyan at the Board, but he endorsed the earlier report and informed the would-be producer that 'toning down the violence would be unlikely to change his mind'.[11] Kubrick, having in the meantime read the book and realised 'it might make a great film', bought the rights from Litvinoff and Raab, who secured the interest of Warner Bros. (who were producing *Performance*) to the tune of $200,000 with a lucrative 5 per cent profit clause. Southern again offered his screenwriting services to Kubrick (as did Burgess himself), but the director decided, for the first time, to develop the project alone.[12] He employed as his source the American edition of the story, thus eschewing Burgess's original (humanist) ending, and began experimenting with screenplay layout, completing a first draft by 15 May 1970.[13] According to John Baxter, the director was 'a good four months into work on the film when he found out the author had intended a radically different ending. But Kubrick, the auteur, brusquely dismissed it as "completely out of tone with the rest of the book" and carried on regardless'.[14]

The genesis of this project reveals by now characteristic strands in the emergence of what would later become cult films of the period. One is the roll-call of familiar names in the intimate coterie – the new 'Chelsea set' – of artists, film-makers, dilettantes, fashion people, actors, musicians, advertising executives, entrepreneurs, pornographers, PR agents, and underworld criminals who controlled and produced the cutting-edge cinema of this brief era. Secondly, we must note once again the (substantial if short-lived) financial commitment of Warner Bros. to radical British film-making at this time. Thirdly, it will be necessary to consider the impact of personnel changes within the British Board of Film Censorship crucial

FIGURE 7: 'Viddy well . . .': the voyeuristic vaudeville violence of
A Clockwork Orange
[WARNER BROS/THE KOBAL COLLECTION]

to the green-lighting of the film. And finally, the creative potentiality of that filmic moment – in which *A Clockwork Orange* was almost *bound* to be filmed by *someone* – must be measured against the long gestation of Burgess's concept.

The writer's story had originated following an assault on his pregnant wife by a group of American GIs in London in 1944, became grounded in the popular culture of the late Fifties' Teds and milk bars, was fuelled by the first confrontations of Mods and Rockers in Brighton at the beginning of the new decade, and linguistically inspired by a visit to Russia in 1961. One reason for the text's longevity of course is its futuristic projection (to an early 1970s setting), but another is the way in which its themes of youth subculture, urban violence, social disintegration, state bureaucracy and moral decay are made timeless through artifice. I shall be examining the picaresque qualities of the film – derived faithfully from its source – in due course. Suffice to say here that it presents contradictions which remain unresolved.

On the one hand, the artifice of both novel and film radically denies violence the mitigation of particularised circumstance. In other words, there is no attempt to justify it on the grounds of social realism. Rather, the work forces us to confront violence through its stylised representation and to deal with the problems as entertainment that entails. As we shall see in the next chapter, this *double articulation* of response to the text appears to be a recurrent and problematic dialectic in cult films. In Kubrick's narrative the viewer is implicated in Alex's violence, drawn into the subjective fantasies of his vivid imagination. On the other hand, it charts with uncanny perception the way in which the bourgeois radicalism and liberalisation of 1968 had begun by the 1970s to permeate working-class culture, with potentially more dangerous effects and the palpable threat of an establishment backlash. Kubrick's film, for all its stylisation, was prescient in the way it rendered the visceral impact of that shift.

Visual Style

Whatever the merits or otherwise of Kubrick's bleak treatment of his source material, the film is indisputably as conspicuously designed and architecturally achieved as Burgess's book.[15] This attention both to detail and to overarching concept, celebrated throughout Kubrick's oeuvre, is nowhere more apparent than here, as several critics have divined. '*A Clockwork Orange* contains one of the most highly determined theatrical spaces in contemporary film', writes Mario Falsetto.[16] 'Kubrick's adaptation . . . is depicted in three segments . . . Each of the three sections has a distinctive colour palette and camera style . . .'[17] Falsetto goes on to elaborate the way in which parts one and three are based upon mirrored scenes, as Alex re-encounters figures (cronies and victims) from his past following his aversion therapy.

Stephen Mamber points out that in addition to these mirroring scenes which traverse the three phases drawn from the novel, the screen time devoted to the first and third sections is almost identical. Kubrick also draws heavily on Burgess's distinctive dialogue in which key phrases ('Do I make myself clear?', for example) recur in each phase.[18] Then there is the symmetry of the number two across the three sections: two days of violence, two years in prison, two weeks of 'treatment' and two days of retribution at the hands of former victims.[19] Everywhere is evidence of Kubrick's determination to render not merely the spirit or tone of the original, but that which is so often sacrificed in filmic adaptations: the artistry of the source. As Falsetto notes: 'No Kubrick film before or since has incorporated such a variety of devices, including different film speeds, visual distortions, extreme angles, varied shot sizes and others, to create a theatrical space and communicate character point of view'.[20]

Such analyses clearly cast *A Clockwork Orange* as a modernist work of considerable formal stature. Not only might it seem appropriate to invoke the idea of the auteur in this case, but moreover, Kubrick's achievement appears in its unique orchestration to avoid many of the generic pastiches and narrative incongruities that we have come to associate with cult films thus far.[21] To divine its cultish attractions we must therefore look further into its visual style and performance strategies.

'I am deeply involved in the administration, because it is in this area that many creative and artistic battles are lost', Kubrick told Alexander Walker in an interview during the film's production.[22] Walker also elicited this revelation from the director regarding the careful planning of the visual design:

> I purchased ten years of back issues of three different architectural magazines and spent two solid weeks with my art director, John Barry, turning and tearing out pages. The material was put into a special display file, manufactured by a company in Germany, called Definitiv. The system encompassed various signals, coloured, alphabetical, and numerical, which were displayed when the file was hanging in a rack. These signals allowed the material to be cross-referenced in almost an infinite number of ways.[23]

This illustration of Kubrick's working practices is instructive. His (almost obsessive) attention to detail and concern with 'administration' matters which are usually systematically devolved to the production team meant that his creative control was almost total. However, while his hand is most conspicuous in visual design, lighting, camerawork and editing, in two important relationships absolute authority was impossible. Significantly, Kubrick never supplanted Burgess as the author of *A Clockwork Orange* (and the writer's intervention was instrumental in the film's controversial reception). And, as important, the precocious performance of Malcolm McDowell also exceeded the director's ambit, as I shall outline later.

As with previous films we have looked at, *A Clockwork Orange* was shot almost entirely on location (in London and the Home Counties during the winter of 1970/1), with Kubrick's Hertfordshire home providing studio and post-production facilities. And the painstaking researching and decoration of particular buildings chosen for their architectural style is particularly important in the achievement of the film's aesthetic look. From the DeLarge apartment in the newly developed Thamesmead area of south-east London, Brunel University's Ludovico Medical Facility and an old theatre on Tagg's Island (the derelict casino), to a transformed American Drug Store in Chelsea's King's Road (the record boutique) and the futuristic property 'Skybreak' near Warren Radlett in Hertfordshire (the writer's house), each carefully chosen building is dressed to achieve a certain kind of theatrical space. But how shall we characterise those spaces?

One idea that bears consideration is the Baroque. Christopher Isherwood reminds us of camp's origins in the Baroque: 'High Camp is the whole emotional basis of the Ballet . . . and of course of Baroque art'.[24] Three elements in the film constitute what may be considered a Baroque style: the theatrical proscenium framing employed in master-shot composition; a highly choreographed, balletic physicality in performance; and a preoccupation with flamboyant pop art iconography. In addition to employing the most vulgar and kitsch icons of contemporary modernity in the decoration of these spaces (in a sort of fluorescent, comic-strip parody of the arty 'scene' of *Blow-up*), their geometric angles, smooth, impervious, plastic surfaces and pneumatic, playground scale denote interiors sterilised and insulated for the permission of adolescent 'play': Alex's flat (especially his room), the writer's house, the Korova milkbar and the record boutique. While the old casino's dereliction (faded Baroque) represents the neglect of the classical tradition (its music and art) in this brash, urban jungle, the empty shell of the Cat Lady's rococo mansion is adorned with the most conspicuously obvious kinds of erotic modern confection. Yet this pop art influence is more than a chic inflexion, or an assumed manner. It establishes a visual iconography which is both seductive and dangerous, promising plenitude yet proving to be hollow. Nowhere is this motif more conspicuous than in Liz Moore's Allen Jones-derived, white female nudes, arched into impossibly extravagant crabs for tables in the Korova Milk Bar. They are what Robert Hughes defined in a 1971 article for *Time* magazine as 'cultural objects cut loose from any power to communicate'.[25] They are eternal signifiers, full of noise yet signifying nothing; rather, stuck in the loop of endless iteration, hyper-signifying. The plastic and the spherical, with their smooth, impermeable surfaces without edge or opening, are space-age objects of a kind of infinite, sterile doom. Moreover, it is not merely a matter of choice objects carefully arranged; scale and dimension are critical too. Consider Alex (Malcolm McDowell) battering the Cat Lady (Miriam Karlin) with a giant plastic phallus or racing at impossible speed through the country night in the 'toy' sports car. Such objects have the power to distort our perceptions of reality, to loom as potent profane icons, dangerously alluring to our impressionable consciousness. It is a further instance of a radical new attitude to the world of objects liberated disarmingly from their familiar ideological constraints. And the consistent exploration of the moral line between belief and delusion is the underlying dialectic of the film and the fault-line from which violence erupts. Furthermore, it is worked not only through visual iconography but through performance style as well.

Performance

The highly stylised and systematically erogenous spaces of the film's first section are fashioned as a grotesque fantasy-scape of Alex's subjective imagination, nowhere more climactically than in the privacy of his own room: 'a womb-like cave where Alex can safely indulge his fantasies'.[26]

> We see him end his 'wonderful evening' with 'a bit of the old Ludvig Van' in a highly expressive montage sequence involving the dancing Jesus sculpture. This masturbation scene is edited with precise rhythms, with a rapid-fire series of images of the sculpture and the music stimulating Alex both sexually and verbally.[27]

The sequence also goes on to incorporate intercut shots from 'lovely pictures' inspired by the cinema, including quotations from *Cat Ballou* (1965) and *One Million Years BC* (1966). The self-reflexive culpability of cinema in the pantheon of cultural resources capable of stimulating the imagination to ultimate pleasure is echoed in the cinematic auditorium of the Ludovico centre, where the films he is forced to watch (becoming increasingly unpalatable as the 'treatment' takes effect) prompt his reflection: 'It's funny how the colours of the real world only seem really real when you viddy them on the screen'. This remark – a gift from Burgess to a filmic interpreter – anticipates the way in which *A Clockwork Orange* itself might be seen, and it is a triumph of Kubrick's visual mastery (as much as Burgess's linguistic achievement) that the work also contains its own self-conscious reading as a commentary on the vicarious pleasures of cinema.

In a very important sense also, this is a film about the cultural production of a media moral panic. Through Alex's own (retrospective) voice-over narration and the institutional forces which confront him (his parents, the social worker, police, the novelist, prison authorities, psychiatrists and politicians) we follow his 'case'. We witness with Foucauldian precision his diagnosis, treatment, recuperation and rehabilitation. We witness how dissent is neutralised in a liberal democracy. And A Clockwork Orange (like Oliver Stone's Natural Born Killers [1994] almost a quarter of a century later) is shrewdly prescient even in anticipating its own controversial reception – too clever almost for its own good. But Alex's comment is more than a pointed example of cinematic self-reflexivity; it has subjective significance too. It contains echoes of a Wildean camp aestheticism and art's ability to transcend the quotidian: literally to make the real supra-real by heightened transformation. It points to the vividness and the vibrancy of this Romantic quest to feel alive amidst the tawdriness of the ordinary. The final shot of the film, following his 'cure' is one of pure, Romantic imagination. Alex's ultimate social entrapment at the hands of the manipulative politico-media machine is simultaneously the means of his imaginative escape into triumphant sexual fantasy before an enraptured society audience. This is the final antidote to his enforced humiliation by the invited experts at the Ludovico. It is no coincidence, of course, that the desire to achieve self-realisation through identification with transcendent icons, the need to escape the institutional constraints of the everyday and the will to ecstatic sexual power, are the provinces both of teenage rites of passage and of the cinema experience itself. And it is no accident that Kubrick treats Alex's dubious, comic-book heroism with what might be termed a picaresque lightness of touch. How is this achieved?

The achievement of this sublime subjectivity depends not only on the projection of Alex's fantasy-scape into the visual design, but also on the persistent use of perceptual point-of-view shots. Falsetto shows how scenes such as the attempted suicide and the Ludovico public exhibition 'are intensely involving and operate in a heightened, hyperbolic way . . . often characterised by the use of a wide-angled lens or other distorting device . . . [by means of which] the spatial field is always connected to the character's field of vision'.[28] Other visual techniques such as slow motion or undercranking, extreme angles or square-on theatrical framing and slow zooms or tracking shots, constantly reinforce both the aestheticisation of the diegetic world and its subjective contingency. Both these aspects are underpinned by the extraordinary soundtrack, Alex's Burgessian voice-over narration and the highly choreographed physicality.

Malcolm McDowell's 'seductive charm' is rooted in the juxtaposition of Alex's verbal dexterity, his knowing eloquence and his physical poise.[29] His vulnerability itself is a coquettish mannerism drawn from his unique style vocabulary. He keeps himself clean and he knows how to behave, to say and do the right things in order to keep the world at one remove, to preserve his own creative-imaginative space, to keep his subjective world of sensation pristine. As such he is a curiously impervious and impermeable figure. His violence is meted out through the stick that is his staff of office, his sex through a strap-on codpiece or a giant work of art. He despises the 'filthy, dirty old drunkie'; Billy Boy is a 'globby bottle of cheap, stinking chip oil'. Alex's violence, like the starched white of his uniform, is clean, rehearsed, and nonchalant. Contrast this with the violence he receives at the hands of others – the broken milk bottle that gives him a bloody nose, the policemen's punches, the eye-drops, salivation and gagging of the Ludovico technique, the bloody beatings and near drowning of the turncoats Dim and Georgie. When he arrives back 'HOME' at Mr Alexander's (the surrogate father who is writing his story in 'A Clockwork Orange'), Alex is drenched and his face is besmirched with blood and mucus. He wants to keep tidy and dry in a world that is a dirty, messy place. This much speaks of his juvenile, regressive tendencies: his need for order, the pursuit of instant gratification, pleasurable self-indulgence, unease when out of uniform.

It is perhaps a tribute to the verve and élan of the opening twenty minutes that the middle section of the film, and especially the prison sequence, is the least successful part. Indeed, it might be argued that the beginning of the film creates so vividly, so enticingly, Alex's hermetically subjective world, that the realist world of police station and prison (all an invention of Kubrick which Burgess's novel glosses over) is, in its 'wearisomely complete detail', little better, as Nick James remarks, than 'Porridge . . . without Ronnie Barker to humanise the poor wit'.[30] Certainly the central longueurs serve, among other things, to offset those more memorable and iconic aspects of the film's visual world. And it is chiefly the opening sequences that fans refer back to, notwithstanding their sympathy for Alex's subsequent plight.

Yet Alex's corrective trajectory is wonderfully Foucauldian, since it is measured most graphically in the systematic disciplining of his body (see below). First, in the Prison Induction Unit, there is the surrender of personal possessions with the fastidious enumeration and documentation of every item, then the stripping of his body and the physical, oral and anal examinations. Secondly, the Ludovico medics straijacket his body and wire him into the head cage with electrodes and eye clamps that ensure he cannot avert his gaze. Later, he is abused before an invited audience. Thirdly, upon his release he is hounded and physically beaten up by many of his former acquaintances. Finally, he ends up immobilised, in plaster, in a hospital bed, at the whim of politicians and captured on the cameras of the media. What is particularly interesting in this extreme (and ultimately unsuccessful) process of socialisation is its production (and, as Foucault would remind us, the celebration) of the juvenile delinquent as a physical type. Alex's local heroism has been reproduced, first as an anonymous statistic, then as a medical case study and finally as a media celebrity. Yet all along, for an audience, his ultimate triumph has never really been in doubt. Even through his ordeals of betrayal, torture, imprisonment, correction, persecution and convalescence, the narrative voice-over 'spoken with a chirpy and engagingly familiar Midlands accent' assures us of Alex's heroic endurance.[31] Indeed, the stylisation of language, costume and physical repertoire are the key attributes by which Alex sets himself apart (even from his fellow droogs) and is transformed into an icon.

Malcolm McDowell admitted in interview that there was little preparation for the part:

> I did not know how to play Alex . . . until I arrived on the set . . . I was absolutely at a loss. I'd read the book hundreds of time. I had a script of sorts. But I just didn't know.[32]

And the actor's ignorance was compounded by the director's approach:

> Stanley's the kind of director who wants you to give him ten variations – just like that. Just at a snap of the fingers. And you do it, you know . . . You make it up, any way you can.[33]

More recently McDowell has credited his mentor Lindsay Anderson with providing him with the key to the role:

> In a very simple way he helped me enormously. He told me to play Alex like a close-up I did in *If . . .* when I smiled defiantly at the head boy as he was about to cane me. He said, 'There's a close-up of you

just looking at me and smiling. That's the way you play *Clockwork Orange*.' I never mentioned this to Kubrick.[34]

The actor in fact credited both directors for the experimental space they created on set:

They can create this atmosphere where you're not inhibited in the least. You'll do anything. Try it out . . . Lindsay and Stanley give you this degree of freedom in different ways.[35]

Kubrick's method was to use the music of Beethoven as a stimulus:

which made me go into this absolutely mad fantastic look. I got twigged on by music as the character of Alex. So the look gave him a schizophrenic feeling, as well. I was rather embarrassed about it at first, but it worked. I remember saying, 'Christ, Stanley, isn't it rather too much? I know it's fun but . . .' Yet he was sure it was right.[36]

It is not insignificant that music should have provided the stimulus to the camp excesses of McDowell's charismatic performance.

Music

The film's music is always an aesthetic, often an ironic, counterpoint to its visual flair. Music, as the most direct channel to our receptive unconscious, is crucial in all cult films (many of which are either generic musicals or contain strong musical performance elements). The early scene in the old casino, where Billy Boy's biker gang are subjected to a dose of balletic ultraviolence to the tune of Rossini's *Thieving Magpie Overture*, has its companion piece at the writer's house where the rape of his wife is accompanied by Alex's dulcet rendition of 'Singin' in the Rain', while the high-speed orgy (again a pastiche of a scene from *Blow-up*) with the two girls he picks up at the record boutique (lasting approximately forty seconds at two frames-per-second) was inspired originally by Mozart's *Eine kleine Nachtmusik*. 'As it worked out in the film,' Kubrick told Penelope Houston, 'the fast movement of [Rossini's] *William Tell* was more suitable to the purpose of the scene', and, one might add, also brings the popular cultural connotation of *The Lone Ranger*'s TV theme to a comic bedroom scene worthy of the *Benny Hill Show*.[37] What these surreal juxtapositions consistently achieve (even when anticipated on repeat viewing) is what might be termed a *trompe l'oreille* effect. The dislocation of image and sound is perhaps the most radical and disturbing technique in the repertoire of cinema. And, as the Surrealists were most conspicuously aware, it is the disruption of our cognitive sensibilities that gives rein (indeed reign) to the unconscious.

Perhaps the most distinctive original contribution to the soundtrack, however, is the (then groundbreaking) use of Moog synthesiser developed by Walter (later Wendy) Carlos and Rachel Ellkind, who had pioneered electronic versions of Bach and the choral climax of Beethoven's Ninth Symphony as well as writing original scores such as 'Timesteps' – a piece inspired by Burgess's novel. Carlos and Ellkind approached Kubrick when they learned he was filming the book and sent him recordings of their work.[38] Kubrick instantly admired their ability 'to create a sound which is not an attempt at copying the instruments of the orchestra and yet which, at the same time, achieves a beauty of its own employing electronic tonalities'.[39] The electronic score, both symbolically and emotionally, bridges the film's central juxtapositions of high art and popular culture, of the refined and the savage, the rich western tradition and austere sci-fi future, art as beauty or pure sensation. As Robert Hughes observed:

> The kind of ecstasy depends on the person who is having it. Without the slightest contradiction Nazis could weep over Wagner before stoking the crematoriums. Alex grooves on the music of 'Ludwig van' . . . which fills him with fantasies of sex and slaughter.[40]

Indeed, 'the fact that the men who ran Auschwitz . . . played Bach and Beethoven' informs not only Burgess's questioning of 'the old Leavisite notion that art humanizes', but moreover establishes that while 'music may not civilize Alex . . . it is an essential mark of his good taste and of his enemies' lack of it', viz.: Dr Brodsky at the Ludovico Medical Facility.[41]

Violence

The problematic relationship between art and violence which is at the philosophical heart of *A Clockwork Orange* has also drawn the attention of Walter Evans, who reminds us 'that Beethoven's art . . . is both profoundly violent and profoundly sexual', while Vivian Sobchak asserts that 'Art and Violence spring from the same source; they are both expressions

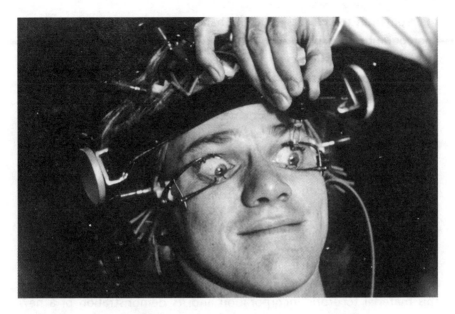

FIGURE 8: Alex (Malcolm McDowell) prepares for
the Ludovico treatment
[WARNER BROS./THE KOBAL COLLECTION]

of the individual, egotistic, vital, and non-institutionalized man'.[42] Yet perhaps to dwell upon these Romantic (and semantic) conceits is to consider the film at a theoretical remove, whereas its experience (so closely allied to Alex's own) is played out across an emotional dynamic of visual and aural sensations of a register much more closely aligned to the rituals and anarchy of comic-strip cartoons. As such, whatever the merits of its aesthetic conception and filmic realisation, it is first (and most controversially) an intensely visceral experience rendered with a picaresque lightness of touch.

The highly stylised, and therefore morally ambivalent, presentation of violence has long been the most controversial aspect of *A Clockwork Orange*. But in its most violent acts the film is also most revealing on the subject of male anxiety in respect of women. Violence against women in *A Clockwork Orange* is choreographed and cartoon-brutal. Moreover, it presents a prurient fascination for the female form as *other*. In each instance, the camera dwells upon the female body with a novice's raw mixture of abhorrence and lust. Note the way in which the gang rape of the woman in the old casino at the hands of Billy Boy's bikers is lit and choreographed as a performance on stage, exposing her full-frontal to an invisible audience (the viewer); consider also the rape of the writer's wife (Adrienne Corri) where Alex cuts breast holes in her dress with scissors – an act of misogynistic humiliation certainly, but also one of adolescent play. Similarly, when forced to demonstrate, before an invited audience of society dignitaries, the success of the Ludovico reform technique, we share Alex's prostrate view of the overwhelming breasts of the naked model looming above, tantalising, half-desirable but repugnant and beyond reach. This unresolved horror/fascination for the anatomy of female difference is the regressive trait throughout.

And this attitude is totally new in British cinema. We are not concerned here merely with the screen exposure of what was previously taboo – full-frontal nudity, sexual violence, rape. Doubtless all that was already available to those who sought it in Soho. It is rather the *resistance* of this material to erotic incorporation and its demonstration of a new problematic. Hitherto, sexual difference in bodily display had been repressed, policed as a matter of public and private morality; in this film it becomes politically inscribed, volatile, a site of visible struggle.

Reception and Censorship

While most early reviewers were complimentary about Kubrick's filmic achievement, many raised the same moral quandary. Jackson Burgess (presumably no relative) condemns the way in which 'Alex is made charming while the Home Secretary is thoroughly contemptible.' Indeed, he considers:

> The means by which Alex is celebrated are simple enough: he is
> not made into a morally significant figure but into a comic hero.
> He is comic because he is so completely and manically what he is,
> and he is heroic because no other character is much of anything
> at all.[43]

Though Burgess's assessment may be wayward at times ('I guess their comic hero is supposed to hold something or other up to ridicule, although I can't imagine what'), he is disarmingly acute about the film's emotional appeal: 'The technique of the picture *is* the technique of brainwashing: emotional manipulation on the visceral level of feeling'.[44] This insight (almost accidentally, one fancies) captures what other contemporary critics missed.[45] Gordon Gow praised McDowell's performance of 'perfect balance . . . extrovert enough to be hateful, introvert enough to be pitiful', thus missing the point that Alex, for an audience, is actually neither.[46] Philip Strick is aware that Kubrick's use of subjective shots 'ensures that Alex constantly has our sympathy', and insists 'despite the occasional extremism of his high spirits, he remains . . . merely the misunderstood victim of social injustice'.[47] Jan Dawson in the Monthly Film Bulletin was nearer the mark in concluding: 'Kubrick controls his audience with the same calculated precision that he imposes on his material, obliging us to shed our humanity that Alex may acquire it'.[48]

If contemporary critics' concerns about the moral ambiguities presented by the film retained a balance and tacit admiration for Kubrick's achievement, the popular reception of the film was less measured. That the director himself had anticipated the furore is evidence of 'the same calculated precision' that Jan Dawson noted elsewhere. 'Variety reported in 1972 that Kubrick maintained a level of virtually unprecedented input with Warner Bros. regarding the release pattern for the film. His office amassed two years' worth of data on every theatre in every city covered by Variety's weekly box-office reports . . . It opened on 19 December 1971 and in its first two weeks of release, the film broke house records in New York, Toronto, and San Francisco'.[49] Furthermore, Kubrick shrewdly allowed the X-rating the MPAA had put on the original cut to stand for the first nine months of release, then replaced 30 seconds' worth of the most explicit footage from the high-speed ménage à trois and the gang-rape film Alex is forced to watch with more innocuous material, thus gaining an R-rating which benefited from the high-level-publicity and word of mouth generated by the initial release for its Christmas 1972 reissue.[50] Though it was outstripped at the Oscars in all three nominated categories (Best Director, Best Film and Best Screenplay) by The French Connection (Friedkin, 1971), it won the New York Critics' Best Director and Film of the Year awards.

In London, where retiring censor John Trevelyan spoke of it as 'perhaps the most brilliant piece of cinematic art that I have ever seen', incoming Secretary Stephen Murphy passed it uncut with the customary 'X' certificate (in a decision he later agreed was hurried). It was released in February 1972 and became the first film ever to run for more than a year at the Warner West End cinema.[51] By this time it had gained sufficient notoriety for its February 1973 nationwide distribution to send it to the top of the UK box-office charts for four weeks.[52] In retrospect the highly sensitive climate created by outspoken campaigners such as the Festival of Light and Mary Whitehouse's National Viewers' and Listeners' Association can only have heightened the film's exposure. To his credit Lord Harlech stoutly defended the Board's decision, particularly in high-profile press publicity of criminal cases linked to the film, but several local authorities chose to ban the film. It was erroneously reported that the Home Secretary, Reginald Maudling had sought a private screening, but, according to Robertson, he 'had called to seek an explanation from Murphy as to the reasons behind the BBFC decision to make no cuts'.[53] Indeed, the Board's sympathetic treatment represented a complete volte-face from their 1967 judgement on the project and subsequent cuts imposed on The Devils (1970). The moral panic encouraged press linkage of the film with unconnected instances of violent crime and gang behaviour of which there were several reported during 1973. As is frequently the case, controversial cultural texts present a soft target for those seeking convenient scapegoats for complex social ills. However, Alexander Walker offers a slightly different perspective, claiming that A Clockwork Orange bore the brunt of a reactionary head of steam that had actually built up around controversial releases of the previous year (The Devils, Straw Dogs, The French Connection and Dirty Harry) and rumbled on into the mid-Seventies (The Exorcist), by which time Kubrick had surreptitiously withdrawn his film from British exhibition. By this time too Stephen Murphy, the hapless successor to the paternal John Trevelyan at the BBFC, had resigned. During his short four-year incumbency he presided over some of the most difficult decisions in the Board's history amidst a relentless barrage of media criticism calling not only for his own scalp but for the scrapping of the entire Board.[54] Ironically, the director himself was the sole suppressor of A Clockwork Orange, which, as James Chapman notes, 'is probably the most effective censorship of a completed film ever implemented in Britain'.[55] That Kubrick never publicly explained his actions is of only passing interest in comparison to the underground notoriety the suppression subsequently fuelled. The film's cult cachet was sealed with the advent of video and the widespread availability of illicit imports. Following the director's death in 1999, Warner Bros. wasted no time in re-releasing the film in British cinemas and cashing in on its celebrity with a DVD edition.

The passage of time and the ebb and flow of subsequent causes célèbres and moral panics has allowed for more candid retrospectives. In his consideration of twenty years of violence in American films since *A Clockwork Orange*, Michael Eric Stein adjudges:

> Even in the best and most serious violent American films since the '70s, violence is both expressive and exploitative, poetry and fantasy, moral censure and rock and roll.[56]

And in applying this judgement to Kubrick's film he finds 'the central paradox: with violence comes passion and with that passion comes our ability to choose what we love, what we dare, who we want to be – our humanity':

> Malcolm McDowell's face is elfin and childlike – we take delight in his pleasures. The framing of the film is often a reminder of our own voyeuristic complicity in movie violence.[57]

This admirable admission is sustained in other recent critical assessments.

> There is little wonder that the film's violence is in some ways attractive. Not only is it presented with great imagination and skill, but it is also performed by the only character in the film with any degree of charm. This may present some viewers with a moral dilemma. If the film criticises the violent world it presents, why is violence presented with such imagination?[58]

Falsetto's own answer to this question lies in the film's ability to 'strike a delicate balance between involvement and distance':

> Alex may elicit the viewer's sympathy. The audience may even admire his creativity and survival instinct, but if it gets too close to the character emotionally, the film's main critique will be undercut. A degree of emotional distance must be maintained, which is why the internal tensions, performance strategies and visual style are of such importance.[59]

Whilst agreeing with Falsetto's central point about the dialectical operation of these twin impulses of attraction and repulsion (the *double articulation* I shall consider further in the next chapter), perhaps the notion of balance or equilibrium is misplaced here. For surely what we have here is essentially an imbalance, a disequilibrium. The ambiguities played out across this dialectic are weighted heavily towards attraction and involvement. The converse impulses of distance and repulsion act upon an audience very much as a safety-valve, a last-minute mechanism of release, an escape hatch; or, from another perspective, as a means of containment, of contingency, a framing device. Whether the film's 'internal tensions, performance strategies and visual style' do promote 'a degree of emotional distance', as Falsetto claims, is a moot point, and one debated by several other critics in defence of the film's gravitas. For example, Philip French admires this 'masterwork that constructs a significant bridge between the early 1970s and the present' and considers an audience is both 'involved and repelled because the camera presents us with Alex's point of view, while the stylisation distances us from the events'.[60]

Yet I would take issue with such an assumption about the distancing effects of stylisation. Might not stylisation equally have the effect of sanitising violence, of inuring us to its reality? By his own admission, when asked 'Is there any kind of violence in films which you might regard as socially dangerous?' Kubrick replied:

> Well, I don't accept that there is a connection, but . . . if there were one, I should say that the kind of violence that might cause some impulse to emulate it is the 'fun' kind of violence: the kind of violence we see in the Bond films, or the Tom and Jerry Cartoons. Unrealistic violence, sanitised violence, violence presented as a joke . . . There may even be an argument in support of saying that any kind of violence in films, in fact, serves a useful purpose by allowing people a means of vicariously freeing themselves from the pent up, aggressive emotions which are best expressed in dreams, or the dreamlike state of watching a film, than in any form of reality or sublimation.[61]

I would argue that, especially with hindsight, *A Clockwork Orange* displays *exactly* that kind of stylised, highly orchestrated, slapstick violence we associate with visceral action-adventures or more appropriately perhaps, animated cartoons. The passage of time and cultural absorption has largely neutralised its shock. What remains – the lack of realism, the overt theatricality – makes it attractive as a cathartic kind of pleasure. Indeed, as Kubrick himself suggested in the same interview in November 1971, there is a sort of therapeutic pay-off, a kind of relived rite of passage attendant upon our identification with Alex. Moreover, the director also invites us to read him on a subliminal level:

> If you look at the story not on the social and moral level, but on the psychological dream content level, you can regard Alex as a creature of the id. He is within all of us. In most cases, this recognition seems to bring a kind of empathy from the audience.[62]

And he told Paul D. Zimmerman of *Newsweek*: 'Telling a story realistically is such a . . . ponderous way to proceed, and it doesn't fulfil the psychic needs that people have'.[63] The particular needs addressed here are those unresolved issues of resistance and incorporation, of the struggle to realise subjective identity in order to take one's place at the social table. It is just this kind of empathic reading, demonstrating an awareness of the nature of cinematic pleasure beyond a story's social and moral implications, that the distance of time and the eternal rites of passage of unrealised youth bring to the fore.

During the 1970s and the 1980s, critical opinion in the face of hostile media denunciation rightly pursued the rigorous defence of artistic integrity as a justified moral high ground. But latterly, such a lofty principle seems to miss the point. Thirty years on, for cult fans this is a great film precisely for the reasons that conservative voices originally condemned it – because it celebrates violent and sexual transgression and antisocial behaviour as heroic pursuits. Nowhere is Kubrick's own opinion more graphically recycled for the benefit of a contemporary cult audience than in the pages of *Empire* magazine:

> *A Clockwork Orange* cruelly exposes the old liberal line about great cinema making us realize the horrors of violence. *A Clockwork Orange* puts forward a strong case for the symphonic beauty of violence, the glamour of evil . . . Naturally, the boys in the back row of the late show lapped it up. *A Clockwork Orange* may have drawn the art house crowd in the rest of the world; in this country it attracted the lads, the mob, the masses . . . [I]n young Alex every British youth who ever wore the uniform of a teenage tribe could glimpse his own reflection. I was in my mid-teens 20 years ago and me and all my friends felt that here was a film about us . . . *A Clockwork Orange* is the most tribal of films. The violence is ritualised, the dress code is rigorous, the cult is king. It seems appropriate that it should have become the ultimate cult film.[64]

Other recent retrospectives have adopted a similarly productive, historical approach. Nick James, in comparing *A Clockwork Orange* with *American Psycho* (2000) laments the latter's lack of satirical edge:

> Ridicule, irony and sarcasm – the weapons of satire – were the first recourse of UK punk rock . . . The link between the sneering of *A Clockwork Orange* and Johnny Rotten's ranting delivery is obvious and rhetorically they are manifestations of the same voice of British youth discontent . . . It's hard in the neat and tidy new millennium to remember how large crowds of unruly youths did gather in the 1970s . . .
>
> With the 80s came an unprecedented interest in the history of youth style and rebellion that went hand in hand with the new fascination with the rich.[65]

Such cultural populist views as these are useful for the perspective in which they cast the cult phenomenon in contemporary culture. The vast majority of the contributors to the electronic community 'AClockworkOrange2' were not yet born in 1971.[66] Video and DVD may well have been their first point of contact with the film. They celebrate the film in a spirit of nostalgia for its iconic presentation of violence, its visceral nihilism, projecting back to an imagined moment when youth rebellion might have had teeth and been given certain credence. But it is emphatically also a resource: a milestone (doubtless one of many) on their own personal rite of passage. Note the following brief exchange as an example:

```
21 From: <brandinni>
   Date: Wed Nov 25, 1998 2:44pm
   Subject: so happy to see you all

   my favorite quote was i've suffered and suffered
   and everyone wants me to keep on suffering. i
   never read the book, but it looks like i'll have
   to. i totally got the message of the movie
   though. you know how people can do the rocky
   horror picture show thats how i am with a
   clockwork orange. ever since i was 14 the movie
   is something i need to watch atleast once a
   month. i get so much from it everytime i see it!
```

22 **From:** <AlexThDroog>
   Date: Tue Dec 8, 1998 8:28pm
   Subject: Cast for Clockwork...

   Wow, Brandini, I just flashed on something. I am
   a fanatic of both the RHPS, and Clockwork. I am
   a member of a Rocky "cast". I think you should
   try to get a Clockwork Orange cast going. All
   you need is a theater that shows midnight
   movies, and a few good people to act as droogs.
   I bet it would work great! Casts are a whole lot
   of fun. And Clockwork is the baddest and best
   movie in the midnight cannon!

Here it is not only the palpable enthusiasm and commitment of these dedicated fans which is of interest. Their proposal (perhaps not a terribly original one) that *A Clockwork Orange* could become a group performance act like *Rocky Horror* also raises problematic implications and cult promise in equal measure. Perhaps the vicarious pleasures of such identification are enough.

Summary

The themes of Burgess's satire are ongoing, if not eternal: the struggle of the realisation of youth into adulthood, freedom of expression versus social control. The particular contexts in which book and film appeared (at the beginning and the end, respectively, of a decade of upheaval which saw a new social class reinventing hedonistic, Romantic revolution) provided a new, highly charged and visible materiality on which those eternal and personal struggles were staged as social and political acts. The visual style of Kubrick's film – redolent of pop art and psychedelic styles – renders those struggles iconic (both in their eternal and temporal aspects, as personal and political acts) for a generation who feel themselves somehow to be, peculiarly, accessories after the event. For those who feel that particular pang of nostalgia (as if they were, by cruel fate or accident, born out of their right time), vicarious pleasures and second-hand dreams are the weapons by which to hold the present at bay, or to engage with it only obliquely. It is not so much the reliving of a misspent youth as the fulfilling of an unspent one. As Burgess himself insisted shortly before his death in November 1993: *A Clockwork Orange* personifies 'a *style* of aggression, not aggression itself'.[67] For the cultist, self-realisation is, profoundly, a matter of style.

4

THE WICKER MAN (1973)

Introduction

I have suggested so far two possible explanations for the rise of the cult film in Britain. Firstly, the formation of niche taste-communities as a result of the fragmentation of the exhibition industry; this in turn was attendant upon the continuing decline in cinema attendance. And secondly, social changes (particularly in attitudes to sex and politics) concentrated in the rise of a predominantly youth-oriented counter-culture of the late 1960s, which allowed for the treatment of hitherto taboo subjects in new forms across a range of cultural texts. The young American academic Theodore Roszak was one of the first writers to try to define this new radicalism:

> The counter culture is the embryonic cultural base of New Left politics, the effort to discover new types of community, new family patterns, new sexual mores, new kinds of livelihood, new aesthetic forms, new personal identities on the far side of power politics, the bourgeois home, and the Protestant work ethic.[1]

Roszak, as Marwick notes, is typically idealistic in describing both the breadth and depth of this revolt and its unity of purpose. But Marwick here nuances Roszak's bold contemporary account with an important caveat: that there was not a single 'youth culture' of an essential character which somehow detached itself from and set itself in opposition to established institutions and values. Rather:

> What happened in the Sixties is that large numbers of new subcultures

> were created, which then expanded and interacted with each other,
> thus creating a pullulating flux which characterises the era.[2]

This notion is useful, not least because it accords with the institutional
fragmentation of cinema during the period and the emergence of
distinctive audience segments which might be considered as separate
subcultures. But it also suggests the dynamic and interactive nature
of cultural relations: the state of flux resulting from the permeation of
social boundaries that gave rise to the kind of mixed coterie from which
Performance was born.

Gender and Genres in British Films since the Sixties

Certain British films of the late 1960s which have since attained cult
status share a common concern with problems of masculine identity. The
'Swinging London' films of the first half the decade are generally more
taken up with negotiating female admission to a social world of freedom
and empowerment to which men already have access and of which they
remain largely in control.

As the second half of the decade witnessed the rise of second-wave
feminism, 'liberation' legislation (the Abortion Act, the Sexual Offences
Act and the NHS [Family Planning] Act in 1967) and the emergence of the
counter-culture, so identity and image (both male and female) became
transformative sites of self-conscious experimentation and performance
(as *Performance* itself shows).

Elsewhere, Hammer continued to present more candidly the emotional
currents of sexual desires, though these are frequently encoded in phallic
scenarios that ultimately reaffirm penetration (both psychic and sexual) of
the mysterious female other. However, it is instructive to note how low-
budget, formulaic genres like science fiction and horror are able (because
of their fantasy iconography, routine plots and circumscribed narrative
boundaries) to push the limits in matters of sex and violence, and (in
certain hands) to develop a potent vocabulary for expressing less stable
aspects of identity at this time. Yet paradoxically, during the 1970s, the
hitherto secure boundaries of low-budget genres are breached in different
ways (and from quarters as diverse as Pete Walker's exploitation films and
Nicolas Roeg's auteurist interventions). And such shifts also witness, in the
case of horror, the demise of the gothic history so beloved of Hammer
Studios, and a new, if uneasy, emphasis on modernity in, for example,

Dracula A.D. 1972 (1972), *I Don't Want to Be Born* (1975) and *To the Devil a Daughter* (1976). Generic instability, as we established in the *Rocky Horror Picture Show*, also marks the entry of the kitsch and the camp into cult film sensibilities.

'The *Citizen Kane* of horror movies'

The Wicker Man is no more or less a horror film than *Performance* is a gangster film or *A Clockwork Orange* science fiction. And *Get Carter* is a gangster film which draws on conventions of the Western and revenge tragedy alike. Such shared contradictions with regard to generic identity may be seen as characteristic of the cult film, which employs oblique, selective, hybrid or parodic attitudes to genre conventions while never quite shaking off their trappings entirely.

The Wicker Man, though it has been celebrated by *Cinéfantastique* as 'The *Citizen Kane* of horror movies', has only one genuine moment of terror in the final *denouement*.[3] For the most part it is a curious mixture of detective story and folk musical. Though for marketing and critical purposes the film has, perhaps understandably, been pigeon-holed, it manifests a similarly arch distance from its generic characteristics as *The Rocky Horror Picture Show* does. And it shares with that genre parody a camp spirit of carnival too. As I have already suggested, cult films adopt a certain 'take' on popular genres, and it is that attitude, I believe, which not only characterises the films themselves, but also partially determines fans' abilities to engage with the text on a completely different level. It is this second aspect I shall be addressing later in this chapter.

Of course, on one level *The Wicker Man* can easily masquerade as horror. While Christopher Lee (Lord Summerisle) was, by the late 1960s, keen to shrug off his Count Dracula mantle and break new ground, the generic determination of his star persona is not so easily discarded. And *The Wicker Man* also featured a cameo role for Ingrid Pitt who had starred in several Hammer productions. Yet Lee, in playing here against type, also manifests charismatic qualities in performance that were quite new. Indeed, he still considers Lord Summerisle his finest acting role.[4] Again, it is a question of playing beyond expectation, while still being at least partly haunted by familiar roles. And, as we shall see, Lee plays a part which casts him as a 'bad father' figure of considerable allure: 'indeed, a villainous but also charming "persona"'.[5]

Though broadcast on British television several times since the early 1980s, and available on video, it has only been with the advent of DVD that *The Wicker Man* has been available in a full, 'restored' version following the reinstatement of lost or excised footage. The belated issuing of 'directors' cuts', to use the marketing parlance, has been of considerable interest to cult fans, and this format also allows documentaries, interviews and comparative versions to be endlessly debated and discussed.

Finally, it is worth noting that a good deal of the counter-cultural discourse of the late 1960s was expressed through a fascination with paganism and the occult, from the Rolling Stones' *Their Satanic Majesties Request* (1967) and 'Sympathy for the Devil' (1968) to hippy environmentalism and back-to-nature rhetoric, and from the deification of Aleister Crowley to the avant-garde films of Kenneth Anger. As Leon Hunt writes, 'the growing interest in paganism was partly bound up with uncovering a more "authentic" national identity and culture' and further, became 'a way of talking about the relationship between the upheavals of the late 1960s . . . and the backlash of the 1970s'.[6] As an example of that 'backlash', *The Wicker Man*, like Cammell's *Performance*, draws on aspects of the occult and pagan practices for its source material. Film-makers at this time were certainly keen both to explore and exploit the counter-cultural cachet of such influences, usually, as here, ironically. And yet the convincing portrayal of these aspects depends, in this case, to a large extent upon the imaginative use of natural landscapes on location, and upon the employment of convincing local extras.

Production History

The Wicker Man was filmed on location in the Dumfries and Galloway area of south-west Scotland in autumn 1972. But even before filming began, the production was dogged by conflict.

In April 1972 the beleaguered British Lion was sold by Star Associated (a conglomerate owning theatres, bingo halls and discos), which had run the ailing studio for less than a year (retaining John Boulting as Managing Director). The new buyer was tycoon John ('Pretty Boy') Bentley whose operation Barclay Securities invested £7.5 million, apparently on the strength of the development potential of Lion's Shepperton Studios site.[7] However, partly to appease union fears of peremptory asset-stripping,

FIGURE **9**: Lord Summerisle (Christopher Lee) in
The Wicker Man: a cult film about a cult
[CANAL+IMAGE UK LTD/BRITISH FILM INSTITUTE]

it was necessary for the new management to get some pictures on the books. Bentley appointed Canadian independent producer Peter Snell in July 1972, quickly promoting him from Head of Production to Managing Director; Snell brought with him playwright Anthony Shaffer's script of *The Wicker Man* and Bentley approved the proposal virtually on the spot. British Lion's board, however, had its doubts. When they read the script they considered the project unviable, especially in America – a vital market if production costs were to be recouped. But Bentley backed the film, according it a modest £420,000 budget and an on-location shoot that would not trouble the accountants unduly or take up any studio space at Shepperton. Once again, financial exigency clearly determines film aesthetics. These arrangements appeased union fears and underlined that British Lion was making films again. But Bentley's backing rested on one condition: the film had to be begun immediately – tricky in late summer 1972 for a film set in a blossoming Scottish maytime.[8] So, according to

Allan Brown, a mixture of ulterior motives and unseemly haste set the pre-production climate.[9]

Christopher Lee in fact was central to the *Wicker Man* project from the outset. At the end of the Sixties he had approached Anthony Shaffer with an interest in his play *Absolution*. But Shaffer (riding high on the stage success of *Sleuth*) told Lee he'd 'write him an intelligent horror film'.[10] He found what he was looking for in the shape of David Pinner's 1967 novel *Ritual* concerning a police investigation of a child's death and occult witchcraft practices in a remote Cornish village. Jonathan Clowes, Pinner's literary agent, set up a dinner for the pair of them with Christopher Lee. Lee, Shaffer and producer Peter Snell each contributed £5,000 to purchase the rights, and Shaffer began work on what he insists was unpromising material.[11] Declaring he had abandoned any hope of adapting the novel for the screen, Shaffer instead set to work on an original screenplay vaguely inspired by certain events and the occult spirit in Pinner's novel.[12] A more significant source, perhaps, was Frazer's *The Golden Bough*, which provides much of the symbolic iconography and ritual practices of the pagan settlement of Summerisle, the remote Scottish island to which a mainland police sergeant goes to investigate the disappearance of a missing child. Shaffer encouraged Hardy, who was recuperating after a mild heart attack, to research the 'old religion' with a view to constructing a story about the nature of sacrifice. If Hardy developed much of the film's potent symbolism, Shaffer's greatest contribution was arguably his (mischievously cynical) awareness of the contemporary resonance in the counter-culture's enthusiasm for alternative religion, spiritual experiment and moral licence. Reflecting on its cult status not long before his death in 2001, the writer commented:

> It's logical that *The Wicker Man* became a cult movie because it's a movie about a cult. I wonder if these fans are bright enough to realize they're doing to the movie what the islanders did to the Old Religion. They're taking the same comfort and sustenance from it.[13]

It is important in considering the appeal of this film to its fans to note the religious sense of drawing 'comfort and sustenance' from a ritual form. This is an aspect of cult fandom I shall be exploring in more detail later. But first, in order to explain the cult status of *The Wicker Man*, it will be necessary both to highlight certain aspects of its production and post-production history which have contributed to its popular critical mythology, and also to consider how incidents in that history have marked the film itself. For, as Eco suggests, a cult film must firstly 'provide a completely furnished world so that its fans can quote characters and episodes as if they were aspects of the fan's private sectarian world'. But furthermore, in order for a fan to engage with it, it must be possible 'to break, dislocate, unhinge it'.[14] I am interested here in how a film which can be so fruitfully disassembled was put together in the first place.

If the now-legendary tales of organised chaos, fractious starlets and whisky-fuelled artistic egos that have grown up around the story of the *Wicker Man* shoot are to be believed, it is a wonder the film was made at all. Certainly the 1977 special issue of *Cinéfantastique* devoted to the film, and the more recent research conducted by Allan Brown, have woven a compelling mythology from the established facts. However, what the catalogues of conflicts and upsets recorded by Bartholomew and Brown demonstrate (beyond their contribution to the film's cult notoriety) is how creative tensions in the collaborative process of film-making produce certain kinds of results on screen.

Perhaps what such instances really highlight is a culture clash between old-style industry professionals who were working on material and in conditions to which they were unused, and new-age, subversive ideas in the hands of inexperienced creative agents. Arguably, such tensions did nothing to inhibit some of the finest features of the film: Shaffer's memorable script, Waxman's photography, fine performances from Woodward and Lee, Flannery's imaginative set designs, Paul Giovanni's lyrical score, Stewart Hopps's choreography, Sue Yelland's costumes. But what the results seem to show (as I shall illustrate below) is an assemblage of individual creative contributions not properly synthesised or integrated by a singular vision (and in some instances actually working against one another, pulling the film in different directions). If this last point is a tendency noted by early reviewers of the film (see below), it is partly a product also of the editing process.

Post-Production, Exhibition and Reception

Post-production work began at Shepperton in February 1973 against a backdrop of further change within British Lion. The tycoon Bentley who, according to Alexander Walker, had had his 'eye on the British Lion subsidiaries, Pearl and Dean, which had an exclusive contract with EMI's chain of ABC cinemas to provide screen advertising for their movies until the year 1987, and on Mills and Allen, which owned prime-site poster hoardings', was himself the subject of a take-over by the financial services group J. H. Vassaveur.[15] They appointed two new men: Michael Deeley as Managing Director and Barry Spikings as his deputy in an umbrella company called Lion International, and a sell-out to EMI was mooted. In March, Peter Snell was told he was to be replaced. By November, though a print had been made, The Wicker Man remained unreleased.[16] Then took place the celebrated private screening for Mr and Mrs Christopher Lee, after which Lee allegedly told Deeley that he had enjoyed the film very much but there was lots missing and Deeley branded it one of the ten worst films he'd ever seen.[17]

Before it was available for preview, and prior to his departure from British Lion, Snell had set up a promotion at the Marché at Cannes, utilising the remaining wicker effigy in a stunt which drew enough attention to attract the interest of Roger Corman, veteran American independent producer.[18] He offered Deeley $50,000 for the rights to distribute the film in America and cut it to his specification.[19] A print of the original 102-minute cut was duly shipped to Corman in the States. Corman returned a letter to British Lion suggesting how the film might be slimmed down because it lacked pace. Eric Boyd-Perkins, following instructions, completed the edit overnight removing some 15 minutes from the running time. His version significantly cut the film's opening scenes on the mainland, removing the initiation of Ash Buchanan and reducing the narrative time from two nights to one.[20] This 84-minute cut was released to British audiences as a (by then unfashionable) double-bill with Don't Look Now (1973). It previewed in London's Victoria Metropole in December 1973, before its official opening on 21 January 1974 at the Odeon Haymarket.[21] As I shall argue below, the truncated version of the film known as the original theatrical release only compounded the narrative incongruities which were in part the results of the difficulties of the shoot. And this disunity was a weakness which contemporary critics noted.

Most reviewers recognised the film's concept and damned its execution, praised the script and the calibre of the actors, but deemed the whole less than a sum of its parts. The Financial Times was not alone in its claim that the film's 'fascinating ingredients do not quite blend'.[22] Dilys Powell in the Sunday Times conceded: 'one must admire the playing and the distinction with which Robin Hardy has directed'.[23] The Sunday

Telegraph said the film lacked the balanced 'inter-relation of the ordinary and the extraordinary that marks the best fantasy fiction'.[24] When it was previewed at Burbank Studios in Hollywood on 3 May 1974, Alan Howard in *The Hollywood Reporter* complained, 'Hardy completely botches the scenes in which villagers sing and dance more like music hall professionals than the cosmic worshippers they're supposed to be'.[25] Such negative reactions not only reflect the common difficulty in locating the movie within established generic conventions, they point to the very narrative incohesion which, I want to suggest, gives the film cult appeal. British Lion's own press pack declared (not without a hint of despair) that the film 'defies conventional classification. If one had to give it a label perhaps "a black thriller" would be a fair description, for, if comedy can be black why not thrills?'[26]

The Secretary of the British Board of Film Censors, Stephen Murphy, was perplexed by correspondents who were troubled by the film's anarchic themes, despite its 'X' certificate. He confessed he found it

> a funny old film; part of the viewing public takes it as an occasion for mirth and a few people seem to take it very seriously indeed. There can be few people who do not recognize this film as simple phantasy. Inhabitants, even of spoof islands, in the United Kingdom are not really given to burning constables and cattle.[27]

The American story was no less tortured than the British experience. However, it is here that the cult aspects of the film's exhibition history really emerge. Corman, despite his early interest and influence, found his modest offer rejected by Deeley. The backers Film Finance who had put £85,000 of the film's budget would require a more significant deal (something in the order of $400,000 gross) in the American market in order to break even.[28] Then, Beachead Properties, whose aim was to offset their proposed investment against tax (the now outlawed practice known as tax-sheltering), put up $150,000 and secured a deal with National General (worth $300,000) to distribute *The Wicker Man* in America. Disaster struck however when a matter of days later National General was declared bankrupt after American Financial (their backers) decided to withdraw from the film business. Warner Bros. took over the deal, marketed the film's horror elements with a lurid advertising campaign and sent it out around selected drive-ins.[29] The studio claimed their tax losses, the film bummed and was soon forgotten. At least, almost.

In spring 1976, Abraxas, a partnership of New Orleans-based Stirling Smith (a film lecturer and local TV personality) and John Simon (a 25- year-old Harvard graduate who was writing film reviews for the local paper) contacted Warners with a view to acquiring *The Wicker Man*. The complicated arrangement with Beachead and National General proved no obstacle to Abraxas securing a lucrative option on a film no one really wanted.[30] Smith and Simon raised $100,000 from investors and put up $20,000 for the sub-leased rights from Beachead in a deal that guaranteed Abraxas a 60:40 split on future profits.[31] At this point Robin Hardy, through his lawyer, heard that a new company was planning to distribute *The Wicker Man* in America and flew straight to New Orleans. He told Smith that somewhere there might exist his approved, 102-minute cut of the film. With cultish determination Smith vowed to track it down and release only Hardy's approved cut.[32] This however, proved far from easy. Spikings and Deeley (now both high up in EMI) were less than helpful. Peter Snell (now with the Robert Stigwood Organisation) was enlisted to make enquiries at British Lion's vaults. No negative was found. Then Spikings revealed the now mythological story that the 368 cans of *Wicker Man* negatives had been inadvertently disposed of along with trimmings from the cutting-room floor and were very likely buried in the foundations of the M3 motorway, close to Shepperton Studios.[33] In the saga of mixed fortunes that characterises *The Wicker Man's* history, this tale is perhaps the most extraordinary and the most significant in the cult canonisation of the film. It is fuelled by outlandish conspiracy theories (propounded chiefly by Christopher Lee himself who has said 'I believe somewhere in this country . . . there are maybe two or three people who know where it is, who have been sworn to silence').[34] Editor, Eric Boyd-Perkins and producer Peter Snell agree, more realistically, that a careless accident is the more likely explanation for the disappearance of the film's negative.[35]

Meanwhile, Snell told Smith about the 102-minute print which had been forwarded to Roger Corman. Corman's company New World located what was very likely the only print of the original version in existence and showed it to Smith who declared it a masterpiece.[36] Simon then took the print to Los Angeles and, under the supervision of Robin Hardy, set about the tricky process of reconforming the internegative of the positive print, which, though successful, resulted in some degradation of the image.[37] Uncertainty remains, therefore, as to why the version which was finally put on theatrical release in late 1977 in selected cinemas across the southern States was shorn of its opening mainland sequence and ran to only 96 minutes, though Robin Hardy recalls that he approved the cut at the time.[38] It wasn't until Media Home Entertainment released the film on home video and paycable in 1993 that the full 102-minute cut first saw the light of day.[39] Mysteriously, and in the best traditions of *Wicker Man* controversy, the colour internegative made by Hardy in 1977 from the Corman print has been lost, so further prints of the 102-minute cut must come from existing prints, resulting in further loss of quality, though technological improvements in the conversion process now redeem this somewhat and the version cut and distributed by Warner Bros. on DVD in 2003 is noticeably better than many earlier available prints, transferred as we are told from the original 1" analogue telecine master. [40]

The 1977 American release of the film was aided by a celebratory issue of *Cinéfantastique* devoted to the *Wicker Man* saga. From unpromising beginnings, by the time the film finally hit screens in the States it had become something of a cause célèbre. Hardy, Shaffer and Lee all played their parts in promoting the movie in the States and, trading on the film's already chequered history, it enjoyed a popular run. It opened in New York on 26 March 1980 and takings on the first night were the second highest in Manhattan.[41] Hardy and Shaffer published a novelisation in 1978, which in its way inaugurated a plethora of fan literature inspired by the film that receives its latest incarnation in Allan Brown's thorough, journalistic study, *Inside 'The Wicker Man': The Morbid Ingenuities*. Such popular studies (together with journal/fanzines like *Cinéfantastique*) are instrumental in generating the mythology (rooted in fact) of the film's misadventures. And this mythology constitutes the liturgy of fan knowledge all initiates must learn. But if this kind of demonstrable contextual expertise is the stuff of internet cult fan debate and seemingly endless rehearsal, it is but as background to the minute dissection of the film text itself, in both its available versions.

The Cult Text

The complicated history of the film's different versions begged a definitive 'Director's Cut' that Hardy was only too pleased to endorse. Such flamboyant marketing ploys are designed to appeal to the film buff, the cultist and the collector – to rebrand a past product with classic status. It is significant therefore that the new DVD edition of *The Wicker Man* (released in 2002) offers both the 84-minute and the 102-minute edits. Important to cult fans is the existence, side by side, of different versions that can be compared, replayed, debated and dissected. Like the record collectors' world of limited editions, coloured vinyls, alternative sleeves and misprinted labels, the cult film fan thrives in a fundamental sense on *difference*. So what of the differences? And wherein does *The Wicker Man's* originality lie?

The purpose of the opening mainland scenes (102-minute cut) is surely to establish Sergeant Howie's dour, spotless 'Christian copper' (Edward Woodward) and to ridicule him, using his 'long-haired' subordinate McTaggart (John Hallam) and the saucy postman (Tony Roper) as representatives of normality. Shaffer's script extended this pre-Summerisle sequence to include Howie's evening patrol of the local taverns, witnessing with undisguised disgust the debauchery of drinking and whoring amidst squalid backstreets. While the script's opening descriptions of the 'scum and effluent that floats on the disturbed surface of the water in the harbour' is metaphor enough for the 'fallen' world Howie polices alone, Shaffer endorses the cut, concluding that, 'It's better the way it is, just with Howie walking past the "Jesus Saves" graffiti. You play against the grain from the off, you don't give the story to the audience'.[42] That said, the differences point up subtle, but significant, shifts of emphasis in these various narrative beginnings. If the mainland appears to be as debased and un-Christian as the Summerisle we discover, then corruption is universal (not either simply urban, or remote). Similarly, this scenario condemns Howie from the start. It seems to me the chief argument in favour of the truncated opening (84-minute cut) is that Howie is an unknown quantity *until* he reaches Summerisle. We have no pre-judgements about his character except (crucially) the assumptions we might have about a policeman (whether that be as an agent of reactionary state authority or, more likely, a reassuring embodiment of sober reason). It is important that, at least to start with, we are *with* Howie; we discover this strange island through his eyes. If Howie is damned from the outset, his entrapment is surely less beguiling.

The other major narrative change in the shorter version of the film is the conflation of the two nights Howie spends on Summerisle into one, and the excision of the initiation rite of Ash Buchanan (Richard Wren). The three-day term Howie endures under the influence of the islanders' Pagan practices, which builds towards his May Day sacrifice, carries a weight of religious symbolism the shorter version loses. And the ritual offering of the virgin youth to the landlord's daughter Willow MacGregor (Britt Ekland) establishes her (over and above the bawdy barroom celebration of her sexual charms) as the siren Howie must resist in the second night's encounter. Furthermore, we are denied the introduction of Lord Summerisle (Christopher Lee) who brings the boy to her window, with his elegy to fecundity and the promise of tomorrow's 'somewhat more serious offering' – an intimation that the capture of Howie (body and soul) is not merely planned in advance, but, more sinisterly, predestined.

The remainder of the reduction from 102 to 84 minutes' running time amounts to the trimming of Howie's exchanges at Lord Summerisle's home (shedding some of what Lee considered to be his best lines on the relative merits of different varieties of apple) and the perhaps more significant loss of some ritual iconography from the build-up to the May Day procession leading to the film's cliff-top climax. The dramatisation of Pagan practices, with their rich, symbolic suggestiveness and colourful carnival spirit, is arguably the most celebrated and successful ingredient in this curate's egg of a movie. Not only were these elements painstakingly researched in the planning stage by both Hardy and Shaffer, they are also among the best dressed, best staged and imaginatively shot scenes in the whole film.[43] True, the difference that one more phallic symbol might make could be considered marginal in a film already replete with totemic charms. However, in my view, the shorter version hurries the final build-up, sacrificing the self-conscious lingering upon ritual elements that constitutes Robin Hardy's signature. Certainly, Shaffer and Hardy agreed that while often outrageous and sometimes shocking, it is crucial to the film's credibility that the Pagan world of Summerisle be believable. If Howie is duped by this alien culture, then an audience surely must be complicit in the elaborate fooling. Herein lies the moral balance of the film, between our identification with Howie as a representative of reason (despite his narrow creed) and our sympathy with his sacrificial humanity, and the seductive religious rhetoric of this alternative community which must continue to intrigue even as it appals. In short, it commands a certain devotion on the part of the audience.

Yet beneath this there is also a strong psychosexual subtext which surfaces in the repressed policeman's resistance to the siren charms of the seductive Willow and his other erotic encounters: copulating on the village green, sex-education at the local school, breast-feeding in the ruined churchyard, catching Ingrid Pitt at bathtime. His initiation into Pagan practices is as strongly rooted in its procreation creed as it is in its death rituals. No accident then that his final 'sacrifice' in the cage of the Wicker Man's abdomen should symbolise a return to the womb for this man who has, on religious principle, thwarted his own entry into the phallic community. The symbolic androgyny of this defining moment is plain: fatal incarceration within a male womb. It marks both the culmination of the profound anxiety about earthly sexual difference which is conspicuous throughout the film, and the spiritual transcendence (in Christian orthodoxy) to a realm in which sexual difference doesn't matter. To this extent, the film's playing across the dynamic of sexual permission and repression rehearses a familiar adolescent rites-of-passage initiation, just as, at another level, it exposes the political and generational divide between the policeman's authority and the counter-culture's liberation.

I want to highlight now some of those self-conscious elements in the narrative which seem at first sight to jar, but (particularly on repeated viewing) have a resonance that propels them into cult appeal. These are moments in the text I have dubbed 'nodes' and 'interstices': elements which seem either to stand out in bold (sometimes incongruous) relief from the narrative texture or to reveal the cracks in its surface. These manifest themselves in several ways: in symbolic reference, in acting styles and body language, in the use of music and in the juxtaposition of certain camera shots. But together they conjure a sort of dissonance which might be termed *the spirit of play*.

This playful subterfuge begins from the moment Howie sets foot on the island and is met with denial by the harbour-master's inscrutable cronies, and continues with postmistress May Morrison's (Irene Sunters) resistance to the idea that her own daughter is missing – she has a daughter, not Rowan, but Myrtle, whom she introduces. Then when Mrs Morrison intervenes in his questioning of the girl to offer him tea, though he accepts, the scene ends and we cut to The Green Man Inn later that evening.

The barroom drinking song disrupts the impetus of Howie's investigation just as he has intruded upon their bawdy entertainment. There is a distinctive slapstick style about this musical interlude, involving as it does the whole company in an obviously rehearsed set piece which impinges radically, if playfully, in the diegesis, and wrests power from Howie's serious purpose. Indeed, the incongruity of the film's musical set pieces (pared down from the demands of the original script which freely plunders Cecil Sharp's Victorian folk-song anthology) was endorsed by the composer himself.[44] Paul Giovanni said he 'felt right from the beginning that what I was doing was not stylistically in keeping with the screenplay'.[45]

In this scene the rational disruption is compounded further by the camera's dwelling upon the missing harvest festival photograph and Willow's pointed retort that 'some things in their natural state have the most vivid colour', after Howie complains about the unappetising appearance of the tinned food he is served for supper. Later, as the hapless Sergeant takes the air before retiring, he witnesses couples openly engaged in sex on the village green. This sequence is shot in a stylised slow motion which conveys the drowsy, hypnotic sexual power which has descended upon the villagers with nightfall. They are undisturbed by his incredulous observation.

The initiation of Ash Buchanan introduces Christopher Lee's Lord Summerisle whose body language is curiously stiff throughout, as if he were wearing a corset. There is something strange about the way he holds himself: the lower back, neck and shoulders. He is, we might say, a living totem: his physical power (and thus his political status amongst the islanders) is expressed symbolically (rather than actively) in this rigid, muscular, constrained posture. There is something sensually alluring and gratifying in his physical symmetry and command. Indeed, his whole body resonates with phallic power. This has to do in part with the contrast between his intimacy and aloofness. Examples in this play of proximity and distance work across an opposition of attraction/repulsion, of what is at once compelling and repugnant. Here brief recourse to theory may be useful.

The semiotic work of anthropologists Ray Birdwhistell (1970) on kinesics and Edward Hall (1963) on proxemics is especially instructive on this matter. Hall's studies of social behaviour codes and physical proximity parallel Birdwhistell's vocabulary of body movement and gesture. One of Hall's observations of interest to the cult film scholar is that, like verbal language systems, proxemic behaviour is not only culturally inscribed, but is arbitrary, despite its iconic appearance:

> Its arbitrariness is not obvious at first, because proxemic behaviour tends to be experienced as iconic – eg a feeling of 'closeness' is often

accompanied by physical closeness – yet it is the very arbitrariness of man's behaviour in space that throws him off when he tries to interpret the behaviour of others across cultural lines . . . *The iconic features of proxemics are exaggerated in the minds of those who have not had extensive and deep cross-cultural experience.*[46] [my emphasis]

This last point seems particularly pertinent to the study of filmic language, since I would argue that non-verbal communication works (in mainstream narrative realism) iconically, whereas it is disrupted (in the ways I have outlined) across cult texts in aberrant forms. The spectatorial feeling of being thus 'thrown' is both exhilarating (permitting the abandonment of dominant social codes) and disturbing (sanctioning antisocial behaviour). It may even be the case that cult film fans (those who are especially prone to profound emotional investment in and reaction to certain film texts) are 'those who have not had extensive and deep cross-cultural experience'. This is a suggestion I shall return to later.

Summerisle's controlled posture contrasts markedly with Howie's increasingly frenetic physical activity. Despite at first his measured economy of gesture and the policeman's military deportment, Woodward's Howie is a squat figure of progressively nervous sensibility which is captured in frequent point-of-view reaction shots and in the frantic May Day search of the town which culminates in the pursuer becoming the pursued. Furthermore, Howie's waning authority is echoed in the literal stripping of his body: first, as a sexually tormented figure sweating in his pyjamas at Willow's potent dance, then the donning of the Fool's costume stolen from Alder MacGregor (Lindsay Kemp), and finally in being attired in a plain, messianic shift at the point of sacrifice. Indeed, the ritualistic ridiculing of Edward Woodward's Howie is relieved and redeemed only, yet profoundly, in his death – a moment of genuine and enduring tragedy which evokes a line from another Scottish drama: 'nothing in his life became him like the leaving of it'.[47]

From his fruitless discussion with Summerisle, Howie receives permission to exhume the body of the missing girl Rowan Morrison (Geraldine Cowper). The sequences in the ruined churchyard at Anwoth are arguably among the most successful, but highlight two important features typical of the film. In the first sequence Howie discovers a young mother breast-feeding, an egg held in her palm, and clears the stone altar, fashioning a crude cross from apple box wood – a moment redolent with a symbolic strangeness. The second features an encounter with Aubrey Morris's gravedigger whose playing (like that of Russell Waters's harbourmaster and Lindsay Kemp's innkeeper) is wonderfully and irreverently camp. In terms of acting styles the supporting roles are almost uniformly overplayed. Yet what comes across as coquettish in the females' dealings with Howie (Britt Ekland's Willow, Diane Cilento's schoolmistress and Ingrid Pitt's librarian) is played as high camp when it comes to the men. This playful, mocking tendency is borne out in Christopher Lee's own urbane, charismatic charm: there is a mesmeric quality in his low, rather throaty delivery.

The discovery of a hare in the coffin of Rowan Morrison is captured in close-up with an accompanying musical twang from the Celtic harp. This is another repeated technique in narrative italicising – almost cartoon-style – which is overdone throughout. Similarly, there are visual gags such as the lingering close-up on the organ stop 'flute d'amour' at Lord Summerisle's castle which confound narrative verisimilitude. Yet, I would argue, it is precisely such jarring discords (in camerawork and sound) which the cultist adores, and, on repeated viewing, he or she anticipates such self-conscious moments with relish.

In terms of codes of realism, such dissonance is disruptive and (at least in part) deliberately so, as the ineluctable process of Howie's ridicule and entrapment builds to its climactic moment. Yet unlike mainstream horror, which relies for its effects on the accretion of suspense and the corresponding release of genuine shock which are contained within the rhythm of narrative discourse, *The Wicker Man* seems riven with cracks in its narrative structure. This disharmony, which has confounded critics who have sought to place it within the horror genre, is, it seems to me, what makes the cult film unique. At one level, the persistent undermining of Howie's sober narrative of police investigation through the emergence of the discourse of Pagan ritual practices dramatises a clash of cultural values and religious power which remains appealing (not least to cult fans). It was no accident that this remote community's reincarnation of the old religion also draws on the contemporary counter-culture. So, at least theoretically, there is a coherent, perhaps radical, thesis underpinning the film's objectives. However, in the manner of its execution and its aesthetic, the film's sinister purpose and tone is continually disrupted by the elements of play which intervene, often comically, always self-consciously, to delimit our psychological and emotional involvement, upon which the success of horror, as of other genres, depends. As Shaffer told *Cinéfantastique*:

> Our intent was to do an unusual picture in the horror vein, one that hopefully works on the accumulation of details. To a certain extent, you are meant to put it together for yourself. I feel you *must* leave something for your audience to do, you have to [emphasis retained].[48]

Some, if not all, cult films tread these cracks in the paths of narrative engagement in the way they subvert codes of cinematic realism. In so doing, they become celebrated and cherished, as much for their hyperbolic flaws as their visual excesses. Such textual incongruities open up narrative spaces for that fan intervention so peculiar to cult films. They rehearse playful rituals which fans appropriate, re-enact and invest with meaningful pleasures beyond the realm of the text itself. *The Wicker Man*, then, offers the believer the raw materials of religious, sexual and political transgression within the safe, fairytale world of vicarious play. The textual imbalance, the 'glorious ricketiness' of these ingredients, constitutes a large part of the film's cult appeal.[49] But the charismatic allure of performance is crucial here too.

Mesmerism and Charisma

The complex power of Christopher Lee's Lord Summerisle centres on the idea of charisma which has been used to explain the curious appeal of many cult figures. The charismatic figure has important connections with the person and theories of Mesmer. Mesmerism, or the pseudo-scientific belief that the natural forces of the universe could be summoned at the behest of will for purposes of good or evil, has a persuasive logic when applied to what has been described above. Mesmer's claims, originating in the French Enlightenment's fascination with universal theories that might account for (and treat) behavioural and psychological problems, attracted a good deal of medical attention in nineteenth-century Britain. They were one manifestation of a philosophical determination to describe and deal with deviance. Writing on the influence of Mesmerism on the life and work of Dickens, Fred Kaplan suggests a prophetic ambition at work:

> Perhaps Mesmer himself sensed or anticipated the coming psychological crisis of western man, the illness of the nerves and the

FIGURE 10: The old church at Anwoth – a Christian relic in *The Wicker Man*
[AUTHOR'S OWN IMAGE]

nervous system that was to become the characteristic disease of a
society attempting to grapple with the problems of personal and
public identity that the new age forced on many of Victoria's subjects.[50]

This conjecture has some useful resonances. Firstly, it identifies social
upheaval (especially in the relationship of 'personal and public identity')
as traumatic, whether applied to Victorian London or Britain in the Sixties
and Seventies. Secondly, it situates Mesmer on the cusp of Enlightenment
rationality and the Romantic movement at that revolutionary historical
moment when the undisputed authorities of church and state (and their
sacred mysteries) could be swept away by scientific thought and the
power of imagination. Again, one could locate such historical moments in
the apparent contradiction between late-nineteenth-century interests in
folklore and religious fundamentalism, and the emergence of Darwinian
rationalism and the science of psychology (not forgetting that the first
laird, Summerisle's great-grandfather, had been an agronomist – a man of
science). Thirdly, Mesmerism is applied by will-power in a pre-Nietzschean
harnessing of universal energy. It is worth considering Lee's performance
as Lord Summerisle in light of Mesmer's methods.

The mesmeric state was, according to the theory, a form of trance,
hypnotically induced by the operator summoning natural magnetic
forces and applying them physically to the patient. Once mesmerised,
the subject could then be treated, either by interrogation or by physical
manipulation. Despite the medical claims of success in the treatment of
conditions ranging from epilepsy to depression (and even for anaesthesia),
scepticism inevitably loomed large in Victorian London. And, perhaps
unsurprisingly, it focused on the exploitation of power:

> In the public mind, potential sexual power and exploitation were
> implicit in the relationship between the operator and his subject,
> between the strong-willed Victorian male and the potentially hysterical
> female.[51]

Evidence suggests that (as with Freud's psychoanalytic experiments)
patients were invariably female and while some men were treated
under mesmerism, 'success' rates were higher among women. Clearly,
the sexual politics of domination and submission are inherent in the
mesmeric method, as is the implication that deviant females benefit from
its corrective application.

What makes the theory and practice of mesmerism a more fitting analogy for explaining Lord Summerisle's dominion over his people than, say, Freudian psychoanalysis (which could be charged with similar exploitation) is precisely the mesmeric quality of his controlling powers as evidenced especially in patterns of gaze, physical gesture and proximity, and voice. These are the components of a kind of magic, every bit as potent as that practised by charismatic leaders of new religious movements. They also figure in establishment fears about the power of pop icons in the counter-culture of the late 1960s and in the moral right's anxieties about the corrupting influence of controversial film in the early 1970s. At root these events are each marked by the surfacing of naive or debased systems of thought: vulgar science if you will. Perhaps one of the ways in which historical upheavals are negotiated across society is by applying new (or revitalised) knowledge to expose in new ways objects of traditional taboo: sexual difference, cleanliness, the body.

In Arthur Frank's typology of body use in action, he defines the 'dominating body' as 'constantly aware of its own contingency':

> The essential quality of these bodies is their construction of desire as *lack*, a lack which demands compensation. Combined with the body's dyadic other-relatedness, the dominating body's lack produces a fear which is turned outwards on others who are exterminated in order to combat that fear . . . Finally, the dominating body must be dissociated from itself in order to punish and absorb punishment. Dominating bodies are overwhelmingly *male* bodies . . .[52]

What could pass in this sociological study for a description of Lee's physical persona in The Wicker Man (notably its 'self-dissociation') also finds echoes in the social study of charisma. According to Shmuel Eisenstadt, 'charismatic appeal is effective especially when the social order is uncertain, unstable and ambiguous and when the charismatic figure or group offers a value, order or stability to counterpoise'.[53] Weber and others writing of the phenomenon have 'emphasized that feature of the charismatic which distinguishes it from other forms of domination – its affective nature':

> Because the bond between the charismatic leader and his followers is an emotional one he is able to inspire in them that kind of loyalty which is both unquestioning and submissive . . . The leader is thus

seen to offer deliverance; his pronouncements, inchoate though they may be, in some way resonate with the basic feelings, hopes, desires, ambitions and fears of his followers.[54]

This issue of *affect* may be an important aspect of cult subjectivity.

Freud's own intervention in the description of the charismatic leader, perhaps unsurprisingly, draws on the representation of the primal father-figure in the Oedipal scene. He suggests that the charismatic group, with its idolatry of the alternative father-figure, offers an outlet for the repressed guilt which is the legacy of the socialised containment of Oedipal resentment. Such a model seems attractive to understanding the role of Lord Summerisle in *The Wicker Man*, with Sergeant Howie his virginal, sacrificial scapegoat. Emotional release is attained not so much by the leader, as displaced in the follower (and viewer) in the licentious permission this 'bad father' grants. In the case of Lee also, much of the charismatic charge is invested in physical poise, a certain suavity and the power of the look. If we can speak in terms of a cult 'look', then this is it, in all its seductive power. And much of its magnetism is also signified in the vocal register and tonal qualities of Lee's delivery. But what is the attraction? Returning to the influence of mesmerism and charisma, we can locate our disrupted reading within a trance-like surrendering of our own objectivity. This is what Freud called 'the possibility of self-loss through merger', and might equally stand as an epitaph for *Performance*.[55] But how shall we relate these issues of affective spectatorship to the matter of narrative disruption outlined above? And how does the location of alluring performance function to secure our viewing positions within such broken texts?

Double Articulation

In her seminal article 'Visual Pleasure and Narrative Cinema', Laura Mulvey calls for 'the first blow against the monolithic accumulation of traditional film conventions' by self-consciously freeing 'the look of the camera into its materiality in time and space and the look of the audience into dialectics and passionate detachment'.[56] She argues that such disruptive necessity is the responsibility of 'radical film-makers', and by implication those working outside mainstream popular cinema. Yet ironically, the specific cultural circumstances of Anglo-American commercial film-making from the late 1960s provided opportunities for the radical treatment of visually explicit material (which had hitherto been the territory of avant-garde and exploitation cinema) to emerge into the mainstream. How is it that such material (itself implicitly as misogynistic as anything emanating from Classical Hollywood) might be considered 'radical' in terms of Mulvey's conception of cinematic scopophilia? I believe the answers to this lie on two levels: in the cultural sphere, and in the realm of film aesthetics.

At cultural moments when the themes and treatments of certain texts are (in Raymond Williams's term) emergent – that is in advance of pre-existing, dominant or residual social codes – their impact may be sufficient to disrupt (that is both to make visible and to disturb) pre-conscious cultural sensibilities regarding the conventions of a particular medium.[57] Earlier I proposed, for example, that *Performance* and *A Clockwork Orange* ushered in new perspectives on the world of material objects. It is here that cinema breaches what Mulvey calls its 'relationship to formative external structures'.[58] How does this take place? Essentially it occurs on two levels. The censorship of, and popular critical reaction to, a certain film text will define the contextual parameters of its cultural intervention. And these too shifted considerably during the 1960s. Such conditions are likely to produce one kind of 'distancing awareness in the audience'.[59] The other kind of radical disruption of audience perceptions which can be attributed to certain films of this historical period concerns visual style. Whilst mainstream narrative cinema, according to Mulvey's criteria, disguises its aesthetic operation, accommodating culturally dominant subject-positions, avant-garde filmic practices provoke a self-conscious detachment, resisting culturally sanctioned access to familiar reading positions. Across this viewing spectrum, a third type of film (of the kind I am considering) deliberately exaggerates and manipulates popular generic expectations. It promotes a heightened sense of identification through power-pleasure. At the same time, it thwarts and disrupts that pleasure via a variety of means: the double articulation of excess and incongruity. An audience is required to adopt a dialectical relation to texts which display a double articulation of visual pleasures through strategies of engagement and distancing, of abandon and control. It is across this dialectical relation that the problematics of sexual identity, in particular, are played out, because such strategies subvert secure subject positions by presenting extreme (fantasy) practices of sexual difference and radically contesting them. Why might the protocols of double articulation apparent in many films of this period subsequently appeal to cult fans? To try to answer this, let us return to the nature of performance.

Goffman, Interactionism and Performance

In his work on performance and interactionism, Erving Goffman provides an analogy which may be useful for understanding the production and consumption of the cult film text. In discussing the way in which social performances are (by mutual acknowledgement of actor and audience) necessarily idealised, or restricted to their summary meaning, Goffman indicates that on occasion gestural signals or other peripheral signs intended to corroborate and anchor the communicated essence of the main performance can, conversely, disrupt, negate or undermine this essential presentation, with sometimes humorous, sometimes embarrassing or shocking effects. Such situations may, he argues, be either the result of poor, unorchestrated performance, or inaccurate audience interpretation, or both. Either way:

> As students of social life we have been less ready to appreciate that even sympathetic audiences can be momentarily disturbed, shocked and weakened in their faith by the discovery of a picayune discrepancy in the impressions presented to them. Some of these minor accidents and 'unmeant gestures' happen to be so aptly designed to give an impression that contradicts the one fostered by the performer that the audience cannot help but be startled from a proper degree of involvement in the interaction, even though the audience may realize that in the last analysis the discordant event is really meaningless and ought to be completely overlooked. The crucial point is not that the fleeting definition of the situation caused by an unmeant gesture is itself so blameworthy but rather merely that it is *different* from the definition officially projected.[60] [emphasis retained]

In *Performance*, *A Clockwork Orange* and *The Wicker Man* I have detected what we might call moments of slippage in the performances of key iconic and charismatic figures (Jagger's Turner, McDowell's Alex and Lee's Lord Summerisle in particular). Such examples of narrative incongruity in a film text can result in an imbalance either in the consistency of one particular creative ingredient (such as acting style), or in the relationship between one constituent and another (such as editing and music), or in the balance and arrangement of the mise-en-scène. It may be tricky to establish to what extent such inconsistencies are truly 'unmeant gestures', deliberate 'jokes' (as in *The Wicker Man*) or radical artistic strategies on the part of the creative agents (as in *Performance* and *A Clockwork Orange*) – this will usually be determined by the production conditions as it was seen to be in the cases I have highlighted. But in an important sense, for audiences, this doesn't really matter. Indeed, the dramatic hiatuses forged by such performative incongruities open up spaces for audiences so minded to speculate and fabricate explanations of their own. And sometimes the surfacing of these fissures can be seen to go totally beyond the aim of the original producers, depending, as it often does, on historical distance or repeated viewing. For the unconscious of a film text may emanate not merely from the accidents of its production, but from cultural contingency too. A Freudian slip in one age might be negligible to succeeding generations, and 'sometimes a cigar is just a cigar'. But the most sombre of dramas can be rendered hilarious if rehearsed often enough. Whatever the case, Goffman's key observation that might be applied to cult audiences is their tendency to reject 'a proper degree of involvement in the interaction'. In the case of cult fans of *The Wicker Man*, this degree of involvement is, indeed, often 'improper' in the extreme. By which I mean, of course, in excess of cultural norms.

'Wicker-Heads'

Due in no small measure to the mythology which has developed around the film as a result of its traumatic history, the 1980s have seen a steady growth in fan activity (first in America and later in Britain). Generated partly by college campus screenings and partly through cable TV, video and BBC *Moviedrome* re-releases, an active and dedicated fan culture has emerged, initially around print fanzines such as *Summerisle News* and *Nuada*,[61] location tourism and television documentaries, and latterly on the internet with newsgroups debating releases of soundtrack and DVD, literature, memorabilia, merchandise and collectables.[62]

What has been dubbed 'Wicker Week' is an annual event held around May Day and the feast of Beltane at The Ellangowan Hotel, Creetown, which provided the interior scenes of the film's village inn, The Green Man. This convention was inaugurated by landlord Bill Christie in 1999 and has since attracted a congregation of the Wicker Man Appreciation

Society to this, the adopted centre of Wicker Country in the Dumfries and Galloway area of southern Scotland. There, hundreds of fans and devotees of the film gathered to tour the now well-documented locations in which the film was shot, attend workshops given by Wicker aficionados such as Gail Ashurst, editor of the Wicker journal *Nuada,* and enjoy entertainment provided by, amongst others, Ian Cutler, the film's violinist.[63]

If the annual meeting of who *The Sun* calls 'Wicker-Heads'[64] is the centrepiece of their social calendar, there is an enthusiastic correspondence on subjects as diverse as comparative aspect ratios of the film's different versions, new-age Paganism, and Geraldine Cowper (the child actress who played the missing girl Rowan Morrison) appearing in *EastEnders,* regularly posted across a plethora of dedicated internet sites, numbering, according to Robin Hardy, some 75,000, in the Wicker Man webring.[65] Yet such cult fan appreciation predates wide use of the internet. Dave Lally, who is credited with drawing up the definitive map of Wicker Country, was president of the appreciation society as early as 1980 and published the now defunct *Summerisle News,* which spread stories of fans trading remaining pieces of the original Wicker effigy like relics of the true cross.[66] The film has been the subject of two recent documentaries, made for BBC Scotland (1998) and Channel 4 (2001), and enjoys increasingly frequent television outings. It has been credited as a major influence by comedy writers Steve Pemberton and Reece Shearsmith of *The League of Gentlemen* fame, and inspired the Burning Man festival in the Nevada desert where each year a large celebration of alternative lifestyles culminates in the lighting of a huge human effigy. Since 2001, Galloway has staged its own '*Wicker Man*' music festival. In May 2002 *The Wicker Man* was showcased once more as part of a Fantastic Films Weekend at Bradford's National Museum of Photography, Film and Television, at a special screening attended by Robin Hardy. The director was also present at the University of Glasgow's Crichton Campus, Dumfries, for the first academic conference to be devoted to the film. '*The Wicker Man*: Rituals, Readings and Reactions' was held in July 2003, and has spawned two recent publications.[67]

This mass of evidence demonstrates the entry of the film into a range of critical discourses where it is really transformed into something else: the raw material of a discursive site for creative and critical activity. I have tried to pinpoint qualities in the film which I believe lend it to such treatment and I have endeavoured to locate those features in its production and post-production histories. The question remains, however, as to what critics (be they fans, journalists, broadcasters or academics) derive from such activity. To employ the concept from Bourdieu, what kind of 'cultural capital' does cult fandom produce? This is a big question and one that deserves further elaboration later. But it is worth raising some tentative suggestions in that direction here.

I think there is undoubtedly a sense of devotion manifest in cult fandom which is derived in part from the iconic and ritualistic aspects of *The Wicker Man*. And the quasi-religious quality of this fandom is observed in repeated viewings, the calendar of annual events and the veneration of 'sacred' sites. This is a set of responses both to the themes of the film and their iconic structuring. But it is also an active extension and elaboration of those aspects. Attendant upon this almost religious sense of devotion is also the key expression of difference. Witness for example this brief self-introduction to the *Wicker Man* Digest and the exchange which follows:

> I joined this site out of interest after finding it listed on IMdb. Just seen Wicker Man the directors cut. Thought it was a really good film as unlike most films it wasnt just the same tired formats churned out even allowing for the fact it was made years and years ago. So what kind of stuff do you discuss here?
> Siobhan
>
> ***
>
> Hallo!
> To me, the slightly dated feel to the film is part of its joy; looked at from thirty years' distance the folk-paganism is more nostalgically Seventies than ancient and powerful. And 'It was upon a Lammas night . . .' is a perfect song of the era
> . . .
>   . . . a Lammas night? at Beltane? – but then, it's all just a little bit wonky, it's not too perfect; someone described it to me as 'horrid and a little bit silly'. Which is fine I think; it's a film to be enjoyed. And it's curious that you were so taken by the director's cut. I first saw it in a shorter version and I don't think that it needs all

that stuff on the mainland. Have you seen the short
version too?
Jonathan

***

Hello all,
Thought I'd introduce myself, big fan of the WM,
which makes, by the way, most of my friends think
I'm rather strange. (well to be honest it is one
entry on a list, but that's neither here nor
there).
  Joined the group mainly out of intrest for May
Day, any more new wicker manny goodness in my life
is quite welcome.
  Anyway, I'll be about, and say more when I have
something more to say.
Best and Brightest
erehwesle

***

I have both versions on DVD and on VHS and the first
time i saw the film it was the longer version. When
i bought the tape it was a shorter version and to
me the film was muddled.
  It may not seem like it but the scenes on the
main land help reflect some of Sargent Howies
background.
  I hate that the musical numbers which added to
the atmosphere of the movie, will not be in the new
version.
  It is a Masterpeice
Jonathan

***

The words to corn rigs are by Robbie Burns though,
and old enough even if the tune is not.
Larry

***

Well, I just joined for the same reason, so I'm not
sure what the nominal 'we' discuss, but I did love
the movie.
  Posting a reply to say that the name Siobhan

rocks. I wish I lived in Scotland (though perhaps
it is beaten by Rowan, I must admit)
erehwesle

* * *

Hello
Thanks for the compliment on my name. Being from
Scotland I suppose does give the wicker man that
extra little bit of interest for me.

Apparently my mum lived in Dumfries and saw the
actual wicker man being constructed.

Ii havent seen the shortened version but I think
the small part on the mainland really is important
to the film as it does help us to understand Sargent
Howie.

I am a complete aethiest so I find most religions
fascinating and especially liked some of the ideas
used in the film.

As for the soundtrack that should not be taken
out! Its an essential part of the film.

And I DO NOT think they should be remaking the
wicker man fair enough holywood wants to do a cult
orientated movie but classics should be left to be
just that.
Siobhan

* * *

His name is Robert Burns (or Rabbie, if you must),
but never ROBBIE.
Regards
Jamie Stuart
Galloway
Scotland

* * *

Have to agree Jonathan. The longer version is
imperative towards the film as you don't understand
why he was coming into land in the beginning of the
shortened film. I am sure everyone who has the dvd
knows of the Easter Egg in it. If not after a few
clicks here and there you get to some footage of
the cast sitting in the recording studio doing the
commentary. By the way I am from Northern Ireland

```
so I am glad to see someone with a lovely name like
Siobhan in the group!
Neil
```

```
                              * * *
```

```
Do you think had they not killed Seargant Howie that
Rowan would have had to be sacrificed?
   Just a random thought
   My name seems to be popular here must be the whole
celtic thing and people liking the wickerman.
Siobhan
```

Not only does a spiritual intensity denote the depth and seriousness of one's fandom, it also separates it from other kinds of fandom, from other texts, even from other fans of this text. Paradoxically, while cult fans enjoy sharing their enthusiasms with fellow devotees, they manifest highly competitive expressions of their fandom and often seek to protect the privacy of their own appreciation. So the enmeshing of fandom in the fabric of ritual demarcates it from fandom in general, and aims to prevent its corruption, to keep it pure. Yet this aim is always hopeless, because there is an essential contradiction at its heart. The expression of fandom necessitates production and interaction: the production and collection of objects, merchandise and memorabilia, and interaction with other texts and fans. These necessities inevitably raise the public profile of the text and publicise its fan-base, resulting in the commercialisation and commodification of fandom, and an increase in the popularity of the text, all of which serves to threaten the sanctity of fandom itself and to destroy its illusion of purity. I suspect that cult fandom exists in this rather vulnerable twilight zone between private obsession and public expression.

Furthermore, a newsgroup like the *Wicker Man* Digest may be seen firstly to celebrate liberation from mainstream tastes in the valorisation and intense celebration of a hallowed text. But in so doing it also apes a sort of critical cultural orthodoxy in the meshing of the practices of close textual analysis, cultural distinction and internet group dynamics. I suspect that the certainties of a rule-based system and their temporary overthrow are key elements in the cultist dialectic which also deserve consideration later.

FIGURE 11: On the *Wicker Man* tourist trail: notice at the campsite at Burrowhead
[AUTHOR'S OWN IMAGE]

Summary

While sharing many of those textual and contextual features which are beginning to emerge as key aspects of cult films, *The Wicker Man* has a different kind of feel to it from the dark violence and nihilism of *Performance* and *Get Carter*. Tragic and at first shocking as its dramatic conclusion is, the film is imbued, like *A Clockwork Orange*, with a more enduring spirit of play. The picaresque playfulness of the pagan rituals, music and dance extends, as we have seen, to the film's jaunty, idiosyncratic structure. This is what permits access to its rich and suggestive vocabulary and inspires fan response. This is also redolent of the camp performance style of *The Rocky Horror Picture Show*, though arguably *The Wicker Man* occupies a more hermetic, less permeable diegetic world. Perhaps this is why location tourism has become such an important part of Wicker fandom and why ritual gatherings and festive celebrations are more appropriate than camped-up midnight screenings. Certainly the religious aspects of the story inspire fan devotion worthy of pilgrims of yore, and understandably the *Wicker Man* Digest attracts membership and interest from pagans and new-age enthusiasts amongst others, tracing a lineage back to the counter-culture which partly inspired the film.

As the Seventies opened out, the counter-culture took on a more diverse, insular and fragmented character. If this re-evocation of the pastoral was one facet of this escapist trend, another was the picaresque qualities of play, dressed up in an increasingly flamboyant, Baroque manner (evident both in *A Clockwork Orange* and our next film, *Tommy*). But *The Wicker Man* plainly demonstrates a key aspect of cult films. Its performance of transgression has inspired cultists to engage, in diverse ways, in the production of conspicuous difference which seems to be at the heart of fan devotion.

It is fitting perhaps to conclude by addressing the problems of the textual experience of the cult film *in culture*. I am arguing throughout this book not only for the essential difference of cult films from other films which accrue widespread, sometimes lasting, popularity. I am also suggesting that the central texts of British cult cinema arose in a historically specific period (primarily) during the late 1960s and early 1970s, for cultural reasons beyond the fragmentation of studio production, the decline in cinema-going and the relaxation of censorship (though these were all material factors). Anthropological and psychoanalytical theories can, as we have seen, provide useful interpretive models for charismatic leadership and its role in group behaviour, but too often lose specific historical context or fail adequately to explain differences in human behaviour in their universal or social accounts. Semiotics has already been invoked to try to conceptualise what I perceive to have been a new attitude to the world of objects at this time, and fundamental tensions within the language community. I have suggested that cult films address these new attitudes and tensions through what I have called hyper-signification: an excess of symbolic elements whose interrelationship is neither completely determined nor ever totally resolved by the narrative process. Yet again, it is difficult to square the circle of semiotic theory in terms of historical change. An explanatory model is needed which, as Williams began to suggest with the idea of 'structures of feeling', can account for how 'specific feelings, specific rhythms' emerge from their material, historical context.[68] This is something I hope to move towards in this work.

CASE STUDY 2:

Monty Python and the Holy Grail (1975)

Monty Python had an established following on the strength of four television series (1969–74) and a feature-length spin-off compendium, *And Now for Something Completely Different* (Ian MacNaughton, 1971), well before the release of this, their first original feature film.[69] Indeed, their fan base can be said to have grown as much as a result of extensive live performance tours and the release of five LP records (between 1970 and 1975), besides books and other merchandising.

So genuinely 'cross-media' was the Python 'phenomenon', it is no surprise that each new creation should become a cult object in its own right. In this way, it is perhaps more accurate to define Python as a collective 'treatment of' a particular medium (in this case feature film). Consider, in *the Holy Grail*, the sustained visual jokes about film-as-form, expressed in a range of self-reflexive gestures and structuring devices throughout what is essentially a period narrative. Thus, the film exemplifies (albeit for comic effect) the rare intervention of modernist film practices into mainstream, popular cinema.

Inspired in part by Pasolini's *Canterbury Tales* (1971), which modelled a 'style and quality of shooting [required] to stop it being just another *Carry On King Arthur*', period realism, paradoxically, was central.[70] Indeed, much humour emanates from the juxtaposition of ancient legend with an awareness of the impossibility of rendering historical reality in film. First-time co-directors, Terrys Gilliam and Jones, 'both had the idea of doing an antidote to the Hollywood vision of the Middle Ages . . . really dirty'.[71] But this shared vision proved difficult to realise.

Location filming (during April and May 1974) in Glencoe, on Loch Tay and at Doune Castle assisted in achieving a certain bleak authenticity. Budgetary constraints (old film stock bought cheaply) also contributed to the overall effect.[72] But, like *The Wicker Man* and *Withnail & I*, this was a difficult 'rookie' shoot, which produced uneven results. An investors' preview showing in October 1974 was, according to Michael Palin, a gloomy affair: 'The film was 20 per cent too strong on authenticity and 20 per cent too weak on jokes'.[73] Before the UK premiere on 3 April 1975 a substantial re-edit and the addition of pre-recorded music (which 'lifted it into the area of swashbuckling parody') were required.[74] But its critical and commercial success was instantaneous, grossing £19,000 in its first week in London and breaking box-office records in New York later that month, taking $10,500 on the first day.[75]

Monty Python and the Holy Grail reimagines Arthurian legend as utopian playground.[76] This echoes the cultist nature of hypothetical alternative lifestyles across a range of other contemporary film and television fantasies, from *Zardoz* (1973) and *The Wicker Man* to *Survivors* (BBC, 1975–7) and *Arthur of the Britons* (HTV, 1972–3). Such fantasy utopia, whether serious or comedic, whether futuristic or historical, allows free rein to the 'serious play' of cult sensibilities. Thus, a decade before *Withnail & I*, the Pythons' transgressive humour gave a generation of adolescents scripts to memorise, rehearse and intone like the mystic liturgy of some obscure, clandestine sect.

FIGURE 12: A quest with a purpose: *Monty Python and the Holy Grail*
[PYTHON PICTURES/EMI/THE KOBAL COLLECTION]

5

TOMMY (1975)

Introduction

While Ken Russell's film version of The Who's 'rock opera' *Tommy* did not reach cinema screens until the mid-1970s, it spoke of earlier times. It harnesses and exploits the same spirit of nostalgia evident in *The Rocky Horror Picture Show* which was released in the same year. But while Sheridan and O'Brien's musical romp drew lovingly on the American B-movie horrors and sci-fis of the 1950s, *Tommy* harks back to a British post-war austerity which casts a longer cultural shadow. Though it is as camp and flamboyant at times as anything emanating from the Transylvanian convention, its seaside postcard realism eschews out-and-out fantasy and its narrative preserves Pete Townshend's impressionistic, *Bildungsroman* trajectory. Yet on another level *Tommy*, like *Rocky Horror* in its contemporary glam-rock style, is also attempting to deal with the more recent cultural legacy of the late 1960s. On its belated release even the most enthusiastic of reviewers asserted: 'It is a film that *should* have been made around 1970 . . . when it was immediate'.[1] And the *Hollywood Reporter* described it as offering 'the kind of audio-visual "trip" that the movies of the 60s never succeeded in as well as the music of the era'.[2] It is widely accepted that popular music was the chief vehicle of the 1960s' cultural revolution. During the second half of the decade, the spectacular flowering of that audio spectrum drew visual inspiration from Surrealism, Dada and Pop Art. However, cinema, not unusually, lagged behind the times by perhaps as much as five years. Thus, as we saw earlier, efforts to bring *A Clockwork Orange* to the screen began in the mid-Sixties, but its post-1968 depiction of violence could be rendered more explicitly and with a vibrant, pop-ish, picaresque attitude by the early 1970s. Similarly, the distance between The Who's *Tommy* (1969) and Ken Russell's film of 1975 incorporates a nostalgic, sometimes parodic, and frequently hyperbolic, rendition of the source material. We might characterise this *post hoc* situation in terms of patterns of cultural slippage. In each case, I suggest, the space this opens up within the film texts is a playground for cultish sensibilities.

With hindsight, the film of *Tommy* is a spectacular celebration of the visceral directness and energy of The Who's rock music and the dazzling surface appeal of Ken Russell's pantomime, pop art iconography. In the film's best sequences, the vibrantly photographed physical performances and visual style are orchestrated in an editing technique (Stuart Baird's) that provides an energetic counterpoint to the rhythms of Townshend's technologically advanced, quintophonic sound recording. If such audio-visual dynamics have, since the advent of the pop video and MTV, become a commonplace, Townshend and Daltry agree that credit must go to Russell for foreseeing such potential and sustaining it (if unevenly) across a feature-length format. As Townshend recently remarked, 'It seemed to me that he had that kind of pop video approach – he just seemed to be perfect'.[3] But the film also warns of the transience of pop's instant gratification, a mistrust of false idols, and the mistake of looking to popular culture's seductive, hypersignifying images for life answers. Like *The Wicker Man*, *Tommy* is a film about fake religion, moral transgression and alternative spiritual cults. Like *A Clockwork Orange*, it deals with physical and psychological exploitation, the abusive and authoritarian nature of public and private institutions and the recessive, unrealised masculinity of a vulnerable, if charismatic protagonist. But *Tommy* alone makes visible, perhaps above all, the cultural fault-lines of the 1970s. Specifically this is rendered in music: on the one hand 'serious', heroic rock and on the other frivolous, dispensable 'pop'. But it is also apparent generally in the way in which it foregrounds the double standards of the abusive, exploitative family and their heedless pursuit of material wealth as a substitute for genuine social values.

The enduring success of *Tommy* (first-run theatrical release, television outings, soundtrack album sales, stage version, video and now a '2-disc collector's edition' DVD) reflects several combined factors. It was a film pre-sold on its musical credentials. It worked as cross-over product. It gained solid, if limited, backing from its producers. It had both the creative potential and the formal boundaries Ken Russell requires in order to achieve his best film work (*Women in Love* [1969], *The Devils* [1971] and *Tommy*). It combined a pop-synthetic retrospective of the Sixties generation with state-of-the-art sound reproduction and forward-looking, MTV-style visuals that set a trend in pop music films for the next ten years. And, though its post-production history has none of the skeletons-in-cupboards form of other, less fortunate if more celebrated cult contenders, textually *Tommy* has those qualities which, for hardcore fans, make it special, as recent newsgroup contributors demonstrate below.[4]

> **From:** <liszka_pet>
> **Date:** Tue Mar 21, 2000 3:22am
> **Subject:** Stuff about me
> Well, if no one else is going to do this besides
> you, then I will too! ^_^ I don't know when
> exactly I got into the Who. Maybe it was during
> my trip to LA when a girl friend and I heard
> "Squeezebox" for the first time. All we could
> remember was the chorus "in and out and in and
> out . . . " So our friends who didn't hear it
> thought it was a pretty dirty song. ^_^ Not long
> after that I saw a behind the scenes/making of
> Tommy. After that I just HAD to see it so I
> looked long and hard for a copy of it and just
> loved it! It was sort of before my time, what
> with me not quite 21 here, but I've always been
> an individual.
>
> **From:** <docbb_4469>
> **Date:** Wed Mar 22, 2000 6:32pm
> **Subject:** Re: Stuff about me
> That's good, one should always strive to be
> an individual. I didn't quite fit in with my
> age group either when I was younger. The Who
> cross boundaries, I think, of age, gender,
> class, etc. I have lots of favorite Who songs,
> not just from "Tommy," but other albums as well.
> Have you ever heard of the albums "The Who Live

at Leeds," or "The Who Sell Out?" Way before
your time, but interesting, non-the-less.
And of course I like "Quadraphenia," and
"Who's Next."

From: <liszka_pet>
Date: Sat Apr 1, 2000 6:46pm
Subject: No one answered the question!
Hey there all! Having a blast up here in the
north . . . thought since no one had answered
the question, I'd answer it. I quite liked
cousin Kevin . . . and I loved Tina Turner
as the Acid Queen . . . but my favorite wuold
definitely have to be Uncle Ernie. MY mom loves]
him too . . . he's just so nasty. "Fiddling
abite" and such. ^_^

From: <docbb_4469>
Date: Sun Apr 9, 2000 9:37pm
Subject: Re: No one answered the question!
Well, I must have missed something, but if we're
talking favorite characters, I'd definitely have
to go with Tina Turner/Acid Queen. Cousin Kevin
and Uncle Ernie also have their charms, though,
I agree.

From: <liszka_pet>
Date: Sun Apr 9, 2000 11:29pm
Subject: Acid Queen
Ahhh . . . I must say, I do love Tina Turner.
And the Acid Queen get-up was pretty groovy. I
very nearly went as her for Halloween some years
ago. I especially liked how the played the whole
scene of Tommy getting high.

From: <pinball_honey>
Date: Fri Apr 21, 2000 10:00am
Subject: Musical Tommy MERCHANDISE WANTED !!!!!!
Hi anyone out there ! I´m looking for any TOMMY
merchandise esp. from Canada Tour (shirt +
jacket , pin , keychain) but also from any other

```
production ! I´m completely mad about that
yellow/blacl logo  . . .   PLEASE HELP ME ! SEll
me what you have or trade (I have German
stuff to trade  . . .  heehee)or let me know
where I could probably get any Tommy merchandise
!!!<br>THANKS A LOT !!!
YOUR PINBALL HONEY
```

```
From: <my_name_remains_a_mystery>
Date: Sat Apr 29, 2000 5:31pm
Subject: roger daltrey
roger is SO fine . . . hes also the sexiest!
```

```
From: <liszka_pet>
Date: Sat Apr 29, 2000 8:00pm
Subject: Re: roger daltrey
He is certainly that. My friends all say I'm
crazy, because he's so much older, but older
men rule to begin with. And Roger, well, they
just don't come any better. I first became
really aware of Roger Daltrey in 1992 when he
sang at the Concert for Life at Wembley. I think
I was 12. ^_^ Nice to know I'm not the only
person who missed his career that digs
him.
```

This short sequence of postings reveals concerns and enthusiasms not only typical of current *Tommy* fans, but redolent of cult obsessions more generally: pop idols, sexual permission, music, merchandise, youthful nostalgia, gender and generational differences – a fandom which is at once active and contemplative, communal and highly personal. As before, in this chapter I shall try to locate some aspects of these fan preoccupations in the film text itself and its contextual history, elaborating some of the larger themes which are emerging as we proceed.

Tommy – the 'Rock Opera'

The original album entitled *Tommy* was released in 1969. In the intervening years The Who's stage show (at concert halls and opera houses) and, from 1972, Lou Reisner's full orchestral production attracted large audiences on both sides of the Atlantic. The new decade inaugurated the theatrical extravaganza that traded on the hedonistic excesses and the unfulfilled spiritual yearnings that were the immediate fall-out of the post-hippy era. The abolition of the Lord Chamberlain's jurisdiction in 1968 paved the way for the likes of *Jesus Christ Superstar*, *Hair* (also both produced by the enterprising Robert Stigwood) and the cult of *The Rocky Horror (Picture) Show*. Once again, these productions were the brain-children of a relatively small coterie of creative talents and they marked a cultural retrospective on the previous decade. As Alexander Walker remarked of David Puttnam and Ray Connolly's David Essex double-bill *That'll Be the Day* (1973) and *Stardust* (1974), the early Seventies heralded 'the start of a revisionist view of the Sixties'.[5] However, these films presented a jaundiced, social-realist view of young, male ambition. Other kinds of responses indulged the glamorous excesses of the kitsch and the camp, in a celebration of the permission the Sixties had ushered in and the early Seventies pushed to new extremes or parodied with ironic detachment. But to see the cynicism of the Essex films as a conservative reaction and the flamboyant excess of Ken Russell's work as merely the heedless, hedonistic pursuit of further self-indulgence would be wrong. Both kinds of text contained their elements of nostalgia and placed popular music and the icon of the pop star firmly at the centre of youth culture. And even the most outlandish examples of glamorous excess shared a serious underlying preoccupation with spirituality, and the search for personal values in a barren world of moribund social structures, fast money and fleeting sensation.

The composer Pete Townshend reflected on the origins of *Tommy* and its relevance to youth culture in a 1975 interview to coincide with the film's release:

> *Tommy* is, if you like, a blanket cross-section of now, of the way people are now, of the way society is, of the way young people clutch at anything which seems as if it might help them along a bit quicker, whether it be rock 'n' roll, drugs, revolution, or whatever. They all want the short cuts, the easy way out, nobody's prepared to admit that life has a purpose, as such. Nobody's willing to admit that the individual is to blame for anything.[6]

Townshend's rather despondent overview stands in stark contrast to the utopian possibilities heralded by Roszak's counter-culture of 1968. Yet

The Who's songwriter was completing *Tommy* at that time. The work was a combination of Townshend's desire to develop the format of the popular song beyond the commercial strictures of the single and the album towards a unifying thematic concept, and a personal expression of a spiritual route from the watershed of 1967 (via the teachings of Indian mystic Meher Baba):

> I realized that there was a parallel in the shape of the autistic child . . .
> This was a straightforward analogy because the word 'illusion' is used
> by Meher Baba in a mystical sense. In other words the illusion that
> we live in, is one where our senses are fully functioning – we have our
> five senses and we have our emotions . . . but these are whole chunks
> of life, including the whole concept of reality, which escapes us . . .
> So I decided that the hero had to be deaf, dumb and blind, so that,
> seen from our already limited point of view, his limitations would be
> symbolic of our own.[7]

Spiritual doctrine aside, this idea of sensory alienation is interesting. It points to the adolescent's concern with being *in* the world but not *of* it, which is analogous to the achievement of socio-sexual identity. Pop culture and fandom play a crucial role for many teenagers in negotiating this formative transition. This is a matter I shall return to below. But before exploring in any depth the thematic issues inherent in *Tommy*, it is first necessary to consider the commercial aspect underpinning the success of what became known, from this time, as cross-over product.

Tommy – the Film

Ken Russell's film of *Tommy* (1975) was produced by Robert Stigwood, the Australian music entrepreneur who was keen to reach a wider audience with products that would transcend discrete media. The rock album/stage show/feature film triptych of formats became an extremely popular and lucrative commercial enterprise from this time. As a contemporary review in *Photoplay* put it:

> In just five years since Pete Townshend and The Who's rock-opera
> *Tommy* revolutionised the music scene, world-wide sales of the LP
> have topped the ten million mark. And anyone who has paid out for
> a double-album record is more than likely to go and see the movie.[8]

This straightforward economic projection was a trend some in the movie business were slow to latch onto. Ray Connolly complained that:

> Although you and I may have known for years that the people who buy records in large numbers tend to be the very same people who enjoy going to the pictures, it appears to have come as a recent revelation to the film industry . . . For 20 years, while rock has been establishing itself as the contemporary music form of the second half of this century, film-makers have continued to view it with suspicion and not a little distaste.[9]

But *Variety* speculated that this cross-over audience indeed presented a bright new future for Hollywood. It noted that 'Disk marketing methods have changed radically and, as with films, albums have become product that can be profitably promoted via television . . . and musical adaptations aimed at customers pre-sold on the music':

> Of interest, in this connection, is the fact that the UK is a self-sufficient and highly profitable disk market which helps to make such domestic pix as *That'll Be the Day*, when sold in association with an album, viable propositions . . .
>
> Heartening news though that may be for the British film trade, Stigwood is looking for bigger things from *Tommy* . . . [He] is gambling on the international clout of British rock names for an extra profit dimension. He is pitching the film offshore on a territory by territory basis (Columbia has it in the US) . . .
>
> Stigwood, after *Jesus Christ Superstar* . . . now heads a whole corps of music industry personnel who are looking to get into films. Stigwood's organisation operates a films and television division (under Beryl Vertue) with offices in London, New York and Hollywood.[10]

The film's marketing strategy was also underpinned by other key production decisions. John Walker reports that 'Part of the [$3.5 million] finance came from Columbia and the stipulation was that it should include American stars. Hence Ann-Margret as Tommy's mother and Jack Nicholson as a doctor', together with US singer Tina Turner as the Acid Queen.[11] As well as The Who themselves, named British rock stars included Elton John (as the Pinball Wizard) and Eric Clapton (as The Preacher).

The following year *Variety* reported that Columbia's marketing preview survey in the USA recorded the success rates of this strategic plan. In the

20–24 age group there was a 77 per cent awareness of the *Tommy* music in record and concert form and the 'bulk of interest in the film is generated by its rock personalities . . . rather than the film actors'. However, 'Movie stars give the project more legitimacy among movie fans without dulling anticipation among rock purists'. The majority of moviegoers on both sides of the Atlantic were attracted primarily because of The Who's music: 'Nowhere is there mention of the fact that *Tommy* was directed by Ken Russell'.[12]

Inspiration for the film project indeed originated with Townshend and The Who's then manager, Kit Lambert, as early as 1968. The band were quoted as saying that Russell was their first choice as director of a possible film version from the start and Lambert went so far as to draft a script, though no direct approaches were made to Russell at this time.[13] In his most recent reminiscences, Pete Townshend recalls a certain degree of creative struggle over the film proposal:

> When we were first recording it which was 1968, what I didn't realize was that Kit Lambert who was The Who's producer and manager, together with his partner Chris Stamp, had the hope of becoming a film maker, of making films about rock 'n' roll. And as soon as I started working on *Tommy* he was very encouraging in making it as ambitious and as broad in scope as possible. It was his idea that the story should span more than a lifetime and incorporate the two world wars. By the time it was finished, he had already written a screenplay. But I blocked that movie. I think I was very close to him emotionally and very dependent upon him at that time and thought that he would fly off to Hollywood. So Kit didn't get to make that movie . . .
>
> Subsequently, what caused Ken Russell to become interested in the movie . . . was the fact that I gave permission to Lou Reisner to do an orchestral version. And the orchestral version was what gave Ken Russell the way in. The first offer that we got was in fact through Hammer Films (and that was with Chris Stamp). Chris Stamp then talked to Stigwood about it.[14]

Once Russell was on board (having been approached by Robert Stigwood and attended a performance of the Reisner orchestral version by the London Symphony Orchestra at the Finsbury Park Rainbow), some preliminary meetings with Townshend (chiefly about classical music) were sufficient for the director to fashion a screenplay, which itself incorporated elements from several recent, abandoned projects.

In the year after *Savage Messiah* (1972) Russell was involved with a number of new schemes, none of which came to fruition. He allowed the intrusion of several authors into his life (the most insightful being John Baxter's first full-length biography, *An Appalling Talent*, 1973), and did a number of interviews for journalists. He accepted offers to work again in television (a BBC documentary on Vaughan Williams), and even agreed to be the subject of a Southern TV biography, *Man of the South*. He best summed up this period of hiatus in his own words:

> I'm going through a pessimistic 'down' stage, I think. At the finish of that last film I wasn't well, as you know. I was going through some terrible mental battles and I think it was reflected in the music film [the aborted potted history entitled *Music Music Music*]. So the best thing to do is just forget it. I thought, as a bit of therapy, I'd do a couple of documentaries . . . I think I need recharging my batteries.[15]

Yet 1973 saw neither television project realised. Russell began developing several new film possibilities which included 'a pop musical called *Rachel Lily Rosenbloom* to be directed by him on Broadway . . . a version of Rabelais's *Gargantua and Pantagruel*',[16] a proposal 'to direct Peter Maxwell Davies' opera *Taverner*' and *The Angels*, which 'combines . . . episodes inspired by George Neveux's *Juliette ou la Clef des Songes*, large chunks of material about racial problems, outrageous satire on organised religion and established forms of government, and cryptic autobiographical references'.[17] While MGM rejected the latter 'in part because they couldn't understand it', it shares with *Music Music Music* similar concerns with the compromised artist forced into commercial sell-out, a media victim of his own success. Futhermore, *Music Music Music* followed 'the adventures of John Fairfax, the composer of a religious rock opera entitled *Jesus on Venus*' who is forced 'to supplement his income by doing to the music for TV commercials' which include 'an incident where a child spews up canned lamb'.[18] It is perhaps not surprising (and by no means unprecedented in Russell's work) to find several of these themes and ideas regurgitated in *Tommy*. Indeed, the director admitted:

> *Tommy* is loaded with material from previous scripts . . . Variations of the baked beans sequence in *Tommy* were in *The Angels* and in *Music*

Music Music, while a variation on the shrine sequence in *Tommy* turned
up earlier in *The Angels* and in *Gargantua*. I don't know what I would
do without my rejected scripts.[19]

Pragmatic as such creative methods may be, what is remarkable is the
way in which Russell's sensibilities seem to have been moving towards
the material Townshend provided in *Tommy*. And The Who had long
envisaged Russell as their favoured screen interpreter. 'I was delighted that
the more I read into the scenario, the more it resembled a screenplay I'd
written called *The Angels* which was about false religions which I was told
was uncommercial and so I couldn't get finance. So I saw that this could
be an amalgam between the two'.[20] While this happy coincidence may
be attributed to a certain contemporary Zeitgeist regarding spiritual and
artistic integrity versus commercial exploitation, the collaboration was by
no means a match made in heaven, and the compromise which became
Tommy the movie is just that – neither completely The Who's, nor Russell's
ultimate vision. If the director 'found *Tommy* unfamiliar, even unpleasant to
the ear the first time he heard the score', he was relatively at home in the
task of finding visual metaphors for the emotional registers of music.[21] On
the other hand, while Russell's treatment develops the narrative background
to the story (for which Townshend wrote six additional songs), fleshes out
the emotional lives of the central characters for the screen, and adds the
sustained mirror symbolism and pinball leitmotif to the elaborate fantasy
sequences, his interpretation emphasises those personal preoccupations
with fake religion, artistic compromise and the corruption of advertising and
material culture perhaps at the expense of Townshend's spiritual dimension.
The composer's reaction on release was indeed somewhat guarded:

> It's not tremendously faithful to the original aim of the original album.
> Also, it's tremendously faithful to the original storyline which is peculiar
> because the story line is quite weak and clichéd . . . Beneath all the
> colourful imagery and the big visual qualities, the same message does
> come through. Ken *does* have a similar sense, a similar spiritual poise,
> even if it's a bit unbalanced.[22]

Reflecting more recently on the qualities Russell's vision brought to the
adaptation, Townshend recalls:

> I felt that if I could achieve anything and it had a spiritual sub-text it
> would straddle the world of pop from which we'd come and this new

hippy world that seemed to be about new-age values. It really felt to me like what he had was a kind of pop art knack – it seemed to me that he was the right man for the job.[23]

Some reviewers, however, felt that the distance between album and film (from the late Sixties to the mid-Seventies) was itself unbridgeable:

> *Tommy* was a child of the Sixties. It fulfilled the audience's need for a work that would validate the importance of rock music. And it was accepted more for its conception than its execution. Truth to tell, it was a superficial, Khalil Gibran-styled parable, redeemed only by The Who's peculiar ability to make even their pretentiousness enjoyable, and by an undercurrent of humour that suggested the band was taking *Tommy* less seriously than the audience.
>
> Director Ken Russell's cartoon-styled screen version of *Tommy* fails above all because he never solves the problem of transposing a Sixties story into the cynical Seventies . . . Even the visual imagery (mirrors, crawling snakes, dramatic colour changes) is tied to a pop view of enlightenment that lost its meaning long ago.[24]

One senses Landau's derisory view is as much a product of *its* time as is the awkward transposition the film is required (and according to him fails) to achieve. By the mid-Seventies the head of steam that would give rise to punk's bitter nihilism was building underground. Through that dark glass, it can be argued, the only way to view *Tommy* retrospectively is within the inverted commas of a pop sensibility. If the 'pop view of enlightenment' was old hat, it was still a newcomer to the cinema screen, with synthesised, quintophonic, Dolby soundtrack and garish, proto-pop-video special effects. It was deliberately both excessive and tongue-in-cheek. Like *A Clockwork Orange* and *The Wicker Man* before it, *Tommy* demonstrated a picaresque, even carnivalesque, Rabelaisian attitude to social convention.

Visual Style

Both *A Clockwork Orange* and *Tommy* share a flamboyant visual style redolent of the fashionable cartoon-strip acrylics of Roy Lichtenstein and the garish, pneumatic plastics of Claes Oldenburg. Transatlantic pop art was ubiquitous in the late Sixties from Andy Warhol's factory screen-prints to Peter Blake's iconic design for The Beatles' *Sergeant Pepper* album (and its psychedelic derivatives) and George Dunning's animated feature *Yellow Submarine* (1968). Yet the early Seventies witnessed a media-inflected cynicism in what had been perhaps a modish, naive celebration of primary colours and comic-book play. The synthetic and the saccharine, the mass-produced and the relentlessly promoted washed over the public consciousness like a wave of collective nausea. By mid-decade, glam-rock had reached new heights of space-age hyperbole, adopting images of variously feminised masculinity.

If the movies discovered pop and pop art rather belatedly, this was an interest shared by very different cinematic talents. Kubrick's and Russell's employment of highly stylised cartoon visuals and synthesised soundtracks are, at least superficially, what *Tommy* shares in common with *A Clockwork Orange*. While their respective approaches to film-making may be poles apart, what each envisioned through the vibrancy of pop art style is an emotional truth rooted in iconic screen performances. We might contrast the scrupulous, exacting approach of Kubrick with Russell's impressionistic, suck-it-and-see trial and error. Furthermore, Russell is famous for short and sketchy scripts (*Tommy* [106 mins] runs to some 65 pages), lack of direction to actors, and multiple takes (30 of Roger Daltry running through a mustard field) in his improvisational, intuitive approach to filming. Yet his particularity in choice of set-ups, set design, and costume, and carefully rehearsed choreography reflect a more deliberate method. The number of different set-ups in *Tommy*'s eight-week schedule suggests thorough planning and extremely efficient shooting, combined with the requisite amount of good fortune.

For *A Clockwork Orange* Kubrick adapted a number of real locations to an extent unprecedented in his films. This lent an immediacy and authenticity to the bleak futuristic world of the film; the future is here and now. Russell adores locations and the imaginative success or failure of a film idea often rests upon his early discovery of inspiring places. In *Tommy* it is Russell's creation of scenes shot in the Lake District as a narrative framing device for the film's beginning and ending, and the use of the Gaiety Theatre on Southsea Pier (together with other locations in and around Portsmouth) that marry the Romantic and elemental with a seaside-postcard, post-war, cartoon-realism. One example of this cartoon approach is the impossibly small beach-huts in which the visitors to Bernie's Holiday Camp apparently live. A lifelong fan of Belgian surrealist René Magritte, Russell's location hunting is also often a triumph of the pop artist's sensitivity to the found object: a naval scrapyard piled with discarded mooring buoys is transformed with silver paint into a nightmarish pinball park.

However, as with John Barry's studied dressing of Kubrick's location sets, so for Russell, visual design is crucial. The key personnel here were Shirley Russell (costumes), John Clark (art direction) and Paul Dufficey (set decoration):

> The costumes have a wonderful pop feel to them and are very individual. I think a lot of them were off the peg. We went round second hand shops and looked for fifties clothes and I think particularly with Ann-Margret the leopardskin look is absolutely phenomenal . . . We had a pop artist called Paul Dufficey . . . and it's largely due to him that the film has its unique look . . . I think it's very important to get an unconventional eye to anything that has a unique quality of its own which I think *Tommy* does. It was set in the fifties, so already we were doing an historical reappraisal of an era . . . I think we really got an era, although it's a fantasy view of it, it's got a unique style.[25]

One of the key techniques Russell employs in order to foreground costume and performance is the flattening of the picture plane. This televisual quality lends an immediacy to physical action, while the garish colour-palette and high contrast anticipate the pop video. Furthermore, the cumulative effect of a concentration on spherical objects (from giant pinballs to silver eyeballs) against flat, geometric surfaces renders this world curiously impermeable, yet endlessly symbolic. The cross and ball icon of Tommy's new religious movement is an oblique reference to the ancient Egyptian ankh, a symbol of new life adopted by the Women's Movement. Smooth surfaces without openings resist penetration. They become visual playgrounds: safe, sterile, asexual places.

Of course, the musical is a film genre that relies above all upon stylisation. In fact, as one critic was quick to point out, The Who's original *Tommy* wasn't even the 'rock opera' it was (half-jokingly) billed as, but rather a cantata (of linked songs) without narrative progression.[26] Russell's film transformation gave the story its thematic structure and fleshed out the characterisation, while retaining the libretto as the sole vehicle of dramatic communication – there is no additional, non-musical dialogue. This device not only preserves the primacy of the music, but also avoids the (sometimes awkward, always self-conscious) gear-change of the conventional musical between dramatic narrative and musical performance. There is an important sense in which *Tommy* is not a musical film, but a filmed performance of a song cycle. This is not to say that it is not sometimes awkward and always self-conscious, but that its particular brand of stylisation marks a departure from the characteristic approach of prior pop film vehicles (Elvis Presley, Cliff Richard, The Beatles, David Essex, for example). Indeed, this ethos was enshrined in the production process which began with a complete recording of the soundtrack before any filming was done.[27] The cast were then required to perform for the camera to the playback of their own recording: a feat which is especially accomplished in the case of Ann-Margret as Tommy's mother. The dramatic effect of this method is to stylise the diegetic world – to render life's only means of verbal communication that of the rock song. To say that the result is dramatically overblown is to deny some of the subtleties of transformation that Oscar-nominated Ann-Margret in particular brings to the performance. But what it achieves consistently, above all else, is an immense, visceral, emotional charge. In *Tommy*, Russell also extended another well-practised shooting technique of playing music on set in order to energise and liberate actors emotionally and physically; here, that occasional device became a structural necessity. But the palpable emotional commitment and energy of the cast creates, in the best-choreographed production numbers, a 'live show' immediacy and impact that is the antithesis of the restrained codes of classical screen acting. And, unlike the standard backstage musical, this all-singing, all-dancing show offers no narrative respite from this pitch of dramatic intensity. As Russell himself has said, 'Above all, it *communicates . . .*'[28]

Performance

The sublime effect of casting stars from the world of popular music in charismatic screen roles invites identification and mistrust in equal measure. Daltry in all his stiff, awkward vulnerability both is and isn't Tommy. The film pities its protagonist and draws our sympathy. Then, it cynically transforms him into the money-grabbing shaman of a fake religious cult. He remains untouchable, sealed in his private (rock star's) world, as if autistic, out of reach.

The central relationship in the story is that of Tommy and his mother; the rest (even Oliver Reed's Uncle Frank) are cartoon caricatures, albeit

Figure 13: My family: Oliver Reed, Roger Daltry and Ann-Margret in *Tommy*
[RBT STIGWOOD PRODS/HEMDALE/THE KOBAL COLLECTION]

nicely drawn (Keith Moon's Uncle Ernie, Paul Nicholas's Cousin Kevin, Tina Turner's Acid Queen for example). But what gives shape, dramatic contrast and some emotional depth to the narrative is the juxtaposition of Nora Walker's guilt-ridden yearning with Tommy's mute impassivity. And plainly the underlying framework (in Russell's augmentation of Townshend's tale) is an Oedipal archetype. As the synopsis outlines:

> Group-Captain Walker [Robert Powell] unexpectedly returns home, having survived his plane-crash after all, and discovers Nora in bed with Frank. In the resulting turmoil, Frank smashes a heavy bedside-lamp down on to Walker's head, killing him. Young Tommy, standing in the doorway, sees the whole horrifying scene reflected in a mirror – and the shock makes him deaf, dumb and blind ('What about the Boy?').[29]

As he matures (and Roger Daltry takes over from the juvenile Barry Winch), his unfeeling body is prey to all manner of exploitation at the hands of others: faith-healers, specialists, relatives, drug pedlars (all false-gods of differing kinds). His accidental discovery of a superhuman talent at the pinball table gives him his one possibility of redemptive self-expression, yet at the film's iconic centre the pinball contest is staged physically as a kind of existential masturbation for social misfits: all supple wrists and thrusting pelvis.

His mother's ensuing role (as her material fortunes are transformed by Tommy's newfound skill) oscillates between bouts of guilt-driven, suffocating affection and careless, self-aggrandising exploitation. Nora Walker's physical performance is plastic, tactile and fluid; Tommy's is dry, hermetically sealed, and remote. Her eyes are moist, expressive, fulsome; his are fixed, unblinking, in a glassy stare. She is sensual, open; he is impermeable, closed. She is lurid, gaudy, voluptuous, all woman; he is clean, white, innocent, and androgynous. Nowhere is this set of contrasts more apparent than in the climactic white boudoir scenes: first with the grotesque bathing in champagne, soap-suds, baked beans and chocolate (all pure Russell) and later, after a futile visit to a seductive specialist (Jack Nicholson), the 'Tommy Can You Hear Me?' and 'Smash the Mirror' sequences. Mirrors and reflections (Lacanian or otherwise) abound in the film's infinite lexicon of pseudo-Freudian hypersignification. But here, in a drunken maternal initiation rite, she performs a frustrated, erotic dance before his heedless gaze, whips her hair across his face and finally flings him through the round-mirrored wall, through which he bursts in a climax that is at once the breaking of a virginity, an emotional release from the claustrophobia of their possessive/dependent relationship and a transformative awakening of his senses ('I'm Free'). Ann-Margret's sensual, physical abandonment is the perfect foil for Roger Daltry's (thoroughly appropriate) catatonic woodenness. Their troubled, Oedipal relationship is resolved only after his miracle cure when he tears off her gaudy jewellery and symbolically baptises her anew.

Two things are of special significance here. Firstly, the slippage apparent in Daltry's untrained acting style which threatens the coherence of his psychological motivation. As we saw with Jagger in *Performance*, the rock star brings to acting an iconic charisma without the unifying and delimiting controls of dramatic training. While Daltry sustains admirably the mute, autistic distance of Tommy's incapacity, once 'cured' his acting is demonstrably uncontrolled and incoherent, revealing an excess of gesture, and a self-conscious presence. Secondly, his relationship with his mother displays an unresolved, adolescent attitude towards the maternal body in which the film is erotically complicit. This attitude to the female as other is very similar to that adopted in *A Clockwork Orange* and is unsettling chiefly for its lack of resolution in specifically erotic pay-off. The way in which explicit violence, sex and bodily display remain ideologically 'unrecuperated' in such films is suggestive of more fundamental social upheaval.

Summary

Narratively, *Tommy* works as a rite-of-passage journey from childhood, through adolescence to manhood; our hero's mute, alienated, insentient condition operates as a hyperbolic metaphor for the universal problems of maturation and socialisation. But secondly, this theme is also historicised in the particularly acute circumstances of World War II babies, early encounters with death and loss, unstable families, post-war austerity and the rise of youth culture, which culminated in the generational rift that opened up the Sixties' cultural revolution. As Pete Townshend reflects:

> What we then have is a story that relates very much to the emergence of the guitar-rock-hero around the early Sixties as a folk-singing observer, a reflecting-mirror to the disaffection and difficulty that young, working-class men in particular were having getting used to the fact that they were having to find a new way of getting dignity, respect and finding a way of establishing themselves in the order of society without being a member of the services. Ken enabled me to grasp the fact that this was very much my childhood story but also it was like holding up a mirror to a whole generation who said: 'Yes, this is my story, this is what I went through' or at least it was an experience that many shared.[30]

Thirdly, Tommy's post-'cure' phase – during which his miracle healing makes him a media celebrity, revolutionary and religious cult figure – concerns both the prevalent interest in alternative religion and spiritual values that was a fall-out of hippydom and the cynical commercial and media exploitation of its iconic leaders. Messianic symbolism abounds in Tommy's 'calling' of fishermen on the beach, his 'baptism' of Nora Walker's Magdalene-whore mother, and the establishment of the Mission.

Finally, the film's open ending leaves Tommy, the pop icon, on the run from renegade fans, in pursuit of a solitary transfiguration. Townshend notes that *Tommy* charts the story of 'the artist becoming the great messiah who then falls from grace, which is inevitable, when the person who holds up the mirror says, "Oh, by the way, I'm not just *like* you, I *am* you – we both share the same condition"'.[31] Tommy remains just as alienated as before, just as unable to achieve a socialised selfhood, because social recognition involves negation. Paradoxically, his iconic status (like that of the celebrity) is another kind of social exclusion, of isolation and impermeability. And this condition is depicted as a direct result of fan identification. Yet, like the risen Christ, though he is physically untouchable, he is in his transubstantiated state, immortal and triumphant. Unlike Alex DeLarge, whose bodily excesses are disciplined, strait-jacketed, beaten and neutralised, leaving him only to the licensed internal fantasies of his imagination ('I was cured alright'), Tommy's lifeless, abused body is re-energised. His final return to the Cumbrian mountaintop where he was conceived, to bathe in the waterfall where his parents embraced, to worship (in a shot redolent of *The Wicker Man*) the eternal rising sun, is a symbolic rebirth to a physical world of natural sensation; but such rites are purely iconic, elemental, antisocial, in fact religious. Indeed, the suggestions of Pagan symbolism here were, according to Ken Russell, sufficient for the ending to be excised in apartheid South Africa.[32]

Though less assured, and exhibiting none of the accomplished guile of Malcolm McDowell, Roger Daltry's hero evinces a similarly engaging vulnerability. Thus, for fans of The Who, the film describes a frail, unconstituted young man *becoming*, through the liberation and empowerment of rock music, Roger Daltry (the consummate, masculine rock icon). He spends the last third of the film naked from the waist up and his physical prowess (incredibly he performed all his own stunts including the precipitous hang-gliding scenes) is photographed and lit almost fetishistically. The promise of psychosexual transformation – particularly noticeable in physical mobility – is of course also what the film (as the music before it) offers vicariously to a willing audience. As much of a paradox as this might appear when one considers the unambiguous demise of the Marilyn Monroe Madonna earlier in the story, and the fate of Sally Simpson (Victoria Russell) later, nonetheless, the film ultimately endorses and celebrates the star persona. As Townshend puts it: 'It has this way of triggering stuff that is deep-seated'.[33] In other words, bringing

FIGURE 14: The pinball wizard as shaman: Roger Daltry (Tommy)
and his cult followers
[RBT STIGWOOD PRODS/HEMDALE/BRITISH FILM INSTITUTE]

to the surface archetypal teenage traumas and showing the star's transcendence of them (indeed, of all material limitations including fan culture itself). Where lesser pop vehicles might settle for the comforts of a straightforward cathartic trajectory with which to identify, this film is genuinely cult: fans are invited to idolise an icon who has transcended commercial popularity and mass appeal to achieve a state of sublime purity in which we can commune privately, without an intercessor, directly through music.

That'll Be the Day and *Stardust* rehearse familiar rites-of-passage crises simply on a social and historical level: Jim Maclaine's insatiable libido is his one dependable characteristic. Later, *Quadrophenia* too brings a gritty realism to nostalgia for period style. *Tommy* problematises masculinity itself (even if the finale is a triumphant display of the six-pack male physique) and ultimately transcends it. It offers, as other cult performances, stimulation and consolation in equal measure. Like *A Clockwork Orange*, *Tommy* demonstrates through the disability of the body in social space and the disorientation of the senses in the emotional sphere, the common problems of psychosexual development and their release. I believe this is what lends *Tommy* a universal cult appeal beyond the nostalgic period pieces of the Connolly/Puttnam films. As Pete Townshend comments:

That's what makes good popular art – making a hole in it so that you can put yourself into the middle of it.[34]

His use of the pronoun is instructive here. Townshend himself (like Kubrick and Russell) is the maker of good popular art, but who makes the holes in it, and whose self may be put into its middle? What he is referring to surely is the kind of access offered to audiences by cult films like *Tommy* through engagement with charismatic performance, sexual violence and erotic possibility. And as we have seen with previous examples, 'holes' are either made by accident or design in the text and its contextual history, which allow audiences that kind of access to subjective pleasures. The nature of those pleasures and their particular subjectivity is a theme I shall be developing further in the next chapter.

6

THE MAN WHO FELL TO EARTH (1976)

Though its cult future seems assured, its immediate chances will depend on audience reaction to its offbeat appeal as a cerebral sci-fier, a sort of earth-bound 'Space Odyssey' with 'Clockwork Orange' undertones – though it remains a very different film indeed. The David Bowie name should help with the youngsters . . .[1]

Introduction

It has become a commonplace that cult films are oddities which somehow don't fit in to the film culture of which they are a part. As we have seen, sometimes this is because they have been marginalised, suppressed or critically debased. But even when they emerge from the canons of established and respected independent directors, or employ stars and visual styles that have immediate currency, or engage with issues of topical relevance, still in some way they somehow do not 'fit'. They are born out of their time. I have been moving towards an explanation for this by endeavouring to make a link between certain kinds of distinctive textual practice and ideological constraints. I have considered generic hybridity and narrative unevenness, authorial traits and visual designs; but I return again here to the issue of performance where, in cult films, all these textual determinants seem to coalesce with particular clarity. Indeed, the central performance(s) in each film I have examined may well constitute the vital, dynamic link between the original text and its subsequent cult appreciation. Certainly contemporary fan evidence supports this view.

Perhaps performance, above all, is the conduit which best allows access to the text. Perhaps this is the 'hole' in popular texts to which Pete Townshend refers; this may be the same hole Turner sees in Chas's face, and, in turn, the hole Chas's bullet makes in Turner's head. It may be, in short, the portal through which cult fans enter the texts of certain films: films that are full of holes, films that will admit them. Of course, if we are serious about such metaphors they will need justifying. In what way might fans be said to *participate in* the film text? *The Rocky Horror Picture Show* and *The Wicker Man* have provided some examples of what might be termed fan *colonisation* in the broadest sense of the text (which might include the conditions of its exhibition or the locations where it was filmed). But, to return to my earlier discussions around the work of Laura Mulvey and my concept of double articulation, we need also to pursue the matter of spectatorship itself, and the act of looking, if we are to propose that cult films are viewed in a different way. It is here, building on the ground cleared by the likes of Richard Dyer and Jackie Stacey, that the function of performance may be examined afresh.[2]

Performance

It is prescient indeed that upon the 1976 release of Nicolas Roeg's *The Man Who Fell to Earth*, *Variety* should have hedged its bets about the film's immediate oddity, while expressing confidence about its future cult appeal. Yet the reviewer accurately divines both the general sense of Roeg's idiosyncratic work being ahead of its time, and the specific help Bowie's star billing might provide in accommodating early audiences. It is, like *A Clockwork Orange*, also another example of an oblique, unorthodox take on the sci-fi genre, though like Kubrick's film its futuristic projection is firmly earth-bound. The casting of Bowie is a matter on which most critics were united in their approval. So apt is he for the part of Thomas Jerome Newton that one might almost conjecture as to whether Nicolas Roeg chose David Bowie or David Bowie chose Nicolas Roeg. Indeed, we have seen with *Tommy*, and later *Quadrophenia*, what is true of a number of other pop and rock vehicles of the period: they are less the works of specific auteurs than they are extemporisations of an artist's or band's existing profile.

John Walker claims that 'Bowie's alien in *The Man Who Fell To Earth*, adrift in a society like his own but still hostile, overloaded with sensory input, is the archetypal Roeg hero':

Archetypes are what Roeg deals in, which is perhaps why he has featured the familiar personalities of rock singers, simple images for a complex world, in several of his films.[3]

Fair enough. But 'simple' and 'complex' will need some explaining. On the other hand, as *The Hollywood Reporter* put it: 'Bowie stars in a futuristic love story that seems like a mere extension of his imagination'.[4] And long before the film was mooted Michael Watts elicited this response in a 1972 interview with the pop icon:

He says he's more an actor and entertainer than a musician; that he may, in fact, only be an actor and nothing else: 'Inside this invincible frame there might be an invisible man.' You kidding? 'Not at all. I'm not particularly taken with life. I'd probably be very good as just an astral spirit'.[5]

This obscure, lampoon profundity might almost be spoken by Thomas Jerome Newton himself. The bizarre but extremely productive interrelationship between star and protagonist is explained by the film's screenwriter, Paul Mayersberg, in terms of its Romantic core:

David Bowie's much remarked bi-sexuality, which may or may not be true . . . transforms this complete romantic ambiance through a definite two-way pull. Everyone is attracted towards Newton so when he becomes threatened we are threatened too, although it is the people who are threatening him who are closer to us.

In his rock music Bowie has used, more than anyone else, the combination of images from romantic stories and pictures from space . . . The breathless, frightened, occasionally ecstatic delivery becoming increasingly like a saxophone is now a hallmark of Bowie's style . . . His style is unique and because it is unique it is vulnerable, like the character he plays in the movie.[6]

Certainly Bowie's alien in *The Man Who Fell to Earth* evinces a hypnotic, hermeneutic charm – a studied fragility, derived from his stage alter egos, at once endearing and remote. And yet, as with Jagger in *Performance* and Daltry in *Tommy*, there is more to these screen performances than coquettish ambiguity or an easy pop image trade-off. For example, in casting Bowie Roeg later remarked:

I didn't just want an actor . . . I think sometimes there's too much acting going on. It's terribly difficult not to . . . Actors play alien people, alien from themselves. It's a very highly skilled and brilliant actor that can get rid of that performance.[7]

This comment relates directly back to my earlier suggestion (derived from Goffman's interactionist perspective) that the 'slippage' or redundancy in acting technique which untrained stars reveal can produce a palpable chemistry with a sympathetic audience. That pop idols like Bowie overcompensate for one kind of professional lack by bringing to the screen the potent symbolism of their stage and recording image is made manifest in the words of one devoted fan, 'Julie':

> I began to think he was a new kind of Messiah. I used to think he was the Coming of the Lord personified and all kinds of things. I really thought he had some kind of infinite power and wisdom.
>
> Almost like Marc Bolan, I suppose, had a mystical quality that wasn't quite of this world or of this time.
>
> Bowie was magic and he was supreme. He had the qualities of a type of ruler.
>
> He was science fiction personified. To me he represented the most bizarre things which were evil and not of this world and completely beyond the imagination.
>
> I really believed he was an alien of some kind. I didn't think he was at all normal, human.[8]

Such responses reveal how, in one fan's eyes at least, Bowie's preexisting personae anticipated the role of Newton. It may also work to precipitate the collapse of the conventional distinction between actor and character, between reality and fiction, because such distinctions are already blurred in the case of artists like Bowie. Indeed, another contemporary reviewer, Alexander Stuart, agrees that Bowie's achievement is thoroughly 'compelling' and the actor/character interface equally incredible:

> Where Bowie stops and acting begins is difficult to determine; to a considerable degree, Thomas Jerome Newton is David Bowie, and vice versa – or if not actually Bowie, then one of the personae he has formulated during the past few years as a rock performer whose prevailing fascination has been space and science fiction.[9]

David Bartholomew elaborates this point about the crossing of reality/ fiction boundaries, or rather, the extension of the rock star's persona:

Like Jagger in *Performance* . . . Bowie can simply fall back on acting
out his own off-screen media-musical image, emphasizing the weird,
other-worldly . . . quality of his stage performance and record album
content. Newton becomes, of course, a recording star at the end of
the film, his initial album called 'The Visitor', not unlike several of
Bowie's own space-y album titles like 'Space Oddity' and 'The Rise
and Fall of Ziggy Stardust and the Spiders from Mars', all of which
further cements the relationship. The role also affords us the luxury of
looking – erroneously – at the film as a pictorialization of how we like
to imagine our rock stars in real life.[10]

That last point is especially important here. For the fan's (voyeuristic) sense
of glimpsing into the private life of a star through a screen performance is
indeed a fiction. But it is also true in the sense that through acting the star
displays and betrays more of himself than is ordinarily regulated by his pre-
existing image. This provides for the fan a new kind of access to the star
image, and reveals in the star a new, and charismatic, kind of vulnerability.
In classical theatre such intimate identification with vulnerability is often
achieved through the plot device of dramatic irony; here, it is grounded
in physicality and intonation, both conveying of frailty.

Tom Milne, in *Sight and Sound*, writes: 'Bowie's presence and performance
suggest qualities that are recognized as common denominators of difference,
of alienness, of – in fact – non-humanness . . . [and] more particularly . . .
a composite picture emerges of vulnerability . . .'[11] This last comment is
especially telling; for the presentation of human/alien difference depends
on the suppression of other kinds of recognisable difference. In pursuing this
composite image of masculine vulnerability May Routh, costume designer
on *The Man Who Fell to Earth*, revealed that because Bowie was so thin
many of the clothes she dressed him in were boy's sizes. However, this was
also a deliberate strategy because 'I wanted to have a feeling like a sort of
school uniform'.[12] It is highly significant that in dressing an alien man, school
uniform should have been an inspiration: for it is at once pre-pubescent and
codified, and thus obscures both sexual difference and individual personality.
Such performances of masculine ambiguity are also thrown into sharper
contrast in respect of their relations to the female and, specifically, with
regard to the maternal body, as we saw in *A Clockwork Orange* and *Tommy*.
And this is a topic I shall pursue here too in due course. But before we return
to issues of performance and fan response let us locate the circumstances of
Bowie's casting in the context of the film's production history.

Figure 15: On another planet: David Bowie in the desert of
New Mexico in *The Man Who Fell to Earth*
[EMI/THE KOBAL COLLECTION]

Production History

Notwithstanding the issues outlined above, Nicolas Roeg's own comments on the casting of Bowie make clear that there was nothing accidental about the apparent ease with which Bowie played himself. While, like Daltry in *Tommy* (a film role for which Bowie was considered) and Jagger in *Performance*, each rock star brings much of his own stage persona across to the screen role, Bowie is a more considerable acting talent than either of his peers (as *Lisztomania* [1975] and *Ned Kelly* [1970] respectively proved):

> A lot of rock stars think they can just transfer their art or their personality to film. David is an exception to the rule . . . He is a performer. His whole magnetism comes out in acting.[13]

Indeed, earlier in his music career he had undertaken some training and was especially influenced by the tutelage of Lindsay Kemp (who played Alder McGregor in *The Wicker Man*) in the art of mime: 'Lindsay was my last mentor, I think. I've not known another till Nic'.[14] Bowie was suggested to Roeg by executive producer Si Litvinoff who knew Maggie Abbott, then agent for Bowie at ICM. Abbott sent a copy of a BBC *Omnibus* documentary about Bowie ('Cracked Actor') which impressed Roeg, largely for the 'reclusive quality' which came across. Bowie brought the right reclusive attributes of his rock star persona and was, fittingly, not an actor, but could certainly act. Creative decisions apart, one senses Roeg's casting of Bowie, alongside American stars Candy Clark, Rip Torn and Buck Henry, was also pragmatically aimed at garnering the promotional appeal of a cross-over market amongst his established transatlantic fan base.

The final ingredient in the cross-over potential of this star package was to have been music. Si Litvinoff explains:

> One of the great things about this from the beginning was David's great popularity in the music world – he was an icon all over the world . . . The original deal we made with David and Bobby Litman who became David's agent, was that RCA which was to do the soundtrack would pay . . . I think it was $250,000 . . . and that would be David's fee. [Co-Producer] Michael Deeley, as I was told it, tried to renegotiate with David and David said 'Up Yours'. When I finally heard the soundtrack I thought it was remarkable . . . As you know the soundtrack is the album that David did called *Low* [1977].[15]

In the meantime, film editor Graeme Clifford assembled the roughcut against a backing track of Pink Floyd's *Dark Side of the Moon*, which 'worked brilliantly' but would have proven 'horrendously expensive to buy. In the end it was John Phillips [ex-Mamas and Papas] who actually put the music together, which came from a lot of different sources'.[16] Phillips's assemblage of small-town country and western and cool urban jazz with the otherworldy purity of Stomu Yamashta, against a dissonant welter of alien sound effects, becomes as much a part of the outsider's subjective perception of the sweep of American history as the barren New Mexico landscape itself, and is equally ironic in its incongruity. Either Floyd or the Bowie of *Low* would have cast a very different, much more cosmic, futuristic effect. But then in an important sense (despite parallels with

The Day the Earth Stood Still) this is *not* science fiction (of either the techno-epic or the paranoid-thriller varieties).[17]

Screen adaptor Paul Mayersberg dispels the sci-fi trappings with the comment that 'there is at least as much nostalgia for the bicentennial as there is future shock in the film'[18] and Nic Roeg insists that what attracted him to Walter Tevis's 1963 novel was that 'it still has a human story to it . . . it's not just sci-fi'.[19] As earth-bound sci-fi, several commentators have seen the film 'as a visual essay of American landscape' whose 'nearest equivalent is probably Antonioni's *Zabriskie Point*, another view of America seen through alien eyes'.[20] Certainly the outsider's view is the film's primary, if fragmented perspective, and its particular take may be considered (through Roeg's modernist lens) to be existential, rather than alien (in a science-fiction sense) or of alienation (in a Marxist sense). While its arid, cerebral atmosphere invites comparisons with Camus's *l'Etranger*, Roeg reminds us of the Churchillian paradox of language: 'The English in America are very alien-like because we have that mutual language'.[21] It was as much a personal feeling as a statement of existential angst.

By the mid-Seventies, despite three highly individual, critically acclaimed features (*Performance*, *Walkabout* and *Don't Look Now*), and following a successful career during the Sixties as a revered cinematographer, Roeg was still considered too avant-garde for the tastes and pockets of Hollywood financiers. The furore over *Performance* with Warners was not likely to change American studio minds in a hurry. But following the success of the safer *Walkabout* (produced by Si Litvinoff and distributed through Fox) and *Don't Look Now* (as a joint-funded Italian/British production put out by British Lion and Paramount in the USA), Roeg was building a British-based creative and commercial team committed to his uncompromisingly independent cinematic vision.[22]

On the basis of *Don't Look Now*, Barry Spikings and Michael Deeley who had taken over the ailing British Lion (soon to be incorporated into the EMI conglomerate) were persuaded to finance Roeg's next project (to the tune of £1.75 million). Deeley and Spikings (instrumental in the *Wicker Man* post-production debacle) typified a new generation of film financiers: frequently showing themselves to be shrewder judges of the colour of money than of film aesthetics. Nonetheless, they took a significant gamble in supporting Roeg's American project on the back of a go-it-alone policy which withdrew British Lion from the leaking umbrella of parent company J. H. Vavasseur, and depended more upon the hard-pressed purse of the

NFFC than 'a conditional undertaking from Paramount to acquire it for distribution for $1.5 million'. Later, when Paramount's head of production Barry Diller saw the preview with Mike Deeley he was astounded: 'You promised me a linear narrative,' he complained. Deeley subsequently admitted that he hadn't heard the term before; needless to say, the deal was off. Deeley and Spikings had already begun talks with Bernard Delfont of EMI at Cannes in May 1975 and soon the Lion was returned, for its own safety, to captivity.[23] EMI's takeover of British Lion is typical of the absorption of independent film production interests by major recording and broadcasting conglomerates on both sides of the Atlantic during the 1970s and reveals several important strands in the economic determinants of film funding at this time. The first of these is Deeley and Spikings's 'committed internationalism',[24] while domestic production resided with bread-and-butter television comedy spin-offs for no money. Secondly, the 1970s' succession of cross-over film/music products reflects the financial interests of different arms of the parent corporation. And thirdly, ad hoc funding practices supplanted any consistent, long-term studio strategies, which fostered diversity (and enabled a degree of experimentation), but resisted sustained development.

So it came about that The Man Who Fell to Earth went into production on a precarious basis with no Hollywood backing or distribution deal, employing an entirely British crew on an all-American location shoot. A first in British screen history, cinematographer Tony Richmond recalls: 'We were aliens'![25] Yet the conditions in which the film was shot were important to its overall look. One should not underestimate the outsider's perspective afforded by this creative isolation and the crew camaraderie that grew from it. The team took advantage of New Mexico being one of the first states to declare a right-to-work policy permitting the use of imported labour and brought families along for a vacation on location. However, the strangeness of this remote American landscape is palpable in the film itself and alienation is the dominant point of view of its main character. Both these features of the finished film represent considerable departures from its literary source.

The Adaptation

Novels tell but films show. If Stanley Kubrick's distillation of Burgess's A Clockwork Orange still flaunts its precocious literary invention in the declamatory performance of Malcolm McDowell's Alex DeLarge, Roeg's *The Man Who Fell to Earth* uses its source as raw material. Part of the filmic transformation of that material is achieved through the pared-down screen adaptation of Paul Mayersberg; the rest resides in the modernistic visual style of its director. The paradox of Walter Tevis's intriguing story is that its third-person narration explains Newton's subjective motivation and records his point of view from a rational perspective with which we are comfortably familiar: an alien's tale told in a down-to-earth realism. James Leach spells out the basic problem with the straightforward transfer of such representation to film: 'The creation of an alternative world is the central concern of literary science-fiction, but the application of this idea to film often results in the merely spectacular . . . [T]he visual details of the alternative world tend to drown out the ideas that this world might be intended to represent'.[26]

In Roeg's film, Anthea remains only an occasional remembered world in flashback: a place of departure and strange nostalgia in the imagination of Newton. The film is resolutely terrestrial, which accounts for its double narrative enigma: firstly, we are compelled by the presence of an unearthly stranger in the midst of a familiar social world; secondly, we are compelled to view this familiar world anew through the fragmented perspective of the alien himself. Yet, this is a feature also of the strange, arid snowscapes of the alien planet Anthea. It is infused with a melancholy and nostalgic longing beyond the subjectivity of the alien's memory: an idealised, pre-lapsarian state of reproduction without intercourse, pleasure without penetration.

Roeg knows only too well that the most potent fantasy resides in the realms of the possible, which in turn casts the certainties of the everyday in a new light of provisional contingency. What is cinema but a parallel universe of the possible, strangely like our own? Newton is endearingly human in aspects where we would anticipate strangeness: social manners, business acumen, emotional sensitivity, language, intelligence and authority. Yet he is perversely strange on a more superficial level: an English accent and passport, gold rings for currency, orange hair and a green dufflecoat, an albino androgyny, physical frailty, jet-lag. And indeed, while the film's distorted vision of American society implies satirical critique, Newton's genius and power are ultimately contained by corporate and political interests and he is seduced (not least by alcohol) into forgetting his mission – literally, in the film's own terms, losing the plot. Nowhere is this transformation to earthling more graphically symbolised than in the attempt by medics to forcibly remove his false human eyes, which under X-ray have become permanently fused. As we know from *Un Chien Andalou* (1928) onwards (and explicitly in both *A Clockwork Orange* and *Tommy*), the eye is not only the perfect symbol of cinematic self-reflexivity, but it is at once that most vulnerable and powerful organ; quintessentially human, it is our mark of identity and the conduit of social power. Witnessing the eye and its look on screen is also one of the most profoundly self-reflexive experiences of spectatorship.

Returning to the adaptation, the film jettisons most of the novel's explanatory context, reducing Newton's motivation to a simple, if obscure, plot device. It also marginalises the elements of detective mystery and political intrigue, in favour, paradoxically, of a greater emotional force and human sensitivity, which serves to foreground the unresolved masculinity of the central protagonist. Paul Mayersberg discusses the development of Dr. Bryce (Rip Torn) from the novel's 'very ordinary tale of detection' where Bryce 'begins to doubt Newton almost at the outset'. During script revisions

> we substituted the idea of Newton as a query, rather than a quarry . . . We turned Bryce into a friend of Newton's rather than a foe . . . As in some of Graham Greene's writing, surprising friendships between men take on the suspenseful movement of detective yarns. The friendship between Dr. Bryce and Newton becomes dangerous because, as well all know, friendship is the most profound form of detection.[27]

To his own surprise, the idle, philandering, washed-up chemist Bryce is chosen as a disciple by Newton who elects, with suitably messianic mystery, to reveal his origins to the bewildered but intrigued scientist. It is a strange encounter, latent with homoerotic intimacy. An earlier, and similarly intimate meeting occurs between Newton and patents lawyer Oliver Farnsworth (Buck Henry). Mayersberg explains:

> What Nic Roeg did was to devise the entire scene . . . between the two men as an almost romantic encounter, at least in photographic terms. The set was warm and brown. The lamps cast a faint orange glow. Newton's face was bisected by a shadow . . . [like] the archetype of the mystery woman arriving in the office of the private eye . . . Somehow the mystery of Thomas Jerome Newton, who he is, what he really wants, was passed on into the whole look of the scene.[28]

Later, as he rises to run the World Enterprises empire and is eventually needled by the obscure but malevolent politico-economic heavies, Farnsworth's close relationship with Newton is eclipsed by Bryce, just as Bryce supplants Newton in the affections of Mary-Lou (Candy Clark). If the political forces remain shadowy and enigmatic, this change from the original novel was equally calculated:

> The book, which was published in the year of John Kennedy's assassination, conveyed an attitude which today seems somewhat naive. The actual presence of a President of the United States in the novel . . . seemed, after the saturation of Watergate and CIA exposures, to be unconvincing . . . However, it is impossible to tell an interesting story about the United States today without referring to a social and political context. So I rewrote areas of the film to try to come to grips with what one might guess were the State Department's attitudes towards the existence of Thomas Jerome Newton . . . I . . . invented a character who did not exist in the novel. Was he a Government figure? A man from the Mafia, or what? . . . In order fully to grasp the social significance of this character, who only has three scenes in the movie, he has actually to be seen. A decision of Nic Roeg's about his appearance changed this whole aspect of the film . . .[29]

This mysterious figure becomes the only witness to Newton's arrival on earth in an early shot high on the precipitous slag heap of the disused mine where he camps. As with much in Roeg's work, such appearances seldom work on the level of narrative realism alone – they are also suggestive, emblematic. He is the nameless 'watcher': 'a person who sits in attendance on the action, much as the audience does', mute, impassive characters who 'often influence the dynamics of his compositions'.[30] It is an idea Roeg returns to frequently: 'It's very difficult to avoid someone knowing things about you that you didn't want anybody to know'.[31] At the end of the film Newton insists: 'Nobody saw me, I came alone'. And for almost the first time an audience has the advantage of him; his intellectual power is dissipated, his earthly history known.

A further aspect of the novel's screen adaptation is the increased weight given to the central, wonderfully unlikely, relationship between Newton and Mary-Lou. Yet the Romantic situation of the lone (and lonely) figure in an indifferent world has been well established in advance of their alliance.

Mayersberg notes that 'the picture of the solitary figure on the rim of the hill is romantic mystery incarnate, whether it appears in a Western or in a social documentary . . . The style not only of the photography . . . but of the performances, is romantic in the grand nineteenth century manner'.[32] Evoking, as this attitude does, an emotional essence through photographic and performance styles, a 'structure of feeling', Candy Clark's simple, down-home girl is much more than the condescending cliché might convey. '[T]here is something strangely affecting about both the gentleness with which they treat one another and their mutual incomprehension'.[33] There is an honesty and truth about her (just as there is a sympathetic humanity in Farnsworth and Bryce, for all their foibles). She is an evocation of a long cinematic tradition, from the Western onwards: 'Everybody needs something to believe in, some meaning to life. I mean, when you look up at the stars at night, don't you feel that somewhere there's gotta be a God? There's gotta be!' This is no cliché. It is as impassioned a plea from the fallen for divine reassurance as she can muster. But her simple faith is too much for a Newton nervous of commitment and betrayal. At the end of the film, when a guilt-ridden Bryce asks the drunken Newton (whom he and Mary-Lou have betrayed to the authorities): 'Is there no chance then?' Newton replies cryptically: 'Of course there's a chance. You're the scientist, Dr. Bryce. You must know there's always a chance'. The statement is at once a religious absolution and a commitment to scientific probability in an uncertain future.

Indeed, as James Leach has indicated: 'It is in their treatment of the future and of time that novel and film diverge most extremely'.[34] Where the novel's extended time frame is at least ordered chronologically (set in the USA between 1985 and 1990), the film depicts a world of mass communication (including space travel) where time is both a relative and subjective concept, 'fragmented and unpredictable'. We are aware (through the ageing process of Bryce and Mary-Lou from which Newton seems immune) of a passage of time, but have no measure of it. Chaotic narrative interventions abound: flashbacks, repeated or mirrored leitmotifs, a welter of TV images and other pointed symbolic referents, disjunctive cross-referencing and edited ellipses. Roeg's idiosyncratic deployment of montage renders the spatio-temporal diegetic world conditional (often to the point of impenetrability). As ever, he emphasises the subjective commitment required to make sense of the world, to complete the frame. Thus, as sterner critics have frequently made clear, the film's theme of alienation is reproduced in the experience of watching.[35] Yet an audience's ability to access Roeg's narratives is never disabled by his dazzling visual complexity. It may simply be that the ways in are different and defy common expectation. For example, if psychological motivation is relatively obscure here, it is compensated for by an incredible emotional candour: passion, eroticism, violence, intoxication, listlessness, boredom, nostalgia, romance, sadness, loneliness, excitement, fear are demonstrated across a vast, delicately calibrated emotional register. Similarly, editorial composition serves narrative linearity less obviously than it does visual impact. Roeg's mise-en-scène is densely packed, richly suggestive, atmospherically charged in terms of framing, colour, light and tone. His method tends to foreground these aspects of visual and emotional pleasure at the expense of conventional narrative strategies:

> The omission of much of the novel's narrative detail forces the viewer to examine the way in which human relationships develop in the face of the collapse of conventional certainties; what the film adds to the novel is this greater concern with human relationships, especially sexual.
> ... In the film, the problem of human contact becomes involved with the frustration of not being able to live securely in the present.[36]

The terms of this commentary are revealing. Uncertainty about human relationships, the breakdown of conventions, concern with sexual identity, the problems of human contact and 'the frustration of not being able to live securely in the present' might equally be a commentary on western society in the 1970s, the 'symptoms' of any teenager, or perhaps some preoccupations of the cult film fan?

Alien Bodies

> Roeg sees the scene of their first union as one of psychological revelation, Newton's innocence prior to it ('like a boy discovering') is contrasted with Dr. Bryce's succession of joyless and selfish sexual encounters with teenage girls. Only after his 'fall' does Newton come to understand the type of phallic sexuality that dominates Bryce. Roeg hopes that people will draw confidence from the way in which the film explores emotional intimacies of sex rather than its cosmetic surfaces and performances.[37]

Despite its imputation of a didactic purpose on the part of the director for which there is little evidence, this reading is otherwise perceptive on the matter of Newton's sexuality and its potential therapeutic effects, and draws a useful distinction between the 'emotional intimacies of sex' and 'its cosmetic surfaces and performances'. In particular it emphasises the scenario of Newton's alien being essentially pre-sexual in a phallic world with the implication that his Anthean family are the products of an advanced procreative order in which reproduction is possible without penetration. Thus, Newton's terrestrial life charts his sexual initiation into the phallic order and as such, mirrors the process of adolescent maturation.

In this rite-of-passage journey, Candy Clark's Mary-Lou performs the whole range of female role-models from mother to lover, whore and wife. She is an evolution of these circumscribed male stereotypes of woman. At their first meeting in the hotel she has to physically carry Newton from the lift (after the vertical motion disturbs his sensitive bodily equilibrium) in an extraordinary scene in which she handles him in girlish, breathless panic as if he were a broken doll. Here Bowie's emaciated, bony fragility is markedly evident; it seems as if he will break in her hands. His immediate recovery from this trauma and Mary-Lou's faithful attention is intercut with repetitive, repulsive scenes of Bryce's student conquests; Newton and Mary-Lou's discovery of one another is altogether more innocent, almost pre-lapsarian, certainly adolescent.

They drive out to the aptly named Land of Enchantment, where earlier Newton's space capsule landed in the lake. It is here they build their home and arrive at their first intimacy. Sitting topless on the bed, she lights candles. 'I can't seem to get dry', Newton says, removing his robe, 'I'm still wet'. It is a boy's plea to his mother to help manage his body. Their gentle love-making is adolescent, touching, exploratory, as if mutually fascinated only with the surfaces of each other's bodies, their plasticity, contours and ability to tessellate. But he is unable to sustain interest in her homespun domesticity (managing his clothes, the house, home baking), and they fall out.

Newton's rejection of the faithful, uncomprehending Mary-Lou seems heartless and cruel. He announces he is leaving, providing for her needs. Interestingly, she has donned a straight, black, bob-cut wig, echoing the oriental décor of their house and adopting her own kind of alien disguise. Without realising her own double entendre she rounds on him: 'You're an alien! You know what will happen if they find your visa has expired?' She pleads with him, whispers sweet nothings, fingers his crotch trying to seduce him, and he is repulsed as only someone who is sexually alien could be. She attacks him, tearing the shirt off his shoulder and he stands, cowering, palms against the wall, bony, feminine shoulder and V of throat exposed, vulnerable yet reclusive. We never think him capable of genuine male aggression. Their row is interrupted by the oven-timer for the cookies she's baked. In what is a fit of pique rather than a temper tantrum, he knocks the baking sheet out of her hand propelling cookies into an azure sky like flying saucers. Then, locking himself in the bathroom he studies his own reflection, the fake nipples and stick-on human lenses. Worn down by her persistence he unlocks the door and at last reveals his alien self to her in one of the most memorable science-fiction moments in screen history. Their night of genuine discovery is intercut with scenes of Anthean erotic pleasure. Sealed in weightless, amniotic fluid, their bodies mingle, smothered in a kind of viscous milk. It is as if an impermeable membrane has been breached. 'I lifted you up once,' Mary-Lou remembers, as if her maternal nurturing were the only kind of explanatory knowledge she can bring to bear. 'You must believe me, Mary-Lou,' he responds in earnest. Her tentative, fearful caresses of his fine, dry surface are juxtaposed with the lubricated embraces of his Anthean memory/imagination. In what appears to be an unassisted orgasm, Mary Lou shrieks and runs naked to the kitchen where we see her, distorted, through his alien cat's eyes, crying 'Why, why, why?'

On his departure she ventures: 'You must hate me.' 'No,' he replies, 'I don't hate anyone, I can't'. Presumably he cannot love either. Theirs is the fate of two people who never should have met, but did – a curiously human dilemma, within an alien explanatory system. But, as with other futuristic elements in this film, it is visiting the human dimension from an alien perspective that illuminates the everyday anew. And this familiar story of unrealised sexuality, of thwarted intimacy, of an unlikely, freakish alliance that was never meant to be, is confirmed by the curious old-flame, one-night-stand encounter of their reunion and the corresponding playful, drunken abandon of their aggressive passion. The alienation of the sexes is such that only by artificial means can intimate pleasure be achieved – all that play with underwear and a pistol.

Let us now bring together the observations about Bowie's performance with this analysis of sexuality to consider the nature of fan response.

For a youth audience, such sexual role-play is both stimulating and reassuring. Intimacy involving role-models offers an intense vicarious pleasure; while the safety-net of artifice offers protection from self-exposure. It is clear that this central performance combines a physical vulnerability with considerable charismatic appeal while the narrative describes a sexual initiation with all the human frailty and awkwardness that may entail. Here 'Julie' describes her response to Bowie's screen role:

> Eventually, when I saw him in *The Man Who Fell To Earth*, taking off his clothes and seeing him in the nude, I began to realize I fancied him even more.
>
> And then it actually became a little more normal and channelled itself into something more erotic, because I was kinky about the fact that he was so thin and he was like a woman. He seemed the perfect vehicle for my sexual needs and fulfilment.
>
> . . . When I saw *The Man Who Fell To Earth* I got influenced by the idea of skins peeling and the fact that skin can be taken away and produce juices of a kind that can reveal themselves at the height of sexuality.
>
> So that when you make love you actually destroy certain layers of skin and form a liquid mass together.
>
> It was incredibly sensuous and very wild at the same time.[38]

The way in which 'Julie' expresses the screen revelation in terms of the discovery of and coming to terms with her own sexual self-awareness is palpable here. It may well be, I suggest, that popular cultural icons perform a kind of decathexis function in the rehearsal of attachment transition. By this I mean that the star icon is a sort of transitional object in negotiating the entry into sexual maturity. He displays the command of parental authority, a mystical otherworldliness and a sexual charisma in a 'relationship' to the fan which normally exists in the realm of make-believe. Though fantasy, it nonetheless has real pay-offs in the dividends of cultural competence, social acceptance, fashion, grooming and self-image development. Certainly filmic renditions of their emotional vulnerability and physical dependency must act as reassuring symbols of identification revealed beneath their idealised star personae.

Child psychologist John Bowlby's work on mother–child attachment behaviours is illuminating here. He establishes how dependency rooted in physiological needs (food, warmth and protection) and social education (observational learning) exists in changing form throughout childhood, but that sexual behaviours (certain aspects of which attachment behaviour shares) are directed outwards from adolescence towards new kinds of attachment:

> As a result individual variation, already great, becomes even greater. At one extreme are adolescents who cut themselves off from parents; at the other are those who remain intensely attached and are unable or unwilling to direct their attachment behaviour to others.[39]

But Bowlby also considers circumstances where:

> A school or college, a work group, a religious group or political group can come to constitute for many people a subordinate attachment – 'figure', and for some people a principal attachment – 'figure'. In such cases, it seems probable, the development of attachment to a group is mediated, at least initially, by attachment to a person holding a prominent position within that group.[40]

Though Bowlby doesn't discuss this directly, it is worth considering here also the role of the pop group or football team and that of charismatic pop idols or sports stars in teenage fandom as forms of 'attachment figures' which also permit the public display of certain sexual fantasies to be projected onto them. And at the centre of such fictive relationships is the ambiguity between intimacy and strangeness, between serious commitment and playful disregard – the intense preoccupation which is also just a passing phase. To employ a Freudian concept, this is a *fort/da* game of emergent self-recognition. It is just this kind of play that the performance of David Bowie provokes in *The Man Who Fell to Earth*. And in his charismatic vulnerability he acts as both an erotic stimulus and a reassuring displacement for an audience's own sexual anxieties.

I want next to develop this notion of spectatorship, speculatively, in two directions. Firstly I want to consider more fully the distinctive model of cult spectatorship this scenario implies. And secondly, I want then to try to locate this model, provisionally, within a broader social perspective that might be considered one of phallic crisis. Lacanian theory in particular may assist us in this purpose.

FIGURE 16: Aliens make love too (*The Man Who Fell to Earth*)
[EMI/THE KOBAL COLLECTION]

The Phallic Order

The ambivalent subject positions constructed across cult film narratives suggest spectatorial relations of a particularly fluid nature. The strange narrative unevenness and lacunae, and the visual density and signifying abundance of the cult film text both entices and distances the viewer. And the charismatic performance at its centre is frequently both seductively open and frustratingly remote (Bowie, Daltry, Jagger, McGregor). Or else it is disturbingly attractive and alluring in its very malevolence and violence (Fox, Caine, Lee and McDowell).

What I have termed double articulation is effectively a dialectical mode of spectatorship, offering stimulus and reassurance, pain and consolation, in equal measure in the same text. It is thus that cult films are textually aberrant, neither comfortably mainstream nor radically avant-garde. They come from culture in that they retain trace elements of familiar genres and incorporate popular stars and themes. Yet their treatments and procedures (narrative incongruity, hypersignification) frequently break with culture, calling into question our relation with language. Let us consider now the specific subjectivity of this implied viewing position in relation to the idea of the phallic order.

In different ways each of the films under consideration here denies the symbolic reassurance of the phallic order in their manifest disinterest in, or rejection of, traditional sites of male authority. In matters of visual style and performance they all parade camp experimentation with self-identity and image, and flaunt ambiguous sexual excess. They refuse to anchor masculinity according to psychosexual and social convention. In this way each resists entry into the phallic order. Their narratives offer instead both temporary solace and endless stimulus; yet their pleasures, like those of the fetishist, are contradictory, perversely unresolved. This is because each film is densely constructed upon patterns of reiterated signification (in visual codes and performance styles) in which the signifiers are never able to rest, in the Lacanian sense, around loci of *points de capiton*.

This idea must be explained more precisely. According to Lacan: 'While there are no fixed signifieds in language, signification within the symbolic order is made possible by the privileging of certain key signifiers to which the drives, organised around non-incestuous, heterosexual sexuality, become attached'.[41] These *points de capiton*

> act as nodal points which link signifying chains to one another and
> prevent an indefinite sliding of meaning. Via their attachment to the
> drives, which have been organised in a culturally acceptable way,
> these nodal points structure the unconscious in terms of the positions

from which an individual can speak. These positions are organised in
terms of gender.[42]

Such positions are also culturally inscribed within texts in a structured
manner which secures their ideological function and ensures their
subjective pleasure. Cult films, uneven in their structure, hypersignifying,
offer no such security. Rather, their signifying loops seem to fetishise
what Lacan called *petits objets autres* – nostalgic yearnings for those first
objects of the imaginary register 'which are not clearly distinguished
from the self and which are not fully grasped as other [*autre*]'.[43]
These derive their 'value from . . . identification with some missing
component of the subject's self, whether that loss is seen as primordial,
as the result of a bodily organisation, or as the consequence of some
other division'.[44]

What is the reason for this nostalgic lapse and such patterns of
regression in these particular film texts? In terms of Lacanian theory
they point towards an unresolved entry into the symbolic order of
language – an Oedipal crisis. But at once we must acknowledge the
social constitution of language and the cultural basis of texts too. An
inability to enter fully the symbolic order as a social subject depends
upon a rift in what Volosinov identifies as the 'dialectical interplay'
between the psychic and the ideological.[45] Volosinov reminds us of
the *multiaccentual* nature of the sign: how ideology constantly fails to
reduce linguistic constructions to dominant meanings, and how the self
and its social performance is continually compromised and alienated in
language.

How do such rifts come about, historically? It could be argued that the
social changes and cultural developments of the late 1960s effected a
slippage in the ideological purchase upon language. This was manifested
in a variety of ways: for example, the counter-culture's rejection of
traditional institutions and their specific discourses, the overthrow of
conventional cultural forms and the blurring of distinctions between
high and popular art. These were supplanted with a diverse range of new
experiments in self-realisation through language, many of which were
attitudinal, some destructive, most ephemeral. Popular culture itself issued
a plethora of conflicting signifiers challenging ideological consensus. In
particular, cult texts of the 1970s are object lessons in hypersignification,
resisting settlement around ideological consensus (*points de capiton*).

Cult films, I suggest, were but one manifestation of a fundamental anxiety attendant upon these social and cultural shifts. And this crisis of identity is addressed in such films in the pleasurable effects of both stimulation and solace. Yet, their resolution is never finally achieved. Rather, it is as if these films project fantasy worlds where the dominant sexual divisions of the phallic order temporarily don't exist, or wherein the risks attendant on reconciling their pleasures and pains can be imaginatively averted. In this sense, cult texts may be considered at once radical and reactionary. They furnish audiences with alternative subject positions that provide reassurance and identification with models of essential difference. But the solace they afford is that of a shared nostalgia for a lost order, consolation for those who long to belong.

Summary

Let us relocate this theoretical exegesis in terms of performance and reception in *The Man Who Fell to Earth*. In a recent *Guardian*/NFT interview, Nicolas Roeg reflected again on David Bowie's role. He relates a story similar to Malcolm McDowell's report of Kubrick's advice to him about playing Alex in *A Clockwork Orange*:

> It suddenly struck me . . . that the best thing I could tell him was that I didn't know who Mr Newton was either. So I told him, 'You'll help me by not knowing either. Just do it, say the part'. And it was strange – it was better than acting. He was it. He may have been slightly clumsy, and somebody else might have been more together but training would have stopped it. It wouldn't have had the authenticity of the alien, without anything except who he was . . . So the throwing away of the alien disguise was rather like exposing yourself emotionally.[46]

As we have seen, the key to Bowie's success was his untrained manner, coupled with the residual aspects of his iconic image. And key to audience identification with this performance is his emotional exposure in the climactic scene of the film. Nic Roeg usefully reminds us how this scene works as an emblem of sexual initiation:

> In that scene, Mary-Lou and Mr Newton had been together for a while, and though she thought that he was a bit strange and odd, she

had no idea where he came from. Sure he was an alien, but he wasn't a monster. She didn't know that on his planet, it had been planned that he would come to Earth and be among humans, but that they didn't get things quite right with his body. And so when she says that he can tell her anything, which in the human context means 'You can tell me anything and I'll still love you,' and he shows her his method of making love – by exchanging bodily fluids on a grand scale – of course she recoils.[47]

This is the shock of the discovery of sexual difference – that adolescent re-enactment of the primal scene – which makes this a cult film. Only in cult films is sexual identity so explicitly unresolved.

Role-play within cult films is sometimes extended in the realm of fan response too. One internet site has established a role-play game which elaborates the plot and characters of The Man Who Fell to Earth into speculative fantasy worlds.[48] Thomas Jerome Newton becomes an unlikely comic-book hero in fictions which see him besieged by sinister Men in Black, seduced by gothic heroines, and his World Enterprises corporation taken over by manufacturers of weapons of mass destruction. However fanciful they might sound, these various hybrid inventions share two conspicuous links with the film itself. One is a subcultural opposition to, and critique of, contemporary American society; the other is a curiously resilient bond of understanding and mutual respect of difference among the assortment of oddball and alternative characters, centred on the relationship between Newton and Mary-Lou. Subcultural opposition and the bonds of allegiance it fosters, but seldom sustains, are themes common to the last three films we shall consider.

CASE STUDY 3:

Quadrophenia (1979)

Films about youth subcultures are always likely to become cult texts, because they draw upon and celebrate pre-existing styles. The historical specificity of British mods, their memorialisation through the music of The Who, and the nostalgia of a period retrospective unite to make *Quadrophenia* a classic example. But moreover, its success in 1979 (some fifteen years after the phenomenon it recalls) may be attributed as much to the significance of other contemporary subcultures, especially reggae, punk and later ska, as to revival of a particular mod sensibility (for example in the style and music of The Jam).

As Kevin Donnolly relates, the presence of screen cameos by 'new wave' artists Toyah Willcox and Sting is indicative of efforts to articulate mod culture 'along lines that could be understood by a late-1970s punk-influenced audience'.[49] Dave Allen goes further still: 'If there was ever a "pure" version of mod subculture it was in fact not what we know of mods in the first half of the 1960s . . . but the version that was created from the emergence of *Quadrophenia* and Paul Weller. By "pure", I don't mean "authentic" – I mean rule-governed and conventional'.[50]

These concerns were evident at the film's conception. First-time director Franc Roddam was chosen by producers Roy Baird and Bill Curbishley (The Who's manager) ahead of established names such as Ken Russell (*Tommy*). Roddam, noted for his documentary work on television, explained: 'We didn't want it to be just a nostalgia film about 1964 . . . I want it to have some relevance to today . . . What I didn't want to do, is make a stylised film like *Tommy*, where the music carried the narrative'.[51] Thus, only about 50 per cent of Pete Townshend's original 1974 album is employed in the film, though The Who's record company Polygram was the major funding source, and the label cashed in successfully on the record tie-in with the film's release.[52]

Positioned between *Jubilee* (1978) and more populist successors *The Great Rock 'n' Roll Swindle* (1979), *Rude Boy* and *Breaking Glass* (both 1980) and *Pink Floyd The Wall* (1982), *Quadrophenia* marks the crest of a wave of pop music films of the late 1970s and early 1980s. Not only did it become an important locus in the re-emergence of mod culture, its Brighton locations remain the focus of nostalgic fan activity, as is evidenced by the copious graffiti on the walls of a certain alleyway where Jimmy (Phil Daniels) and Steph (Leslie Ash) make love in the midst of the raging street battle.

For all its director's emphasis on dramatic realism however, as a period piece the film is full of holes, riddled with countless anachronisms. And purists are quick to point out that it is, at best, only a film about mods, rather than a mod film.[53] Like *That'll Be the Day* it is overwhelmingly nostalgic – part of a 1970s trend in revitalising past subcultural styles. As a cult object, the film's epitaph says it all: 'A way of life'. But *Quadrophenia* is, between punk and Thatcher, 'purely', a post-mod(ern) text.[54]

FIGURE 17: A way of life: Jimmy (Phil Daniels) with some unwelcome travelling companions in *Quadrophenia*

[CURBISHLEY-BAIRD/THE KOBAL COLLECTION]

7

WITHNAIL & I (1986)

Introduction

The previous films covered in this study were all British-made in the late 1960s and throughout the 1970s. While this is by no means an all-inclusive list of British cult films, I have selected them primarily on the basis of their critical and popular reception from a larger body of films identified by critics and fans as cult. My method has then been to subject these texts to close analysis, to divine what textual qualities they may share, and further, to consider the significance of their contextual histories in the attribution of cult status. One observation that may be made from this approach is that it is no coincidence that certain films from this particular period in British cinema have later become cult objects. I have considered some possible explanations for this from the texts themselves and from their contextual histories, touching on broader trends in popular culture of the period and economic changes in the film industry. But if this is one important time frame for this study, there is also another: the rise of cult itself.

I have suggested that cult appreciation is more often than not retrospective: that it doesn't generally (at least as far as these texts are concerned) emanate from the first release of a film, but later, and sometimes as a consequence of its post-release history as much as its textual qualities. But as with the earlier period (1968–79), we must also consider that there might be wider reasons for the subsequent emergence of cult as a critical category and cultism as a fan practice. And this second period, I would suggest, spans approximately the twenty years from 1976 to 1996. That is not to say that cult wasn't used as a critical term before 1976 – it clearly was. And it is not to say that cult fan practices didn't exist before then either, or indeed continue after 1996. In both instances they did, only not in the same way. I have isolated this period in British film culture for specific reasons. As I shall explain, certain reception conditions pertained which fostered cultism as a critical practice and brought it to wider critical attention.

By the mid-1970s the production industry in Britain was in sharp decline, and its markets had further fragmented (see Tables 1 and 2). While the number of cinema closures continued to increase during the decade, the number of screens remained buoyant due to the practice of doubling or tripling larger cinema buildings (see Table 3). These changes reflected and at the same time made more explicit a marked divergence in audience tastes. As with the first falling-off of cinema attendance in the late 1940s, there appeared a lack of consensus and some confusion amongst audiences, and a mutual mistrust between film distributors and their public. This gave way to a degree of polarisation in taste categories. A typical town centre cinema might offer a family film (say *Live and Let Die* [1973] or *The Return of the Pink Panther* [1976]) alongside an 'X' such as *The Exorcist* (1973) or *The Omen* (1976). In the same week I saw *Swallows and Amazons* (1974), my local cinema was also showing the highest-grossing British film of that year, *Confessions of a Window Cleaner*. This polarisation of the film market is also reflected in BBFC statistics from the Seventies where the percentages for 'U' and 'X' certificates awarded consistently exceed the 'A' and 'AA' categories (see Table 4). However, it may be observed that this differential, along with the percentage of films rejected, diminishes as the decade wanes.

TABLE 1. Cinema admissions in the UK, 1970–9 (in millions)[1]

1970	193.00
1971	176.00
1972	156.60
1973	134.20
1974	138.50
1975	116.30
1976	103.90
1977	103.50
1978	126.10
1979	111.90

TABLE 2. Number of British feature films produced, 1970–9[2]

1970	103
1971	97
1972	90
1973	80
1974	81
1975	80
1976	64
1977	43
1978	49
1979	38

TABLE 3. Number of UK cinema screens, 1970–9[3]

1970	1,529
1971	1,482
1972	1,450
1973	1,530
1974	1,535
1975	1,530
1976	1,525
1977	1,547
1978	1,563
1979	1,604

TABLE 4. Percentages of films passed by category each year, 1974–9[4]

	1974	1975	1976	1977	1978	1979
U	24.01	29.45	29.80	21.73	25.11	27.50
A	14.27	18.91	15.15	18.78	22.27	23.54
AA	12.85	13.27	12.38	16.21	17.69	18.96
X	45.06	34.55	38.93	41.07	34.06	29.58
Rejected	3.81	3.82	3.75	2.21	0.87	0.42
TOTAL	100	100	100	100	100	100

Television was the dominant audio-visual medium of the 1970s and feature film spin-offs of popular series (especially comedies) and sales of feature film back-catalogues to British television companies signalled a growing interdependency. As Jancovich, Faire and Stubbings note, 'By the 1970s television had become the primary site of film consumption'.[5]

This relationship was fully realised with the advent of Channel 4 Television in 1982 and its sponsorship of film production aimed at both TV and cinema audiences (which the BBC immediately copied). Yet well before this explicit link was forged, several independent television broadcasters had established film production wings; for example Southern Pictures of Southern Television and Thames Television's Euston Films.[6] The point here with regard to cultism is that even as the midnight movie circuit declined (which only existed in metropolitan areas of Britain anyway), new markets for viewing neglected and critically debased films emerged on television and also on university campuses. Here, student film societies flourished and film began to be established in the undergraduate curriculum.

The decline in the popular audience for cinema also had the effect of boosting niche film markets on the margins of popular culture. Art cinemas and film societies, sustained by the BFI Regional Film Theatres: sponsorship, grew in number during the decade. This boosted the audience for European art house, avant-garde and classic film reappraisal. Similarly, workshop cinema emerged as a vibrant fringe force in producing and showing political and community films. At the other end of the spectrum, the seventies was a decade which saw, in the wake of the permissiveness of the late sixties, a growth in pornographic cinema, especially those private clubs who could show uncertificated hard-core material. So it may be more accurate to see the Seventies as a decade during which film diversified rather than simply declined, the rise of cultism being but one facet of this new diversity.

A further material change which had a direct impact on the fragmentation of film consumption and the rise of cultism was the development and proliferation of home video (really from the early 1980s onwards, though the technology had been available earlier). Mainstream Hollywood cinema had from the mid-1970s begun to reinvent itself and rise again from the economic doldrums with the development of what became known as the blockbuster package. Part of the strategy for these big-budget, high-profile and extensively marketed films (of which the first and best-known examples were *Jaws* [1975] and *Star Wars* [1977]) was, as in the early 1950s, to differentiate cinema aesthetically from television: to offer an experience that was unique to cinema itself. As this type of film event began successfully to dominate the Anglo-American markets (and British international pictures from the Bond franchise to Agatha Christie adaptations sought to copy the US model), so the space at the margins of mainstream film culture for low-budget, independent film contracted. Perhaps only the film with pop music cross-over potential was sustainable in a market increasingly oriented towards the youth audience. The circumstances were ripe, therefore, for marginalised, neglected or critically debased films to find niche audiences in a range of locations. Additionally, British television companies after 1982 began to invest in the kind of small-scale but cutting-edge feature-length film that had hitherto constituted a single play on television, as well as creating dedicated seasons (such as BBC2's *Moviedrome* from 1988) to declared 'cult' films. This climate, I suggest, was ideal for cultism to flourish on the margins of film consumption. And not only did it rediscover and reify neglected or debased texts, or reappropriate classics from an oblique distance. It also began to discover new films of its own, much to the surprise, in some cases, of their makers.

The next film I have selected for this study is typical of these new consumption circumstances. It is not the only British cult film of the 1980s (or since). But it is significant because of the conspicuous cult following it has garnered; and it is apposite because, like *Quadrophenia*, it looks back nostalgically to the 1960s for its tragic-comic inspiration.

Production History

No one was more surprised at the phenomenal success of the British comedy *Withnail & I* (1986) than its director Bruce Robinson: 'I frankly find it strange that there is so much interest in the film,' he told Louise Brealey on its re-release in 1996.[7] Robinson wrote the partly autobiographical novel that became *Withnail* as early as 1969 when he and Vivian MacKerrell (like his eponymous heroes) were out-of-work actors living in a run-down flat in London's Camden Town. 'The environment started to deteriorate, kind of in parallel to the decade'.[8] Elsewhere, he has reflected: 'All of us in a sense have had these kind of six months or a year intense relationships with someone when you're on a destruct. I certainly lived through that and I'm pleased I got through it'.[9]

It was only after Robinson had gone on to produce a clutch of screenplays during the 1970s – of which the most successful was the Oscar-nominated *The Killing Fields* (1984) – that *Withnail* found financial backing from George Harrison's HandMade Films. Robinson was reluctantly persuaded by American producer Paul Heller to direct (for the first time). Heller raised about half of the £1 million budget from property developer Lawrence Kirstein, while HandMade (which had been formed to support another cult British comedy project, Monty Python's *Life of Brian* [1979]) stumped up the rest.[10]

Robinson admitted that his inexperience behind the camera meant that he would have to rely on the expertise of technical personnel of calibre. Therefore, he and co-producer David Wimbury recruited cinematographer Peter Hannan, Bob Smith as cameraman, Alan Strachan as editor and Michael Pickwoad as production designer. This combination proved extremely successful on several counts. The majority of the film (in common with others in this study) was shot on location. The dependability of his experienced crew freed Robinson creatively to focus his attention on the actors' performance of his script. It also enabled the film to be brought in economically, with very few takes and little wastage. Indeed, the post-Lake District trip back to London, including 'Danny's ingenuous drunk-driving gadget' and Withnail's celebrated arrest, was funded to the tune of £30,000 out of Robinson's own director's fee (£80,000) because the producers considered it superfluous.[11] Furthermore, the crew camaraderie was cemented by the early and highly critical intervention of HandMade's Denis O'Brien. The American O'Brien found it desperately unfunny in production, and seemed neither to understand or trust what Robinson was doing. However, Kevin Jackson remarks: 'As so often, the "artists" rallied against the "suits", and formed a united-we-stand front'.[12]

Ironically enough, for a picture which struggled to find a distributor until 1988 and did very little box-office in its first British run despite favourable critical reviews, it enjoyed much greater popularity in the USA. If the film's initial American success came as something of a revelation, its subsequent cult status continues to belie its modest stature. It is said to have inspired more oft-quoted lines and drinking games in student bars than any other film. *Withnail* is small-scale, but exceptionally well-crafted: Robinson's sharp script, accomplished ensemble acting (Richard E. Grant, Paul McGann, Richard Griffiths, Ralph Brown), and astute costume design (Andrea Galer) are the key factors in a stylish, iconic performance.

The Script

Withnail (Grant) is a public-school tragicomic hero, a man whose delusions of his own greatness are limited only by his frustration at the refusal of a decaying, tawdry, hostile and trivialised world to recognise his genius. Together with flat-mate and fellow thespian Marwood (McGann), he struggles to rise above the detritus of his own personal and domestic squalor, through drink, drugs and any other substance which might temporarily dull the reality of his own circumstances, before fleeing to a Lake District cottage owned by his wealthy homosexual uncle, Monty (Griffiths). Finding the rigours of an unaccustomed country life (not to mention the advances of the reptilian Monty) intolerable, the pair return to London; Withnail is arrested for drink-driving while the more pragmatic Marwood receives an offer of work. A final scene depicting Withnail's drunken suicide (which appears in the original script but remained unfilmed) was considered too negative an outcome for what is essentially a comic drama. Yet, the idea reinforces (as the filmed ending implies) the tragic trajectory of Withnail's ineluctable decline. Histrionic to the last, he winds up intoning a soliloquy from *Hamlet* across Regent's Park. Reviewing the publication of the screenplay for *Sight and Sound*, novelist Will Self pin- points the story's appeal:

> In Marwood and Withnail, Robinson has created an apotheosis of the idea of romantic artistic youth as countercultural rebel. I feel sure that part of the reason for the film's enduring popularity is the sense contemporary youth have that the 60s were the last time when rebellion like this was valid.[13]

In this film cult fans engage with, and respond to, this nostalgic, counter-cultural spirit chiefly through its memorable script and the physical performance and adornment of the body. As one female fan told me in interview: 'What I really enjoy about the film is . . . I love the language. Really clever and funny . . . And it just looks fantastic, visually'. Another male respondent echoed these sentiments: '*Withnail* still looks so special, I suppose . . . because you're dealing with geniuses like Bruce Robinson, who just captured this . . . It's the script isn't it? You read the script and it's just as enjoyable as watching the movie. The sad thing is Richard E. Grant and Paul McGann and Monty – whatever his name is – I wonder if they feel they'll ever reach the heights of *Withnail* again'.

Two factors underpin the success of Robinson's script. The first is that he lived the experience (or something very like it) and it is grounded in reality – or rather the kind of surreality that only certain chapters of life have when viewed from the inside. The second factor is that the author lived with the story and transformed it, from the original novel which was quickly done in the joy and pain of that predicament:

> It was one of the few times in my life I felt I was inspired. I was writing so fast, and crying with laughter as I was writing. I wasn't earning my living writing; I certainly never thought it was going to be published. I wrote it purely for the joy of writing, and I sat there in penury having one of the best times I've ever had.[14]

But having been his calling card for much of the Seventies, it was not until 1980 that

> an actor called Don Hawkins passed the novel to Moderick 'Mody' Schreiber, who liked it, and gave Robinson a few thousand pounds to adapt it into a screen-play. Robinson wrote the adaptation while living in California, and did not enjoy the experience much. Where the novel had flowed freely with the fresh juice of inspiration, the screenplay was more like hard labour.[15]

Crucial here, one fancies, is the subsequent craftsmanship, arduous though it apparently was, which fashioned the screenplay from the source novel. Such processes necessitate changing the mental and emotional relationship to the material. This is a rare transformation for one creative artist, especially if that writer then also goes on to direct his own film of the script. That total possession of the material – as experience and document – is crucial to the candour and honesty of the finished work and its effective realisation. But how does this relate to the performances of the actors and the responses of fans?

Firstly, Robinson himself, it must be recalled, is an actor. Grant reports:

> Robinson says that he *needs* to be in his cups to be able to write as it is such a pain-filled process. Getting it to sound right is like dragging out his guts every time – it explains just *why* he is so meticulous about *nothing* being improvised and all the focus on getting the rhythms right, so that it sounds 'like it does in my head'. It's then the actor's job to make it seem like their *only* of way of speaking. [emphasis retained].[16]

There is a paradox at the heart of such an uncompromising quest for authenticity. If Robinson's working control of the script is reminiscent of the methods of another comedy writer/director, Woody Allen, it is because the single-mindedness of a Withnail or an Allen protagonist is rooted in his thwarted desire to control the world he inhabits through language. His invective and hyperbole, his rhetoric and histrionics, are at once a smoke-screen and defence mechanism to keep the world at bay, and a means of ordering things so as to engage with reality *obliquely*. Paradoxically, in the case of Withnail, our view of him is Marwood's. Robinson's fundamental need for Withnail to be realised faithfully is born of love and friendship. It is not so much a question of authenticity as fidelity. This is substantiated by Grant's account of Robinson's instructions to his film crew. For all his inexperience,

> He has a very simple but strict dictum for the camera crew: everything has to be seen from the I character's point of view. *Nothing* can be shown that strays from this discipline. [emphasis retained].[17]

The reason for this, of course, is because Robinson wants us to share Marwood's intimate view of Withnail, which is also, profoundly, his own. Perhaps cult fans idolise the wayward, uncompromising excesses and the iconic, charismatic self-possession of Withnail, from the safer, more pragmatic vantage of Marwood's point of view – one of love. For Marwood, ultimately, fits in. Much as he loves and admires Withnail, he is at heart a conformist. He escapes their downward spiral of destitution and squalor and finds a job. But it is, predominantly, Withnail's lines that cult fans remember and rehearse. Maybe they identify with, or envy, his mock-heroic ability to see the world obliquely, to keep reality at bay. Maybe the pursuit and mastery of a private, if borrowed, language is a way of doing that for oneself.

Environment and Physicality

The reality of their existence is inescapable. Withnail and Marwood live in conditions of squalor that are as much the product of their own lifestyle as they are the circumstances of their penury. Their cold flat is filthy, their kitchen clogged with decaying mess. When Withnail complains 'You've got soup!' as Marwood spoons coffee from a dish into his mouth, the joke is that what dirty cups and mugs they might possess are irretrievably lost in the morass of the kitchen sink.[18] In a wonderful comic scene they attempt to confront the blocked, stagnant mess armed with pliers and rubber gloves. There is talk of rats, vermin: 'Fork it!' cries the traumatised Withnail in revulsion. That they are overwhelmed, disgusted and terrified

FIGURE 18: 'We've come on holiday by mistake'. Paul McGann and
Richard E. Grant lost in Lakeland in *Withnail & I*
[HANDMADE FILMS/BRITISH FILM INSTITUTE]

by the horror of their own filth marks an important, childlike, psychological
recognition of their humanity, redolent of the best Swiftian scatology.
Moreover, not only is mess beyond human agency or rational purpose,
it also manifests an organic autonomy. Hence, what appals Withnail and
Marwood is not the dirtiness of their kitchen sink, it is the pond-life which,
through neglect, has taken over as a product of their mess. 'There are *things*
in there. There's a tea bag growing,' says Marwood and warns, 'I think
there may be something *living* in there. I think there's something *alive* . . .'

WITHNAIL:	What is it? What have you found?
MARWOOD:	Matter
WITHNAIL:	*Matter?* Where's it coming from?[19]

They have unwittingly created the conditions for another kind of life to emerge from the decaying matter. And that in itself might stand as an appropriate epigram for the narrative metamorphosis of the film. But we are never allowed to linger over latent symbolism, and all this fascination for the unclean is comically set against the class-impregnated mock-urbanity of Withnail: 'We'll never be able to use the dinner service again'.[20] The public-school humour of this dichotomy is captured perfectly in his physical adornment: a feeble, adolescent body in Y-fronts and the ubiquitous Harris Tweed coat.[21] In interview with me, costume designer Andrea Galer commented on Withnail's iconic status:

> You know to me it was a pivotal character that carried the film and you had to walk away and remember his image. You weren't going to be moved by the film – well maybe you would've been moved by the film – eventually you would have been, you know, but its subtlety was essential, but within that subtlety, as far as I'm concerned, that character had to push the boat out. He did push the boat out and I did have a particular idea about that character because I wanted him to appear to be – I wanted to get across his class. I mean after all the class system in the Sixties would appear to be not relevant, but in fact, as is the case in life, it was a superficial thing that class didn't matter, you know, who got on and who didn't get on and so I was trying to recreate a sense that he had found that coat in the attic of his grandfather/grandmother.[22]

The slapstick performance of their physical revulsion conveys a deeper repugnance expressive of pubescent self-loathing. Grant describes his reactions to performing this scene in his own memoir:

> The *manics* have set-in. Feel completely crazed and possessed, combusting with desperation and disgust . . . Painting myself with the cream and wearing the scratchy wool coat sends my system into *irritability overdrive*, which speeds up and motors the *mania* required. [emphasis retained][23]

Their freezing flat drives the increasingly manic Withnail to roll up his coat sleeves and apply embrocation to his emaciated body. And, desperate for a drink against the cold or to numb the pain, downs lighter fluid before throwing up on Marwood's boots. This effort at illicit intoxication is paralleled by the arrival of Danny (Brown) who boasts about the extreme effects of certain chemical cocktails within his narcotic dispensary. 'If I medicined you, you'd think a brain tumour was a birthday present'.[24]

Physical revulsion is important here too. Withnail is fascinated by the newspaper story of the huge, steroid-taking shot-putter, Jeff Wode: 'His head must weigh fifty pounds alone . . . Imagine the size of his balls'.[25] Fear of physical grossness is represented in the obese pulchritude of Uncle Monty, whose promise of escape from their urban squalor is predicated upon his homosexual designs on Marwood. Fear of sex, and especially gay sex, is repeated throughout, from Withnail's railing about the boy who 'lands plum role for top Italian director . . . Two pounds ten a tit and a fiver for his arse . . . '[26] to Marwood's pub encounter with the toilet graffiti ('I fuck arses') and the Irish 'Wanker' of the script: 'I called him a ponce. And now I'm calling you one. Ponce'.[27] To complement this threat is a succession of phallic references: Withnail's failed cigar commercial, the saveloy in the bathtub, Danny's 'Camberwell Carrot' and Uncle Monty: 'I think the carrot infinitely more fascinating than the geranium. The carrot has mystery'.[28]

In *Withnail & I* sex is totally repressed. Indeed, Andrea Galer wanted her costume designs 'to look sexless, so there seemed a bit of mystery . . .'.[29] Withnail and Marwood share an adolescent male friendship which, while it includes physical contact (embracing, sharing a bed against the cold or the fear of intruders), never hints at homosexuality. The film (like their lives) is without female interest. Bruce Robinson has endeavoured to explain this:

> I'll tell you exactly why there are no women in it. If you're in a state
> of extreme poverty when you're young, you literally can't afford
> girlfriends. I wanted to use that, in a subliminal way, as a facet of their
> deprivation. There is no femininity in their lives at all.[30]

Yet we hardly see them lusting after girls they can't afford – there simply are no women, not even glimpsed from afar. I believe something else is going on here. The characters of Marwood and Withnail are pre-sexual, boyish. The best they can do is to shout a juvenile 'Scrubbers!' at a group of schoolgirls as they speed away in the symbolically decrepit Jag from a London in the throes of demolition whether from the IRA, or urban planners or the lengthening dole-queue.

An equally adolescent homophobia is expressed in events which result from Uncle Monty's surprise arrival at the Lakeland cottage. This visitation heralds worse than the Cumbrian elements could deliver, for Marwood at least. For in the dead of night Marwood discovers the terrifying truth that Withnail has gained the freedom of the cottage only by inventing a gay back-story and promising him to Monty in return:

> MARWOOD: I'm not homosexual, Monty.
>
> MONTY: Yes you are. Of course you are. You're simply black-
>   mailing your emotions to avoid the realities of your
>   relationship with him . . . Couldn't we allow ourselves
>   just this one moment of indiscretion?[31]

Escaping the frightening encounter with some fictional improvisation of his own, Marwood is livid at the betrayal of friendship. Monty, rebuffed, flees the next morning. 'By Christ, Withnail. You'll suffer for this. What you've done will have to be paid for', swears Marwood in the cold light of day.[32] And sure enough it is, with the arrival of a telegram offering work and Marwood a way out. *Withnail* is emphatically *not* a female film, it is preter-masculine. It comically legitimises and indulges laddishness (even boyishness). In the negotiation of parameters in respect of crises of class, masculinity and sexuality it may be that cult movies offer different ways of confronting and resolving problems.

Chaos and Dissolution

> DANNY: London is a country comin' down from its trip. We
>   are sixty days from the enda this decade, and there's
>   gonna be a lota refugees . . . They'll be going round
>   this town shouting 'Bring out your dead'.[33]

As with all double-acts, every odd-couple, there is pathos in their parting, born of a bond betrayed only at its breaking. A newly groomed Marwood makes for the station in jaunty trilby; Withnail, under his umbrella, recites *Hamlet* to the wolves in the zoo and wanders off into an indefinite future. Robinson comments: 'Withnail was one of the dead. The symbolism of the very short haircut . . . of the "I" character was based on the horror of Thatcherism [and conformity] coming along.'[34] Yet Marwood survives and moves on precisely because he is willing to conform, to compromise, willing to deal with the mess of life. Galer wanted his costumes to reflect 'the grammar-school boy'.

Uncle Monty, reflecting with pathos on the transience of youth comments earlier: 'It is the most shattering experience of a young man's life, when one morning he awakes, and quite reasonably says to himself, I will never play the Dane. When that moment comes, one's ambition ceases.'[35] There is more to Uncle Monty than sexual predator. His is the voice of Romantic nostalgia, of fading class values, of aesthetic purity, which he captures in this poignant paean to loss: 'There can be no true beauty without decay'.[36]

Withnail maintains his schizophrenic fascination for and abhorrence of mess, refusing to acknowledge his part in it or deal with it. As he quotes from *Hamlet*: 'This most excellent canopy the air . . . appeareth nothing to me but a foul and pestilent congregation of vapours . . .'[37] Withnail's recitation represents a last-ditch determination to play the part (even if only to a company of wolves) and is at the same time his admission of that failure: '. . . what is this quintessence of dust? Man delights not me, no, nor women, neither . . . nor women neither.'[38] Interestingly, his own repetition here may be read as a recognition of impotence – sexual, social, political. What is a rite of passage for Marwood is for Withnail a Romantic quest to find transcendent meaning, purpose, to rise above the dirt and chaos, which he signally fails to do, not least, one might argue, because it is against the spirit of the age. To this extent, *Withnail & I* is a nostalgic piece because it harks back to a time, as Will Self notes, when (if only briefly) transgression was permitted and transcendence a possibility, just as Monty reflects with fondness and pathos on the era of his own misspent youth. Yet as Robinson indicates above, his film rehearses a temporal double-take: for the dog-days of the Sixties read 1979, by which time the climate had changed. It is no coincidence that the waitress in the Penrith tea-rooms, Miss Blenehassitt, should have been chosen by Robinson from the ranks of extras 'to look as much as possible like Margaret Thatcher'.[39]

'Transitional Phenomena'

Such ambivalent fascination and revulsion for the seamier underbelly of existence marks a kind of arrested development or return to an infant psychological state. The schema of this dark play with dirt and mess is linked by David Trotter to the work of child psychologist D.W. Winnicott:

> The part mess plays in the dialectic of illusion and disillusionment
> might perhaps be compared to that played by Winnicott's 'transitional'
> objects.[40]

Winnicott (whose work parallels some of the findings of Bowlby considered in the last chapter) developed his observation during the 1950s that there is a stage in infant development between the use of 'fist, fingers, thumbs in stimulation of the oral erotogenic zones' and playing with the first dolls or teddies when certain objects become sacred to the child (perhaps a blanket or a piece of material) as the first 'not-me' possession, and 'that most mothers allow their infants some special object and expect them to become, as it were, addicted to it'.[41] Such 'transitional phenomena belong to the realm of illusion' yet over time will become redundant ('disillusioned') as the child develops interest in external phenomena, toys. This 'intermediate area of experience', then, 'constitutes the greater part of the infant's experience, and throughout life is retained in the intense experiencing that belongs to the arts and to religion . . .'[42] According to Trotter, not only is the infant's precious object allowed (even encouraged) to become dirty, but the messes we create later in life are indulgences predicated on the same tolerance (as the mother's) of others to accept them as part of our individuality. Winnicott's last claim, that transitional phenomena are maintained in later life (rather than disavowed or repressed), in the intensity of experience we might feel for religion or the arts, is of particular interest here. Winnicott didn't expand on this theme himself, but Matt Hills has considered the influence of his theory on the study of fan cultures.

In adopting Winnicottian theory to account for (cult) fan behaviours, Hills draws the useful symbolic distinction between the primary transitional object '(an actual physical object which the child both finds and creates . . .) and the cultural field which is said to displace the transitional object through the natural decathexis of the object-proper'.[43] In this secondary phase the 'retained object must negotiate its intensely subjective significance with its intersubjective cultural status'.[44] It is within this psychocultural field of 'affective play' that Hills finds Winnicott useful in accounting for fandom. For thus, cult texts

> can be used creatively by fans to manage tensions between inner and
> outer worlds. . . . That fans are able to use media texts as part of this
> process [of negotiation] does not suggest that these fans cannot tell

fantasy from reality. Quite the reverse; it means that while maintaining this awareness fans are able to play with (and across) the boundaries between 'fantasy' and 'reality' . . . It is also important to realize that this process is ongoing and does not correspond to a childhood activity which adults are somehow not implicated in. All of us, throughout our lives, draw on cultural artefacts as 'transitional objects'.[45]

Persuasive as Hills is in expanding Winnicottian theory and adapting it to explain the cultural interface between psychic and social investment in texts, he claims such tendencies are universal (presumably common to all human beings and to all types of cultural artefact – not just 'media texts'). He makes no special case for what might be regarded as the extremes of fan devotion (the end of the consumption spectrum where the cult fan might be thought to reside). Neither does he consider this 'ongoing' adult process as anything other than normal. Could it not be that fans who establish what might be termed an unhealthy fixation upon a certain cultural object have not as infants effectively decathected transitional phenomena, but have repressed them in some way?

It is my belief that the uses to which cult fans put their adopted texts address certain deeply felt socio-psychic needs, be these predicated on lack or disavowal or whatever. And that these are (needs must) particularised responses which do not simply equate with an enthusiasm, hobby, passion, fad, or buffishness that we each might feel about something in our lives. The transitional phenomena of cult films allow the fan free rein to play, get messy through surrogate on-screen selves, and clean up afterwards. We can dabble vicariously in excess, and purge ourselves in disgust. Perhaps cult films in their excesses and incongruities allow us to confront and contest the borderlines between our own fears and desires.

Cult Pleasures

Withnail & I is a spare film, sparsely drawn and located. Its intimacy, its low budget, minimal locations, economic yet dynamically funny script are its strengths, along with the beautifully judged performances of its cameo ensemble. It also had the minor audacity to recall an era anachronistic to its mid-Eighties release, when the Sixties and their legacy were deeply unfashionable, and to make a virtue of that enduring sense of alienation one feels at being out of step with the age. These maverick, oddball traits together lend it special, secret, cult appeal.

Indeed, *Withnail*'s period authenticity, expressed particularly through the flexibility of its costume design, is itself questionable. If it offers serious commentary on the legacy of the Sixties it is the failure of that dream – the gloomy if realistic conclusion that transcendence and revolution reside only in the bottle and joint. They are a phase, a part of growing up. You don't have to have lived through the Sixties to identify with the student spirit of these characters. And Andrea Galer's costumes traverse the distance of that era, as well as its essential spirit. Cult films offer vicarious pleasures within the remit of safe distance. This is textually malleable, re-usable – a film you can take away and play with (in the best and boyish spirit of that other cult clique, the Monty Python clan).

The consequences of such accessibility and popularity are the cult fan's worst nightmares: mass appeal and commercial exploitation. On its tenth-anniversary re-release (which was accompanied by wide film-press coverage) Robinson himself sounded a cautionary note:

> I don't want this to sound bitchy, but there is a downside to re-releasing the film which is that people discover *Withnail & I* and it therefore becomes theirs rather than something that has been marketed and thrust at them.[46]

This comment from the film's own author marks an important point about cult fan pleasure – it is private, essentially anti-commercial. As one cultist puts it, it is an important credential that a cult film 'lacks mass appeal'.[47] This is a point reiterated (albeit tongue in cheek) by David Cavanagh (who dubs himself 'the world's biggest *Withnail* fan') in an article for *Empire*. 'All prospective converts should be discouraged [as this] is not a film to be seen by anyone who is not intense or highly intelligent', or, we might add (since he is eavesdropping on two young women speculating about seeing it), who is female.[48] What's important here, between the jokes and political incorrectness, is the strangely narrow, suspicious, guarded sensibility of the cult fan. Actor Ralph Brown (Danny) sees it as 'a little secret film. I hope all that's not going to disappear now,' he adds.[49] This cloistered celebrity, this precious secret, is under threat from a number of quarters, not least the brewery trade. Oddbins organised a competition using lines from the film on its promotional posters, the first prize for which was a trip to Penrith. Stella Artois sponsored a free open-air screening of *Withnail* on Brighton seafront in July 1999. As commercial interests drain the film of its secret potency, doubtless cult fans will move on, or lie low until the fuss is over.

Faced with this evidence it seems more than ever a mistake to attribute a postmodern sensibility to the business of cult loyalty. There is too much at stake here – cult objects are too precious, too private to be picked over as so much bricolage. They are, for their devotees, sacrosanct. Besides, *Withnail & I* is, for all its ingrained humour, too deeply personal and honest a film to admit irony. This directness, this warmth and a certain (exaggerated) candour, lend it its special appeal.

Costume and Cult Performance

The performance of the film's recurrent themes through its costume design, as well as its ongoing cult popularity were demonstrated at an event staged at the National Trust's Fenton House property in London's Hampstead in June 2003. Attracting an audience of around 150 (most of whom had prior knowledge of the film), there were approximately 10 entries to the competition for the replica Harris Tweed coat, produced by Andrea Galer, samples of whose work for film and television were on exhibition in the house.

The way in which Galer deploys costume work in the context of her own design studio is apparent from her website (www.andreagaler. co.uk) featuring, for example, Richard E. Grant modelling the long coat in a distinctly un-Withnail pose. Yet the use of the coat as costume in the contestants' performances of scenes from the film acted (unsurprisingly) as their dominant signifiers of character. In this way the coat can be seen to operate on a number of interrelated levels: as iconic film costume, as museum exhibit, as fans' dressing-up wardrobe and as advertisement for commercial design. So how does the costume work as a site of meaning exchange across these several levels?

In interview with me Andrea Galer recalled the background to the brief and referred to three important aspects of the film's design ethos. Firstly, she pointed to the iconic aspect of the costume. The fact that Withnail wears the same coat throughout the film transcends period verisimilitude – he's poor and has inherited it, and it's the only coat he has, and he even wears it over his underpants indoors because the flat is cold. It is, moreover, a manifestation of his personality and psycho-sexual immaturity: a treasured transitional object, a Winnicottian teddy-bear. Notwithstanding the poignant *denouement*, there is little in this film so genuinely pathetic and illustrative of physical vulnerability as the sight of

FIGURE 19: A replica Withnail coat on display at the
National Trust's Fenton House, Hampstead
[AUTHOR'S OWN IMAGE]

an embrocated Withnail railing against humanity in only Y-fronts and coat. Whilst again, at the level of social realism, the counter-culture flaunted the flamboyant appropriation of other cultural and period styles (the Afghan coat, the Mexican poncho, army-surplus greatcoats and leather flying jackets), as Galer indicates, Withnail's coat is both more and less than these. It is less overtly 'vulgar' (as much post-1967 fashion was), or 'like something out of Paul Smith' and more aesthetically restrained. But at the same time it is also iconic, ubiquitous and therefore memorable (both to Withnail as a character, and in audiences' identification).

Secondly, the coat's period associations also convey a series of different meanings. There is the Byronesque Romanticism of the high collar and long lapels with its heroic investments of utopian idealism and nihilistic despair. This is overlaid with traditionalism: Victorian quality, Harris Tweed organic naturalism, and Uncle Monty's class dissolution – the twilight of an English aristocracy. And then there is the notion of an inherited heirloom, a coveted possession, reminiscent of a lost boyhood and a painful rite-of-passage, as personal to Withnail as it is universal to an audience.

This leads on to Galer's third revealing comment about timelessness. In order for the film to transcend period recreation, it had both to invoke nostalgia for the loss of that last opportunity for youthful rebellion (in the midst of Thatcher's Eighties Britain) and to reiterate the universal nature of those (thwarted) yearnings. Galer reflected further on this *fin de siècle* theme in interview with me:

> It was a conscious decision on Bruce's part that we are doing a period, we are, you know, end of an era. It was the end of an era. And in effect, although it is precise that era, it's an on-going part of society: anyone can relate to it, even though it was precise – and I personally don't think it's easy to be quite as naive about what your choices are as it was then. You know, it's a sort of sad fantasy, you know upper class and lower class can bond together and we'll all have equal rights – no we don't.

Her costumes for the film's other characters evince the same scrupulous avoidance of stylisation or cliché in their evocation of period and character. In her reworking of traditional fabrics and period styles, Andrea Galer successfully invested in the *Withnail* costumes the film's recurrent feelings of youthful rebellion, Romantic dissolution and thwarted sexuality, inspiring cult fans' personal identification with and ongoing appropriation of the spirit of a lost age.

In its articulation of charismatic identity, Withnail's coat can be seen to occupy an especially evocative space between the distinctive styles of the dandy and the Romantic (as outlined by Joanne Entwistle). Referencing Campbell's (1989) work, Entwistle concludes:

> Thus the dandy style emphasized the artifice of appearance, the self as performed and perfected through self-conscious use of dress and the

body, while the Romantic style was concerned with authenticity and the self as 'genuine' and 'natural'.[50]

The psychic and emotional schisms manifest in Withnail's declamatory physical histrionics can be seen, in this way, as reflecting the struggle between the iteration of the 'authentic' self and its self-conscious performance. Referring back to my earlier point about keeping reality at bay through language, this also is a means of both presenting and hiding oneself. The adornment of the body, its physical deportment, and linguistic repertoire are all devices for achieving this paradox.

It was not merely the accidents of biographies (Robinson's and Grant's) which cast a struggling actor in the role of a struggling actor.[51] There is an important sense in which this film utilises the *performance of* late-Sixties Romanticism as a dynamic bridging device: articulating the space between the psychic and the physical, the personal and the material, 1969 and 1986, the charismatic hero and the cult fan.

Summary

I have focused specifically in this chapter upon the script, physical performance and costume in the presentation of a cult aesthetic. I have further elaborated the themes of matter out of place and Romantic nostalgia as key to the cult sensibility. Finally, via recourse to the work of D.W. Winnicott, I have suggested that through the web of recognition created by these textual attributes, cult films may work as transitional objects, enabling fans to negotiate issues of self-identity, subcultural capital and social marginality. Thus, cult films may be seen not merely as distinctive kinds of text within film culture, but as sites of fan practice which are essentially aberrant. This is neither to pathologize fandom nor to attach pejorative connotations to its deviant practices. Rather, I am keen to establish that cult fandom addresses certain popular texts with a seriousness and commitment essentially antithetical to popular film consumption practices. I shall have more to say about the unusual nature of this film fandom (and its common links with other devoted fan cultures) in my conclusion. But it is worth drawing a distinction here between devotees of *Withnail & I* and the film which coincided (in the pages of *Empire* and far beyond) with its tenth-anniversary reissue in 1996: *Trainspotting*. At that moment cult became 'cult'.

CASE STUDY 4:

Trainspotting (1996)

Doubtless, more has been written about *Trainspotting* than any other British film of the past twenty-five years. But then it has proved to be the second most successful British film of all time.[52] Can it, for all this attention, therefore be considered a cult film? Catterall and Wells remain suspicious:

> *Trainspotting*'s promoters pushed all the right buttons. They colluded with its target audience in a way few British films had done before, utilising already homogenised cults – such as those surrounding Britpop, the burgeoning Retro craze, the Rave scene and Irvine Welsh's novel – to add a synthetic veneer of cultish credibility.[53]

But does this premeditation preclude cult status, or render it merely 'synthetic' rather than 'authentic'?

It seems to me that *Trainspotting* is not a cult film because advertising campaigns for *Starlight Express* and Cobra Sports have ripped off its iconic poster art.[54] Nor is it a cult film because the remote Corrour railway halt on the wilds of Rannoch Moor is the unlikely haunt of fan-tourists, one of whom marked a visit by scrawling on the platform in chalk, 'Doesn't it make you proud to be Scottish?'.[55] And it isn't a cult film just because its brand image explicitly positioned the main characters as members of a band – indeed, as cult figures. In fact, I don't believe *Trainspotting* is a cult film at all. Rather, it is a 'cult' film. Wherein lies the difference? Not simply that between authentic and synthetic. Actually it derives from Danny Boyle's explanation of the film's title:

> The boy's own thing is what the title is really about. It's this thing about lists in the film. Everybody talks in lists. They're always listing their achievements – it's a mentality, an attempt to try to get a fix on the world. Tarantino is an absolute trainspotter. It's a very male thing.[56]

Like *Withnail & I*, *Trainspotting* is a tragicomedy that manifests a cult sensibility. Whether you see it, as some do, as an intelligently subjective view of heroin addiction, or you prefer to go along with producer Andrew Macdonald's insistence that it is 'about friendship and betrayal . . . Not heroin', these are but pretexts. The film's attitude is essentially cult.

Like many of the films in this book, its apparent counter-cultural polemic, its taboo-breaking, visceral attitude, is an elaborate gesture politics: never empty, but ultimately recuperated within the dominant cultural values it purports to overturn. Its 'rebellion', such as it is, is transcendental, sensory, aesthetic, and therefore fleeting, insubstantial.

If *Trainspotting* is for some 'the *Quadrophenia* of the rave era', it is also the *Clockwork Orange* of Thatcherism.[57] It is, in short, an elaborate postmodern assemblage of quotations, drawn from pre-existing cult films, like those of Tarantino. But its self-conscious awareness of its own cult credentials transforms it into 'cult'. By 'cult', I mean post-cult: a film made and marketed and consumed in our own cult times. The question remains: if we are all 'trainspotters' now, can anything truly be cult? The cult is dead; long live the 'cult'!

FIGURE 20: We're all trainspotters now. The cult film goes global thanks, in part, to a successful promotional campaign

[FIGMENT/NOEL GAY/CHANNEL 4/THE KOBAL COLLECTION]

CONCLUSION

Summation

It was essential that we began this enquiry with the text itself. It was necessary to select and scrutinise films which were already defined as cult by fan practices and in critical discourse. The aim here was to elucidate firstly those elements which seemed to distinguish them from popular film in general, and secondly to discover whether these were attributes they shared in common with other cult films. Starting with *The Rocky Horror Picture Show* as a template, it became apparent that characteristics of excess and incongruity were paramount. It was noted that such films display both a Baroque kitsch or camp sensibility and a certain Romantic nostalgia. It appeared that their pastiche of certain low-budget genres (especially sci-fi and horror) was both eclectic and lacking in irony. Yet their iconic tributes were too diverse to adhere to established generic categories, and their narrative disjuncture confounded conventional readings. It was necessary therefore to look for clues in other aspects of the mise-en-scène.

Performance, as its title suggests, led us in the direction of visual style and music. The casting of amateur actors and pop music icons focused attention upon acting techniques, physical deportment and the voice. It was noted here, as elsewhere in *Tommy*, *The Man Who Fell to Earth* and *Quadrophenia*, that iconic stars from the world of rock music bring to screen roles both the signifying practices of their established media personae and the quality of redundancy which is a feature of their untrained screen performance. But such conspicuous allure is not the preserve solely of pop stars. James Fox's Chas Devlin, Michael Caine's Jack Carter, Christopher Lee's Lord Summerisle, Malcolm McDowell's Alex DeLarge, Phil Daniels's Jimmy Cooper, Richard E. Grant's Withnail and Ewan McGregor's Mark Renton all manifest charismatic attraction. Sometimes this is the result of a combination of narrative power with physical vulnerability. In certain cases (*Performance*, *The Wicker Man*, *Withnail & I*, *Quadrophenia*, *Trainspotting*) it rests upon the relationship of a young protagonist to a surrogate 'bad father'. Frequently the timbre of voice, patterns of gaze and physical deportment are constituent factors in this considerable appeal. Finally I proposed in chapter seven that these elements of performance in cult films often create an iconic mask which draws attention to its own charismatic artifice and reveals the hollowness behind it. Its function is both self-presentation and self-protection: a strategy for engaging with the world obliquely as a means of keeping it at bay. To that extent such performances rehearse a kind of disavowal. But in cult films at least, the mask is never a perfect fit – it slips. Its points of slippage are where the unconscious breaks through. I shall return to this idea below.

But how are such charismatic performances rendered so conspicuously alluring in cult narratives? We saw that this has to do with the imbalance between performance and other aspects of the mise-en-scène. Cult films do not produce orderly fictional worlds. Their codes of excess often include violence and the breaking of other taboos. But moreover, they manifest an oblique, sometimes surreal attitude to the world of objects, without resorting to complete fantasy. Realism and fantasy may be poles apart, but they are both comfort zones in terms of fictional space. Dada and the surreal are disturbing or anarchic perversions of reality, because their boundaries are not policed: consider *Monty Python and the Holy Grail*! Time and again, cult films present worlds which contain a surfeit of unincorporated signifiers, potent with polyvalent meanings but devoid of the safe anchorage of context. This is what I have termed hyper-signification. This has not only to do with the objects themselves, but also their physical arrangement within the frame. Take for example the grotesque pop art objects at the Cat Lady's house in *A Clockwork Orange*, or the Magritte-influenced giant silver balls in *Tommy* – impenetrable spheres without fissure. In each case physical disproportion is accentuated by a deliberated flattened or distorted picture plane. We are denied the reassurance of depth of field and the balance of classical perspective. Of course, such incongruity is deployed to sublime effect in *the Holy Grail*, where formal self-reflexivity and comic excess ultimately derails a historically grounded narrative. Sometimes such disorientation is produced by the inexplicable close-up and fast, analytical editing (Roeg's camerawork on *Performance* and *The Man Who Fell to Earth* for example, and Kubrick's photographic tricks in *A Clockwork Orange*). Elsewhere, location backdrops are equally unsettling. The bleak Highlands which double for the England of Arthurian legend, the harsh urban juxtapositions of the Tyneside of *Get Carter*, the malevolent Lake District of *Withnail & I*, the mythical Scottish Summerisle, and the New Mexican 'Land of Enchantment' in *The Man Who Fell to Earth* are each disquieting in their own way.

Next, in terms of the texture of cult films, we need to acknowledge the importance of what we hear as well as what we see. Each of the texts explored here has a unique soundtrack. We considered the pioneering work of Jack Nitzsche on *Performance*, Walter (Wendy) Carlos on *A Clockwork Orange*, Roy Budd on *Get Carter*, Paul Giovanni on *The Wicker Man* and John Phillips on *The Man Who Fell to Earth*. Each of these musical arrangers constructs an aural bricolage based upon definitive source music: blues in *Performance*, classical in *A Clockwork Orange*, folk in *The Wicker Man* and jazz and country in *Get Carter* and *The Man Who Fell to Earth*. Yet each also overlays these roots with disconcerting, impromptu effects from the experimental synthesisers of Nitzsche and Carlos and the harpsichord of Budd, to the aeolian harp of Giovanni, and Phillips's deployment of the eerie dystopia of Stomu Yamashta. *The Rocky Horror Picture Show* and *Tommy* of course count as musicals in their own right. While Richard O'Brien's songs parody saccharine pop to the level of outrageous camp, Pete Townshend's rite-of-passage story is rendered in ground-breaking, quadraphonic monuments of high rock. But each exploits to excess the unnatural rift between narrative and performance endemic in the conventional form. Finally, *Quadrophenia*'s realism is rooted in The Who's edgy, vibrant soundtrack, while *Trainspotting*'s retro and rave soundwall is a collage of counterpoint and ironic commentary. Music is the medium through which social taboos can be breached. It is physically liberating. It allows the unconscious free rein.

The breaching of social taboos seems also to be a common feature of cult films. Some are extremely violent (*Performance*, *Get Carter*, *A Clockwork Orange*, *Quadrophenia*, *Trainspotting* – ultimately *The Wicker Man* too).

Often this is the more disturbing for treating the subject in a detached, sometimes picaresque or analytical manner – presenting violence as spectacle. A similar attitude towards the body is offered in such films' approach to sex too. Once again voyeuristic tendencies are complicated by anxiety and unease. I have proposed that a double articulation of viewing response is implied by such ambivalent presentations of violence and sex. Here again, disavowal comes to the fore.

For all their challenge to codes of permission, however, few cult films descend into anarchy. Rather, they display an unusual respect for rules and rituals. Consider, for example, Sergeant Howie's methodical police inquiry pitted against the alternative religious practices of Summerisle. Or recall the rule-based systems which govern the world of the gangster in *Get Carter* and *Performance*, and the etiquette of subcultural style in *Quadrophenia*. Elsewhere, Alex's droogs are as regimented and choreographed in their violence as Withnail is in his drinking regime, though both are ultimately the victims of the dominant order. Thomas Jerome Newton casts an alien perspective upon human social codes in *The Man Who Fell to Earth*. And Chas Devlin, in breaking a gangland rule of engagement, exchanges one underground system for another, bohemian one, presided over by an equally circumspect, indeed fastidious, Turner. The need for codes of practice is manifest in cult films, though often these are alternative in character: for example, the sartorial rituals associated with mod style in *Quadrophenia* and the litany of lists which punctuate the heroin waste land of *Trainspotting*. Sometimes they are playful inversions of normal social conventions which present a picaresque irreverence for the traditional sites of power, from *The Wicker Man* to Monty Python. Elsewhere they paradoxically govern extremely antisocial behaviour: *Performance*, *Get Carter*, *A Clockwork Orange*, *The Wicker Man*, *Quadrophenia*, *Trainspotting*. Frequently they traverse the hinterland of primary taboos concerning dirt, mess, bodily hygiene and matter out of place: from the 'mud-eating' of Arthurian England to the 'worst toilet in Scotland'. Everywhere they stand as a reminder of the necessity for, but ultimate contingency of, rule-based systems. And they speak of the desire for a framework in which to formulate belief.

With this last point in mind, it is no coincidence that speculative or apocryphal explanatory models also abound. Consider the frequent invocation of mythology, magic, the occult, alternative religion and vulgar medical science in these films. The spectres of Arthurian legend, Frazer,

Ruskin, Charcot, Mesmer, Freud and Crowley haunt these works. It is interesting to note how the historical flowering of such a broad range of interests in the second half of the nineteenth century reseeded itself in popular culture of the late 1960s and early 1970s. Whilst it is beyond the scope of this work to elaborate on this large-scale comparison, it is worth conjecturing that periods of rapid social change may engender a crisis of consensus in the dominant ideology which stimulates radical alternatives at the cultural margins. I shall expand on this theme below. Finally, it may be that common strains of Romanticism resurface to inspire such periods of innovative endeavour, perhaps because of the perceived failure of the collective project or a weariness of Classical verities. Indeed, perhaps it is not too much to suggest that 1968 represents one of those moments of rupture in the Enlightenment principle of governance and order through rational recourse to history.

The Cult in Culture

In the earlier chapters of this book I raised a number of questions about the cultural significance of the late 1960s and around the pivotal year of 1968 in particular. Whilst acknowledging that the term cult had a certain limited currency in popular youth culture before the 1960s, and that there are films which predate that decade which have subsequently come to be considered cult, the Sixties seems to me to have been an important point of departure for a number of reasons.

I have proposed that the diverse set of social changes which brought popular youth culture to prominence at that time, and challenged erstwhile secure cultural boundaries, were not only significant in their own right. They became enshrined in, and exemplified by, a range of popular texts of the period. As Robert Hewison suggests, if we can talk in terms of the late 1960s as a revolutionary moment, then this was conducted almost entirely through cultural production and consumption, rather than at the socio-economic or political level.[1] Indeed, it may be that culture functioned in the service of hegemony as a safety-valve, a mode of displacement for disaffection which (notwithstanding events in Paris, race riots, anti-Vietnam protests or civil rights marches) was largely symbolic. This is not to diminish the import of these upheavals, nor to suggest that the term 'revolution' is misplaced. Rather, it is to draw attention to the heightened significance and burden of responsibility which cultural

FIGURE 21: All that remains of the second wicker effigy
on the clifftop at Burrowhead
[AUTHOR'S OWN IMAGE]

artefacts took on during the period. Cultural texts never simply reflect society in any straightforward way, but they invariably engage with it and sometimes can be viewed as sites both of displacement for fears and desires and for negotiating pressing problems.

One of the challenges implicit in this book has been to develop a model which goes some way towards accounting for the relationship between cultural artefacts and historical change. At a straightforward level cultural texts will always have something to say about the time in which they were made, and their popularity will usually be an index of their influence. But beyond this orthodoxy, two issues are crucial here. One is the role of socio-economic determinants in changing patterns of cultural production and consumption. The other, more speculatively, concerns what might be termed a text's 'unconscious'. By this I mean the textual opportunities which film (perhaps uniquely) may offer for the symbolic displacement of collective unconscious fears and desires.

The Textual 'Unconscious'

I have proposed in each case study that the particular circumstances of production gave rise to a kind of text which was imperfectly rendered, and in which there remains an imbalance in the orchestration of its constituent elements. Sometimes such unevenness is the result of chance as well as creative struggle. Certainly the content and style of many of these films reflects the relative freedom of key agents to pursue radical visions. However, the remarkable correspondences we have noted between these works, both at the levels of form and theme, suggest a more profound source of influence: a rift in ideology.

'History', Yuri Lotman contends, 'is not *only* a conscious process, and it is not *only* an unconscious process. It is a mutual tension between the two' (emphasis retained).[2] It may be useful to see this tension manifesting itself in the spaces between discourse and silence of which all texts are made. By that I mean the struggle between what can be said and what goes unsaid. And what goes unsaid will include both that which cannot be spoken as well as that which is taken as read. Of course, in historical terms this struggle will also be engaged between those who have the power to speak and those who don't. And, as Lotman makes clear, much of the so-called *histoire nouvelle* has concerned itself with the neglected legacy of the latter. But evidence of the unspoken is to be found throughout creative works which are dense, gnomic, allusive, metaphoric, metonymic, provocative and, above all, popular. Indeed, it may be said that because, historically, popular texts have relied on discursive forms and conventions which are accessible to the broadest of audiences, their modes of address are particularly suggestive and open to interpretation, and their structures of feeling are especially acute. It is for this reason that popular texts (and above all popular film) may be seen as the repositories of the collective unconscious. Whilst mainstream popular films may tend to be ideologically conservative and foreclose the range of associations they can sustain, cult films provide access to a remarkably rich repertoire of resources. Both provide evidence of what Lotman calls the 'anonymous processes' of history, as well as the imprimaturs of the creative artists: 'The very essence of the human relationship to culture ensures this: the personality is both isomorphic to the universum, and at the same time a part of it'.[3]

Foucault has addressed a similar theme with his original use of the term double articulation:

> The double articulation of the history of individuals upon the unconscious of culture, and of the historicity of those cultures upon the unconscious of individuals, has opened up, without doubt, the most general problems that can be posed with regard to man.[4]

While not pretending for a moment that we can solve those here, it is useful nonetheless to see the conduits for Foucault's 'double articulation', as with Lotman's 'mutual tension', as being language and texts: the realms of discourse.

Lotman's work also provides us with a profitable model for the way in which moments of ideological rift create crises within the sign system which may be conducive to tropic creativity. For example, he notes that 'the boundaries which separate one kind of trope from another are, in Baroque texts, exceptionally fluid' and constitute 'a means of forming a special ordering of consciousness'.[5] Given that an '"illegitimate" juxtaposition often provokes the formation of a new law', it may be that in circumstances where anxiety surrounds the 'shared context' of signifying elements no stable 'relationship of adequacy' can be attained. Tropic invention may run to what I have identified in cult film texts as hyper-signification. Such cultural texts, I suggest, must be seen as the result of a partial fragmentation in the ideological consensus around language which gives rise to a particularly rich outpouring of creativity. This accords with the contestation of the boundaries between erstwhile secure cultural categories and a rise in experimentation at the margins which occurred during the late 1960s. Lotman describes such a cultural crisis in these terms:

> At a moment when the historical, social and psychological tension reaches the point where a person's world picture dramatically alters (as a rule under intense emotional pressure) a person can dramatically change his or her stereotype, as it were leap into a new mode of behaviour, quite unpredictable in 'normal circumstances'. Of course, if we consider the behaviour of the crowd at such a moment, we shall see a degree of repeatability in that many individuals are altering their behaviour and under the new circumstances are choosing unpredictable modes.[6]

By expressing the effects of social crisis upon individuals in terms of changing stereotypes, Lotman translates psychic responses into behavioural effects which will be culturally visible. At such moments therefore, cultural texts which offer new kinds of stereotype will flourish and have an extremely important social function, depending upon the coherence of their resources. Cult films emerge from the plethora of popular cultural production of the late 1960s as texts which lend themselves to incorporation through their iconic modes of address, yet whose rich resources ultimately fail to resolve themselves into coherent, alternative stereotypes. Thus, they may be seen as particularly precious objects for those individuals who, for whatever reasons, fail to negotiate the transition between their former stereotype and a new one.

The idea of stereotypes is distinguished most profoundly of course around matters of sexual difference and the display of the body. And, as we have seen, these are sites of acute anxiety within cult films. As an adjunct to this point it may seem ironic that the first protracted example of male full-frontal nudity on mainstream British cinema screens, in Ken Russell's adaptation of D.H. Lawrence's *Women in Love* (1969), should coincide with a profound cultural anxiety surrounding masculinity. But Kaja Silverman argues that such instances which seek, in Lacanian terms, to make the physical penis stand for the phallus in an explicit, visible way are signs of the very failure of collective belief in what she calls the 'dominant fiction' – the ideological consensus around the phallic order. In the same way, explicit exploitation of the female form on film is seen as a measure of male disavowal of castration, suggesting, in Silverman's words, 'that female subjectivity represents the site at which the male subject deposits his lack'.[7]

In chapter six I described the relationship of cult films to this ideological crisis using a Lacanian frame of reference, but with due regard to other theoretical models. I suggested that cult films, uneven in their structure, seemed, in their circuits of *jouissance*, to fetishise what Lacan called *petits objets autres* – nostalgic yearnings for those first objects of the imaginary register. In chapter seven I referred to Winnicott's notion of the transitional object as having a similar psychic function. So, cult films may be seen as transitional objects which are used as a means to articulate *retroactively* positions of subjectivity within the (disrupted) signifying system. They present particular kinds of imaginary worlds in which we can (mis-)

recognise ourselves. In order to explain this last point more fully, it is to fan pleasures that I turn attention next.

Cult Texts and Cult Fans

It seems as though certain kinds of cultural texts – ones whose unfinished structure allows remarkable creative agency and psychic investment on the part of the viewer – can be used as displacement for shared subjective anxieties. These examples may exist on an individual basis of course, as Lacan posits in the case of an unresolved Oedipal crisis, but are often culturally inscribed at what Silverman terms moments of 'historical trauma':

> I mean any historical event, whether socially engineered or of natural occurrence, which brings a large group of male subjects into such an intimate relation with lack that they are at least for the moment unable to sustain an imaginary relation with the phallus, and so withdraw belief from the dominant fiction. Suddenly the latter is radically de-realized, and the social formation finds itself without a mechanism for achieving consensus.[8]

Silverman's own case study relates to the figuring of male anxiety as a form of war neurosis in Hollywood films of the immediate post-Second World War years. Sue Harper's work on Gainsborough melodramas of the same period encourages those films to be read as another kind of cultural response to a similar crisis of belief in the 'dominant fiction'.[9] However, interestingly for our purposes, Silverman also acknowledges:

> It has only been very recently that yet another threat has come into play in a politically organized way – that constituted through the representational and sexual practices of feminism and gay liberation.[10]

It seems to me that the specific crisis of masculinity to which she refers here is precisely that which emanated from the cultural revolution of the late 1960s and the rise of feminism and gay liberation which gathered political momentum and profound ideological purchase during the 1970s and 1980s. The impact of debates about gender politics and sexual orientation during this period was also exacerbated by what might be termed a crisis of faith in the family as a symbolic institution. Each of these matters is explicitly addressed, though never resolved, in cult films of the same period. Cult films may be viewed as one kind of textual response to this crisis of masculinity. But why? What psychic needs do they fulfil?

I have proposed that such texts work for fans, both male *and* female, to both stimulate and console. There is ample evidence to suggest that certain males *and* females have profound affective attachments to these films. I would suggest that it is probably a matter of psychic disposition as well as cultural factors which draws certain individuals to cult films as transitional objects in the process of subjective self-recognition with which we are all engaged. Fans use these films as resources through which to rehearse subjective identities and demonstrate cultural competence. The strategies and processes involved are various, as individual needs are diverse. Yet if cultural texts can be viewed, like religious icons, as objects through which we structure our desires in the constitution of our own subjective identities, then cult films are the repositories of fears and longings in the negotiation of sexual difference and subjectivity. They endorse cultural marginality, reassuring their devotees that not 'fitting in' is fine, maybe even heroic. They offer alternative systems of order, symbolic rituals and rites of passage. They provide frameworks for alternative forms of belief.

There is not a direct correspondence between cultural texts and human sensibilities, but there are echoes of one in the other. One of the themes raised in this book has been that of excess: texts of excess and excessive fan behaviours. For Joli Jenson at least, 'Fandom involves an ascription of excess, and emotional display' in contrast to the 'affinity' of the 'aficionado', which involves 'rational evaluation, and is displayed in more measured ways'.[11] If one is describing social hierarchies of taste in terms of audience behaviours, then cult fans do not strictly fit into either category. That is not to say they don't manifest excessive kinds of behaviour: they demonstrate time and again obsessive attention to minutiae and trivia, excesses of emotional attachment and displays of shared enthusiasm or passionate rivalry. They may show extreme levels of response to widely popular texts (e.g. the *Stars Wars* films) or bizarrely 'normal' levels of response to extreme texts (e.g. slasher movies). But the grounds of their obsession and its discursive landscape are also codified and demonstrate 'rational evaluation' and expertise in 'measured ways'. Excess is frequently tempered with restraint, derived from the dual needs for precision and reverence. Control must also be exercised in policing the boundaries of distinction, to preserve the essential separateness of the cult. Like all ecstatic states (religion and sex included), cult fandom is an emotional outpouring which demands self-control: it is abandonment *with* responsibility, otherwise it is nihilism.

Matt Hills proposes that the internet newsgroup constitutes not so much an 'imagined community' as a 'community of imagination'.[12] By this he means that such virtual spaces are not illusory, but real. They are real by dint of the emotional interplay between their constituent members: their 'common affective engagement'.[13] In my own web ethnography of cult film fans I have argued that the terra firma of the film text provides the known grounding for virtual emotional forays and explorations.[14] If for Hills 'affective play' is the description which best fits the 'real-fantasy' nature of fans' subjective pleasures, we might locate this activity socially using an inversion of the term deployed by sociologist Paul Willis.

In *Common Culture*, Willis expounds the notion of 'symbolic work'.[15] This theory helps us to situate cult fan practices within lived culture, as one kind of creative expression which 'is spread across the whole of life. It is a condition of it, and of our daily humanity':

> Symbolic creativity may be individual and/or collective. It transforms what is provided and helps to produce specific forms of human identity and capacity. Being human – human be-ing-ness – means to be creative in the sense of re-making the world for ourselves as we make and find our own place and identity.[16]

Using the resources of cult film texts and the frameworks and discourses of diverse fan practices, cult film fans are engaged in such acts of 'remaking the world' in the cause of achieving a sense of 'place and identity'. This process of interpellation is not merely a function of ideology in any deterministic sense; it is rather a dynamic position achieved through active engagement with and deployment of cultural resources. And its cause is no less than the achievement of selfhood-in-mass-culture. In this way, we may explore the apparent paradox of the cult fan as both outsider and conformist.

In what way are cult fans' demonstrations of outsider status at once representative of the desire to conform? The achievement of cultural distinction through the deployment of cultural capital works on the basis of superiority through exclusiveness. It is anti-populist. It seeks to resolve the myriad paradoxes of popular culture from the individual distinction promised by uniform popular fashions to the illusion of fan intimacy with pop or film star icons. It seeks to capture the moment of enunciation which represents self-assertion through the cultural commodity matrix. Cultural distinction demands initiation rites, secret languages, passwords, membership rights. This may be classed as symbolic work in the service of 'fitting in', because it demonstrates a form of social engagement and provides a ground for symbolic work. This makes the outsider feel that they belong, that they have arrived at the point of articulating a self-within-culture.

Why do cult fans feel they are outsiders? We may speculate about possible explanations from environmental factors to psychological traits. Such feelings may be the product of unresolved Oedipal crises (Lacan) or of having not properly decathected primary transitional objects (Winnicott). Whatever the root causes of their separation, cult fans display the dual tendencies towards excess and restraint. Their behaviours seem marked by the twin drives of obsession and control, of hedonism and propriety, of emotional outpouring and rational debate. These traits are frequently manifested in verbal strategies which reveal emotional commitment, enthusiasm and sometimes seemingly indiscriminate value judgements. These are coupled with a necessary adroitness, a certain savvy discretion. In some ways, such strategies replicate the psychosexual character of eroticism: not so much a game of fort/da, as of peep/bo. It is a type of affective play governed by guarded self-exposure.

One female fan of *Withnail & I* responded in interview to the question of whether there is audience empathy with the protagonists' plight:

> Oh yes, yes there is. Striving for something. And perhaps almost – I have to say it – why some people fit in and why some people don't.

This could just as well be a description of the cult film fan and certainly is part of the pleasure-in-identification which cult fans of the film feel. Another (male) respondent demonstrated his cultish enthusiasm with a typically obscure anecdote:

> That scene in the car that they filmed in the boot on the motorway with Jimi Hendrix playing . . . I bought the CD . . . that's like one of the great rock 'n' roll moments . . . it's just immortal. There is one bit in the film – this is very boring – there's one bit where they're going along the road to London and in the background is a sign that's not 1969, it's got the airport sign and it's not right. And it's the only continuity bit apart from things like Ford Commer vans were a different shape

in 1969. But that bit – and there's no reason to keep it because it's just
– they could have cut it but it's funny just that one idea.

The first response is different in tone and pace from the second. It
is a correct, considered reflection, while the second is an enthusiastic,
committed outpouring with an almost autistic eye for uncanny detail.
Yet, different as they are, both share a characteristic technique of self-
commentary which interrupts or qualifies or even undercuts the main
thrust: in the first case 'I have to say it' and in the second 'I bought the
CD' and 'this is very boring'. Such self-conscious interjection is more than
mere mannerism: it is the acknowledgment of contingency, the admission
of not fitting in. Thus, whether through internet newsgroups or face-to-
face interviews, cult film fans consistently demonstrate the discursive
characteristics of their symbolic work.

The gendered nature of these fan discourses is apparent in the case of
the *Wicker Man* newsgroup, where there is frequently a candour and erotic
charge about female confessions which is very much at odds with male
responses to this film. The following exchange between a female novice
and a male initiate illustrates the point:

```
I saw Wicker Man for the first time last weekend
and I've never been so fascinated by any motion
picture. The mystery and eroticism, combined with
the locale, make for something unique.
    In the scene when Sgt. Howie returns to Lord
Summerisle's home with the hare he's found in
Rowan's grave, there's a shot of the pipe organ and
its keyboard. Just for a moment we see three of the
stops above the keys. Can anyone make out what's
written on them? Somehow I'm sure the names of the
organ stops play into the overall theme of the
movie.

Megan
```

The cautiousness of Megan's introduction doesn't prevent her from
divining the erotic charge in the 'mystery' of this 'unique' film.
Unsurprisingly she then jumps from that general introduction to a very
specific question about an odd detail: the close-up shot of the organ
stops. The manner in which she poses this leading question is coy in the

extreme. One fancies she can make out exactly what's written on the organ stops and has a fair idea how they 'play into the overall theme of the movie'. Nonetheless, the trap is set and regular contributor John (whose minute dissection of the film text is obsessively thorough) comes to the rescue:

```
Hi Megan,

I too was fascinated by the close up of the organ
stops and thought this must be a visual joke. I
asked the same question you did earlier and several
people piped in, pun intended. One even led me to a
website that explained the musical meaning of each
organ stop but not their double entendres. Here is
what I know:
    There are six organ stops that we can see (l-r):
sub bass (16 ft), salicional (8 ft), flute d'amour
(4 ft), lieblich gedact (4 ft), voix celeste (8
ft), and one more I can't read (probably a 16
ft pipe). To me they are visual puns about sex:
salaciousness (the pipe is labelled salicional
but one would assume it's double entendre would
be salacious-something), flute d amor (penis),
voix celeste (celestial voice, during orgasm?) I
don't know about the lieblich gedact but i have my
suspicions. These are all legitimate organ stops,
not contrived.
    I too love the little details like that and have
looked into many of them. You'll find more in the
archives. We haven't talked about the eroticism too
much though. That has been one of the appeals for
me too.
    Glad you enjoy it. We all do.

Cheers,

John L
```

The thoroughness of John's deliberations in tracking down the double entendres is matched by the careful structure of his writing: 'These are all legitimate organ stops, not contrived.' His attribution of sexual associations is executed with almost medical precision. However, in his concluding paragraph two other qualities emerge: a sort of paternalistic encouragement ('I too', 'You'll find more in the archives', 'Glad you enjoy it. We all do'), coupled with a slight hesitation ('We haven't talked about the eroticism too much though') which implies the need for caution in this area.

Naturally, there is here a need to weigh what is said and how, against what is implied in passing or glossed over. Here is the known and secure (the archives) against the unknown and uncontrolled (eroticism). The terra firma of the film text (its incontrovertible substance) provides the known grounding for emotional forays and explorations. Paradoxically, I believe, the mysteries and discoveries are not really being made in the text at all, but in the fans themselves in their testing of emotional boundaries. The film text (which is actually insubstantial and absent) is made, through fan discourse, concrete and present. In some respects it is the only thing of which they are all certain, and certainly the thing these virtual strangers have in common. The rest is play. However, it is serious play which is often expressed through attachment to ephemera beyond the text itself.

Precious objects, whether Winnicottian transitional phenomena or treasured heirlooms, occupy the me/not me interface in our emotional relations with the material world. A wide variety of fan practices surrounds coveted objects and cult film fandom is no exception to this. Significant is not only the *range* of objects – from the film text itself through video and DVD recordings to music soundtracks, collectable merchandise and memorabilia – but also the way in which these are collected, ordered in hierarchies, traded and discussed. Objects constitute a particularly valuable currency in the exchange mechanisms of cult fan relations. Furthermore, cult objects are often also symbolic tokens of those iconic signifiers which are at once present and absent in the film text itself. Take this example of an exchange between two female fans of *The Wicker Man*:

> We have seen an incredible interest in movies like the
> Harry Potter series, and we all know how resourceful
> the advertising industry can be . . . can we expect,
> with a U.S. remake (actually, a totally new story),
> and a new film by Robin Hardy that may or may not
> include some sort of wicker man (called a laddie
> this time), that one Christmas soon, coming to a
> neighborhood near you, that underneath the Christmas
> trees of the world, one will find the most sought

after present of the season, a genuine Wicker Man
action doll, complete with straw and matches? LOL.
Just look how popular Harry Potter paraphernalia has
become.

   Wouldn't that be a kick in the ass?

ophiel_magic, Thursday 22/05/2003

Reading the message, I rushed to grab my Debit card
to buy one on-line!!! I thought you had spotted one
somewhere! Why hasn't anyone thought of it before?
I suppose it's a different world since '73 before
heavy product plugging. I have two Alice Cooper [a
cult pop icon of the 1970s] action figures which I
love, so why not a Wicker man? Imagine a little door
in his tummy so you can place the Howie figure.

   I have wanted to make one out of wicker, straw
etc. but I'm not very good at that sort of thing
so have tried the internet without luck. Can anyone
help me?

queenyfrog, Thursday 22/05/2003

Significant in this exchange is the ways in which these female *Wicker Man* fans seek to distinguish their special film from the merchandising of commercially popular films like the Harry Potter series, thus casting this film as alternative to mainstream commodification. But then, by sleight of hand almost, the second correspondent inverts this rebellion with an affectionate reminiscence about the days 'before heavy product plugging' – a kind of pre-commodity utopian fantasy. Part of this fantasy then becomes imagining a doll-like wicker figure with 'a little door in his tummy so you can place the Howie figure' in a peculiarly girlish regression to a maternal fantasy complete with pregnancy motif. Queeny then concludes by expressing the desire to make a doll from wicker or straw – another anti-commercial, natural, do-it-yourself expression of authenticity which is the antithesis of her opening line about rushing to grab the debit card.

   Such playful engagements with the idea of a collectable object reveal several important issues. Firstly they show how cult fans assert the otherness of their text and its difference from mainstream cinema's commercial environment. Secondly, they then invert this notion with 'what if' speculation about a hypothetical action figure. And thirdly, this becomes a conduit for expressing childlike fantasies and desires for alternative, organic forms of creativity which reassert their personal distinction, indeed, their very 'unmadeness'. Theirs is a world not of manufactured objects but of the imaginative transformation of raw materials. This represents a resistance to a finished, packaged and commodified world view.

If the internet is a forum for allowing such frank (and frankly trivial) disclosures without restraint, it also provides the ritualistic framework and structure which complement fans' attachment to the text itself perfectly. In short, this constitutes a balance of free expression and stimulation with the group dynamics and the subjective rituals of belonging. In this way, cult fandom is rather like forms of religious practice: textual iconography, contextual debate and ritual observance constitute the focus of a shared emotional landscape. Like religious worship, this represents a communion wherein the open expression of feelings which would to outsiders seem strange is not only given credence by like-minded souls, but is given particular form and meaning by the discursive framework of the environment itself. This is why, in the case of *The Wicker Man* especially, the theme of alternative religion is such a powerful explanatory system. Evidence suggests that members of the *Wicker Man* newsgroup are acutely aware of this. Moreover, they use their ritual practice not only as a resource of self-expression but, as the islanders did, as a way of defining their essential difference. Through this discursive framework, they engage with the film's alternative explanatory system to emphasise their 'otherness'. In this way, like mods or Monty Python fans, they are akin to the secret society.

In fan interactions, cult texts promote remarkable candour and rancour; they enable fans to demonstrate canniness about films which are frequently uncanny, and profess devotion to the debased. At the same time, internet identities allow for the orchestrated projection of a subjective self which cannot be exposed as incomplete, unfinished, or socially inept. They enable amateurism to be taken seriously. Newsgroup communications can be a way of producing a symbolic self which is a misrecognition of subjective identity – a mask of disavowal. Finally, the symbolic work which cult fandom enables allows for the fashioning of a text in one's own image. It also fosters the ability to confer order, significance and meaning, and ignore the established categories of critical value. One contextual reason for the cult fan's focus on textual marginalia

FIGURE 22: Fans of *Withnail & I* rehearse a scene from the film
in a competition to win a Withnail coat
[AUTHOR'S OWN IMAGE]

is precisely its lack of critical provenance: it is neither highly acclaimed nor widely popular, but it is imaginatively accommodating. However, as cult criticism and market awareness converge upon the phenomenon, it may already be under threat.

Cult Times

In my opening chapter I proposed that it might be useful to see the cult film phenomenon in British cinema as occupying two overlapping time-frames. The first established the importance of cultural and economic changes during the 1960s in the production of a new kind of film which is later considered cult, and the creation of a film culture which, in the 1970s, is increasingly diverse and marginalised in character and tastes. But in chapter seven I broached the matter of the second timescale. The period of the film cult proposes that cult film fandom – which probably took root during the earlier period – really becomes visible as a conspicuous phenomenon from the late 1970s onwards, and is attendant upon several other important conditions.

An important criterion of cult eligibility, as we have seen with remarkable consistency in this study, relates to a film's critical heritage. It seems to be important that cult films have been critically maligned, suffered at the box-office, been disowned by their own distributors, or otherwise suppressed. If many of these films have their origins in the revolutionary moment of the late 1960s, such tales of woeful neglect and subsequent cult recuperation are stories set in the 1970s and 80s, in the case of these texts. Of course we need to acknowledge, as Greg Taylor does, that such exercises in the critical rehabilitation of debased or neglected works were long ago the stock-in-trade of the likes of Manny Farber and Parker Tyler, and that their standard-bearers in the case of films of the 1970s were their compatriots Sarris and Peary, Rosenbaum and Hoberman, Telotte and the annals of *Cinéfantastique*. Indeed, it is important to note that several of the British films considered here became cult in the United States *first*, thanks to this highly attuned critical response to the vibrant culture of midnight screenings at downtown independent cinemas and the college campus circuit. And yet cult is not simply a matter of the discovery of films which have, perhaps on the strength of their controversial subject matter or lack of box-office appeal, been hitherto marginalised. I have established above that there is more to the cult fandom than the pursuit of subcultural capital through the valorisation of 'trash aesthetics'. How then are we to square debates around the critical provenance of cult films with the conclusions I have already drawn about the uses to which fans put these chosen texts? One part of the answer to this concerns Althusser's theory of ideological interpellation, in which we are hailed by cultural texts and (mis)recognise ourselves in them.[17] But the other relates to the assertion that we live, for better or worse, in cult times. Let me explain what I mean by that idea.

John Patterson recently mourned the passing of the midnight movie and, as he sees it, the resultant decline in the genuinely cultish.[18] Yet what could be more cultish than that nostalgic lament from a film critic in a national newspaper? Paradoxically, as Patterson himself notes, cultism began as the midnight movie gave way to home video, the internet and DVD. Video allowed the ownership of and unprecedented interaction with a film text, only to be surpassed by DVD whose special features and enabling of viewer agency might have been designed with the cult fan in mind. The internet, of course, offers unparalleled opportunities for fan expression and communication, endless dissection and rumination. Even in the cult criticism of Rosenbaum and Hoberman, Telotte and Peary, that seminal cult format – the midnight movie – is already in decline, just as cult criticism is on the rise. When I was an undergraduate in the mid-1980s, cult films were the preserve of student film societies. Now they are the subject of Film Studies courses. And, of course, 'cult films' are now available 'off-the-peg', as *Lock, Stock and Two Smoking Barrels* (Guy Ritchie, UK, 1998), *The Blair Witch Project* (Daniel Myrick, Eduardo Sánchez, USA, 1999), and *Donnie Darko* (Richard Kelly, USA, 2001) proved.[19] Most cult fans view with disdain the recent spate of cult remakes, such as *The Texas Chainsaw Massacre* (Marcus Nisepel, USA, 2003). Yet such flagrantly commercial trade-offs present yet more opportunities – like *Donnie Darko: The Director's Cut* (2004) – for fans to debate the minutiae of critical distinction. It's all grist to the mill. On the magazine shelves in my local supermarket one can buy the monthly guide to cult TV: an oracle of the satellite age called, appropriately, *Cult Times*. But perhaps we should more accurately consider the present time as being, self-consciously, 'post-cult'.

What does all this mean? It indicates that some kinds of cultural consumption have become commodified and fragmented to the point of individuation. Subcultural distinction has been elided through hegemonic processes to the extent that the cult is almost totally recuperated ideologically, and reproduced commercially to feed the personalised media culture. This is why I believe that the established vocabulary of subcultural distinction has lost its critical purchase, at least in so far as this case is concerned. Now cult is just another brand, another niche market, another consumer choice. Like fashion or pop music it trades on the myth of individuation: it promises to make you 'you', to set you apart from the crowd of which you are a part, at a price. This, of course, is nothing more than economic exchange in the service of subjective identity – a sense of belonging. Nowadays, we can each have a personalised cult of our own. And our niche is prepared in advance. We are being hailed – achieving self-recognition through cultural consumption. Cult films have long lost the power to shock. What we have nowadays is 'the schlock of the old'. This is what living in cult times is about. And this book is a peripheral contribution to that culture of the cult. But the idea of cult times also raises a cultural paradox which is as central to postmodernity in general as it is to the cult film phenomenon.

Consider the following philosophical conundrum. In what sense can a cultural phenomenon be said to have existed *before* it entered discourse? In what sense can it still exist *after* it has entered discourse? The answer to the first question used to derive from something called 'authentic culture'. I'm not sure that that idea any longer has critical value, for it is no longer the site where ideological struggles are fought. The answer to the second question is that it can continue to exist only in the warm glow of nostalgia, of something that once was and is already lost, like the midnight movie.

Yuri Lotman has some interesting conclusions on this theme. He writes:

> The interrelationship between cultural memory and its self-reflection is like a constant dialogue: texts from chronologically earlier periods are brought into culture, and, interacting with contemporary mechanisms, generate an image of the historical past, which culture transfers into the past and which like an equal partner in dialogue, affects the present.[20]

It is the power and pervasiveness of this interrelationship which makes those pivotal films of the late 1960s such potent cult objects. They captured and distilled the essence of the Sixties' Romantic spirit for posterity. They enabled subsequent generations of fans to experience that era in the perfect way: vicariously, second-hand, without risk. These films (and fashions and music and literature) are so powerful, evocative and enduring that they have come to symbolise that age more effectively than personal memory can recall or social history recount. They have surrendered their immediate power to shock in exchange for eternal youth. They are Baudrillardian simulacra: truer, more real, than reality ever was. That is why British cult films of the 1970s, from the camp to the picaresque, are so preoccupied with reworking its themes to recapture it. It is also the reason for the success of the unashamedly nostalgic *Quadrophenia* and *Withnail & I*. What is 1986 but a reflection of 1968? But beyond such postmodern conceits, what does nostalgia *really* mean?

The Meaning of Nostalgia

At the beginning of this book, I looked at the *Oxford English Dictionary*'s definitions of *cult*. At its end, therefore, it seems appropriate to consult the dictionary again. The *OED Online* defines *nostalgia* as the following:

> 1. Acute longing for familiar surroundings, esp. regarded as a medical condition; homesickness. Also in extended use.

> 2. a. Sentimental longing *for* or regretful memory of a period of the past, esp. one in an individual's own lifetime; (also) sentimental imagining or evocation of a period of the past.

> b. Something which causes nostalgia for the past; freq. as a collective term for things which evoke a former (remembered) era. Cf. MEMORABILIA *n.* [21]

Nostalgia is considered to be the historicisation of kitsch aptly captured in the phrase 'sentimental longing'. Earlier accounts emphasise its medical derivation: it was literally the condition of home-sickness, a malaise which might retain as much scientific acumen as melancholia or ennui.

In describing 'the contemporary appetite for the past' which we now call heritage culture, Malcolm Chase and Christopher Shaw envisioned: 'The sick man of Europe had taken to his bed, dreaming of a childhood that he had never had, regressing into a series of fictitious and cloudless infantile summers'.[22] This more recent notion suggests that 'the home we miss is no longer a geographically defined place but rather a state of mind'. If it is a place at all, it is an imaginary one, which nonetheless bears all the hallmarks of 'childhood': regressive, 'infantile', a world of long-lost innocence which never actually existed.[23]

Chase and Shaw develop cultural and historical explanations into a sort of general theory of nostalgia: 'In short, it is western societies, with a view of time and history that is linear and secular, which should be especially prone to the syndrome of nostalgia'.[24] Linearity and secularism certainly militate against cyclical traditions, ritual practices and systems of belief. Furthermore, they align this attitude with strains of familiar, post-modernist nihilism: 'We have lost faith in the possibility of changing our public life and have retreated into the private enclaves of the family, and the consumption of certain "retro" styles'.[25]

This cultural explanation is persuasive up to a point. Loss of faith and retreat into enclaves are indeed conditions of living in 'cult times' as I have posited above. But have we retained any more faith in the institution of the family than we have in those of public life? Cult films critique both fairly roundly. However, these authors arrive at what may be a productive principle: 'Nostalgia is experienced when some elements of the present are felt to be defective and when there is no public sense of redeemability through a belief in progress' – or indeed, a belief in anything, one supposes. They continue: 'Nostalgia is a feeling which can operate at many levels'. For instance: 'It may be instrinsic to the life-experience of individuals, as they go through the shifting perspectives of childhood and adulthood'.[26] This particular sense of linking nostalgia to the phases of maturation and rites of passage is useful indeed, as is the earlier notion of the collective failure of what we might call belief objects.

As far as I am aware, Freud is strangely silent on the matter. Yet surely nostalgia is a retrospective fantasy, the memory's utopia. Fantasy, in Silverman's conception, is a powerful necessity 'because it articulates . . . our symbolic positionality, and the mise-en-scène of our desire'.[27] It is bound up, therefore, with ideological self-recognition:

> Belief is indeed a central part of the *méconnaissance* or self-recognition-misrecognition upon which the ego is founded; Althusser suggests that this transaction induces in the subject a sensation whose verbal translation would be: '*Yes, it really is me!*' [emphasis retained].[28]

It seems to me that the nostalgia which surrounds cult fandom is the fantasy-drive towards that place of self-(mis)recognition. The cult text, as we have seen, is a fantasy-resource: a site of symbolic work, serious play, devotional belief and emotional investment. I would suggest that it acts as a fantasy-displacement for nostalgia's ultimate, forever-unattainable goal. For it is in this sense that nostalgia refers back beyond the substitution of the cult fantasy-object to the actual physical home. We know for certain it was real and that we once were there. We know, as certainly, that we are banished from it for good. And this is a physical exile of which, as if by punishment, we are allowed no memory. I am referring of course to the womb – that originary place of union with the mother. For it was there, as almost all psychoanalytic theories agree, that we were once as one, perfectly at home.

To be sure our expulsion is like another Fall of Man, irrevocable, fatal. We fell not only from a state of innocence but from wholeness with the mother, like the oneness with the biblical father which can never be restored (but which is ameliorated by articles of faith and the transitional objects of the liturgy). It is not for nothing that cult films frequently feature relationships between lost or wayward sons, 'bad' symbolic fathers and ineffectual mothers. The fantasy of the wholeness of the perfect relationship with the mother is an absent longing in every cult film, a thwarted nostalgic desire. Yet if we don't all suffer this pain, this original pang of nostalgia, then why should some? Here one can only speculate.

What if those pangs, those longings are strongest in those who for some reason harbour a sense that the present remains but a contingent reality? It may be those for whom the psychic separation which takes place after birth was somehow unresolved, incomplete – cases where, in Lacanian terms, proper Oedipal resolution had not been achieved. Or, following Winnicott's ideas, where, as infants, they have not effectively decathected transitional phenomena, but have repressed them in some way. Whatever the case, the complex relations between the economic, social and cultural on the one hand, and the personal and biological on the other, raise the most profound questions for historians of culture. Ritual fixation upon cultural texts and practices which reassure and stimulate, and which rehearse problematic rites of passage and anxieties about sexual difference may be of particular comfort to some. Over them, nostalgia has the power of the moon upon the tides. Cult films are but temporary shelters along the margins, but they can be made to feel like home.

NOTES

Introduction

1   *The Wicker Man* was my first cult film and the first of my selection to appear on British TV, in Thames Television's 1980 horror season entitled 'Appointment With Fear'. (See http://www.tv-ark.org.uk/itvlondon/thamesmain-new.html, retrieved 5 November 2005.) Since then it has also been shown on TV more often than any of the films chosen here (over a dozen times to date).

2   Julian Petley, 'Review of *Inside "The Wicker Man": The Morbid Ingenuities* by Allan Brown', *Journal of Popular British Cinema*, 5 (2002), pp. 166–70.

3   Karl and Philip French, *Cult Movies* (London: Pavilion, 1999), p. 8.

4   *The Shorter Oxford English Dictionary.*

5   www.oed.com. Retrieved 14 October 2005.

6   Emile Durkheim, *Elementary Forms of Religious Life*, trans. by Karen Fields (New York: Free Press, 1995).

7   Anthony Stevens, *On Jung* (London: Penguin Books, 1991).

8   Louis Althusser, 'Ideology and Ideological State Apparatuses', in John Storey (ed.), *Cultural Theory and Popular Culture: A Reader*, 2nd edn (Hemel Hempstead: Prentice Hall/Harvester, 1998), pp. 153–64.

9   Mary Douglas, *Purity and Danger: An analysis of concepts of pollution and taboo* (London: Routledge, 1966).

10 James G. Frazer, *The Golden Bough: A Study of Magic and Religion*, 3rd edn, 12 vols (London: Macmillan, 1911–15).

11 Mary Douglas (ed.), *Witchcraft Confessions and Accusations* (London: Tavistock, 1970).

12 See for example Christopher Evans, *Cults of Unreason* (London: Harrap, 1973) and David G. Bromley and J. Gordon Melton (eds), *Cults, Religion and Violence* (Cambridge: Cambridge University Press, 2002).

13 Stuart Hall, 'The Centrality of Culture: notes on the cultural revolution of our time', in Kenneth Thompson (ed.), *Media and Cultural Regulation* (London: Sage/The Open University, 1997), pp. 207–38.

14 Douglas: *Purity and Danger*, p. 122.

15   See Alexander Walker, *National Heroes: British Cinema in the Seventies and Eighties* (London: Harrap, 1985) and John Walker, *The Once and Future Film: British Cinema in the Seventies and Eighties* (London: Methuen, 1985).

16   Leon Hunt, *British Low Culture: From Safari Suits to Sexploitation* (London: Routledge, 1998), Andrew Higson, 'A Diversity of Film Practices: renewing British cinema in the 1970s' in Bart Moore-Gilbert (ed.), *The Arts in the 1970s: Cultural Closure?* (London: Routledge, 1994), pp. 216–39.

17   Jonathan Coe, *The Rotters' Club* (London: Viking, 2001), Dave Haslam, *Not Abba: The Real Story of the 1970s* (London: Fourth Estate, 2005), Howard Sounes, *Seventies: The Sights, Sounds and Ideas of a Brilliant Decade* (London: Simon & Schuster, 2006), Alwyn W. Turner, *Crisis? What Crisis?: Britain in the 1970s* (London: Aurum Press Ltd., 2008).

Chapter 1
The Rocky Horror Picture Show (1975)

1   Jay Hoberman and Jonathan Rosenbaum, 'Curse of the cult people – a history of cult film subculture and its central figures', *Film Comment*, 27/1 (January/February 1991), p. 19.

2   J. P. Telotte (ed.), *The Cult Film Experience: Beyond All Reason* (Austin: University of Texas Press, 1991), p. 104.

3   David Chute, 'Outlaw Cinema', *Film Comment*, 19/5 (September/October 1983), p. 15.

4   Gaylin Studlar, 'Midnight S/Excess: Cult configurations of "femininity" and the perverse', *Journal of Popular Film and Television*, 17/1 (spring 1989), p. 8.

5   Mark Jancovich, Antonio Lázaro Reboll, Julian Stringer and Andy Willis (eds), *Defining Cult Movies: The cultural politics of oppositional taste* (Manchester and New York: University of Manchester Press, 2003), p. 1.

6   Ron Pennington, 'The Rocky Horror Picture Show' (Film Review), *The Hollywood Reporter*, 238/14, 24 September 1975, p. 15.

7   Alexander Stuart, 'The Rocky Horror Picture Show' (Film Review), *Films and Filming*, 21/12 (September 1975), p. 31.

8   Burrhus F. Skinner's *Beyond Freedom and Dignity* came out in 1971 and Ronald D. Laing's prolific output during the Sixties centred on the radical re-evaluation of domesticity in such works as *The Politics of the Family and other essays* (London: Tavistock, 1971).

9   Hoberman and Rosenbaum: 'Curse of the Cult People', p. 20. See Umberto Eco, '*Casablanca*: Cult Movies and Intertextual Collage' in *Faith in Fakes: Essays*, trans. by William Weaver (London: Secker & Warburg, 1987), pp. 197–212.

10   Jeffrey Sconce, 'Trashing the Academy: taste, excess and an emerging politics of cinematic style', *Screen*, 36/4 (1995), pp. 371–93.

11   'Indeed, the essence of Camp is its love of the unnatural: of artifice and exaggeration. And Camp is esoteric – something of a private code, a badge of identity even, among small urban cliques', Susan Sontag, 'Notes on "Camp"', in *A Susan Sontag Reader* (Harmondsworth: Penguin Books, 1983), p. 105.

12   http://dictionary.oed.com/cgi/entry/50032066?query_type=word&queryword =camp&first=1&max_to_show=10&sort_type=alpha&result_place=5&search_ id=oSOu-tjMh37-4140&hilite=50032066. Retrieved 10 July 2005.

13   Eco: '*Casablanca*: Cult Movies and Intertextual Collage', p. 198.

14   Alan Jones, 'The Rocky Horror Picture Show', *Starburst*, 36 (1981), p. 47.

15   *Film Review*, 16 (1996), p. 32.

16   Jones: 'The Rocky Horror Picture Show', p. 47.

17   Ibid.

18   Jonathan Rosenbaum, 'The Rocky Horror Picture Cult', *Sight and Sound*, 49/2 (spring 1980), p. 78.

19   Jones: 'The Rocky Horror Picture Show', p. 47.

20   *Film Review*, 16 (1996), p. 32.

21   Jones: 'The Rocky Horror Picture Show', p. 47.

22   Ibid.

23   *Film Review*, 16 (1996), pp. 32–3.

24   Quoted in Sue Clarke, 'Will Rocky Horror Turn You On (Or Off)?', *Photoplay*, 26/3 (March 1975), p. 21.

25   Quoted in *Film Review*, 16 (1996), p. 34.

26   Ibid., p. 33.

27   Ibid.

28   Ibid., p. 34.

29   Ibid.

30   Ibid., pp. 34–5.

31   Ibid., p. 35.

32   Stuart: 'The Rocky Horror Picture Show', p. 31.

33   Ibid.

34   *Variety*, 24 September 1975, p. 22.

35   Pennington: 'The Rocky Horror Picture Show', p. 15.

36   Tony Rayns, 'The Rocky Horror Picture Show' (Film Review), *Monthly Film Bulletin*, 42/499 (August 1975), p. 182.

37   Clarke: 'Will Rocky Horror Turn You On (Or Off)?', p. 46.

38   Jones: 'The Rocky Horror Picture Show', p. 47.

39   Ibid., p. 48.

40   Quoted in Kenneth Von Gunden, 'The RH Factor', *Film Comment*, 15/5 (September/October 1979), p. 55.

41   Ibid.

42   Jones: 'The Rocky Horror Picture Show', p. 47.

43   Von Gunden: 'The RH Factor', p. 55.

44   Rosenbaum: 'The Rocky Horror Picture Cult', p. 78.

45   See Douglas Gomery, *Shared Pleasures: a history of movie presentation in the United States* (Madison: University of Wisconsin Press, 1992).

46   See Andrew Sarris, *Confessions of a Cultist: On the Cinema, 1955–1969* (New York: Simon & Schuster, 1970) and Greg Taylor, *Artists in the Audience: Cults, Camp, and American Film Criticism* (Princeton: Princeton University Press, 1999).

47   For a wider discussion on the midnight movie see Jay Hoberman and Jonathan Rosenbaum, *Midnight Movies* (New York: Harper & Row, 1983).

48   Rosenbaum: 'The Rocky Horror Picture Cult', p. 78.

49   *Screen International*, 353, 24 July 1982, p. 6.

50   Telotte (ed.): *The Cult Film Experience*, p. 104.

51   Robert E. Wood in Telotte (ed.), op. cit., pp. 156–66.

52   Bruce Kawin in Telotte (ed.), op. cit., p. 20.

53   Rosenbaum: 'The Rocky Horror Picture Cult', p. 78.

54   Ibid.

55   Ibid., pp. 78–9.

56   Ibid., p. 79.
57   Quoted in *Film Review*, 16 (1996), p. 35.
58   Chute: 'Outlaw Cinema', p. 12.
59   Ibid., p. 15.
60   Ibid., p. 12.
61   Telotte (ed.): *The Cult Film Experience,* p. 13.
62   Jones: 'The Rocky Horror Picture Show', p. 49.
63   Patrick Kinkade and Michael Katovich, 'Toward a Sociology of Cult Films: Reading Rocky Horror', *Sociological Quarterly,* 33/2 (summer 1992), p. 192.
64   Ibid., p. 199.
65   Rosenbaum: 'The Rocky Horror Picture Cult', p. 79.
66   Ibid.
67   Kinkade and Katovich: 'Toward a Sociology of Cult Films: Reading Rocky Horror', p. 201.
68   Rosenbaum: 'The Rocky Horror Picture Cult', p. 79.
69   See for example: http://beam.to/transylvania, http://rocky-horror-costume.co.uk/ and LipsDownOnDixieFans@yahoogroups.com.
70   Mass-Observation Archive, Spring Directive, 1999, University of Sussex.
71   Ibid.
72   Ibid.
73   Ibid.

Chapter 2
Performance (1970)

1   See Arthur Marwick, *The Sixties: Cultural Revolution in Britain, France, Italy and the United States, c.1958–1974* (Oxford: OUP, 1998), Robert Hewison, *Too Much: Art and Society in the Sixties, 1960–75* (London: Methuen, 1986), Alexander Walker, *Hollywood, England: The British Film Industry in the Sixties* (London: Harrap, 1986) and Robert Murphy, *Sixties British Cinema* (London: BFI, 1992).
2   *Statistical information relating to some aspects of the British film industry* (London: Film Education, 1993), pp. 4–6.
3   Piri Halasz, 'You Can Walk Across It On The Grass', *Time,* 15 April 1966, pp. 30–4.
4   See Sue Harper and Vincent Porter, *The Decline of Deference: British Cinema of the 1950s* (Oxford: OUP, 2003).
5   Murphy: *Sixties British Cinema,* p. 105.
6   Walker: *Hollywood, England,* p. 244.
7   Rank dealt with Disney, Columbia, Fox and United Artists, while ABPC handled Warners, MGM and Paramount releases. Walker: *Hollywood, England,* p. 244.
8   Murphy: *Sixties British Cinema,* p. 105.
9   Quoted in Ernest Betts, *The Film Business: A history of British cinema, 1896–1972* (London: Allen & Unwin, 1973), p. 284.
10   Ibid.
11   Walker: *Hollywood, England,* pp. 244–5.
12   Murphy: *Sixties British Cinema,* p. 112.
13   Sarah Street, *Transatlantic Crossings: British Feature Films in the USA* (London & New York: Continuum), p. 169.
14   Bill Baillieu and John Goodchild, *The British Film Business* (Chichester: John Wiley & Sons Ltd., 2002), pp. 84–5.

15 Thomas H. Guback, 'Hollywood's International Market' in Tino Balio (ed.), *The American Film Industry,* 2nd edn (Madison: Wisconsin University Press, 1985), p. 479.

16 Walker: *Hollywood, England*, p. 338.

17 Ibid., p. 339.

18 Betts: *The Film Business*, p. 284.

19 Baillieu and Goodchild: *The British Film Business*, p. 84.

20 Guback: 'Hollywood's International Market', p. 479.

21 Murphy: *Sixties British Cinema*, p. 112.

22 Walker: *Hollywood, England*, p. 416.

23 Robert Watson, *Film and Television in Education: An Aesthetic Approach to the Moving Image* (London: The Falmer Press, 1990), p. 3.

24 Hewison: *Too Much: Art and Society in the Sixties,* p. xiii.

25 Colin MacCabe, *Performance* (London: BFI, 1998), p. 9.

26 Ibid., p. 17.

27 Ibid., p. 18.

28 Ibid., pp. 16 and 18.

29 Ibid., p. 20.

30 Ibid., p. 20.

31 Ibid., p. 22.

32 Walker: *Hollywood, England*, pp. 415–16.

33 MacCabe: *Performance*, p. 22. Whilst this is probably true, Roeg's track record as a lighting cameraman and director of photography runs an instructive course through key films of the Sixties: *The Caretaker* (1963), *The Masque of the Red Death* (1964), *Dr. Zhivago* (1965), *Fahrenheit 451* (1966), *Far From the Madding Crowd* (1967), *Petulia* (1968).

34 See Scott Salwolke, *Nicolas Roeg Film by Film* (Jefferson, N. Carolina: McFarland & Co. Inc., 1993) and John Izod, *The Films of Nicolas Roeg: Myth and Mind* (London: Macmillan, 1992), Jon Savage, 'Tuning into Wonders', *Sight and Sound*, 5/9 (September 1995), pp. 24–5 and Peter Wollen, 'Possession', *Sight and Sound*, 5/9 (September 1995), pp. 20–3.

35 The Cammell family knew Crowley in Devon during the Second World War and Donald's father wrote a biography of the occultist. See MacCabe: *Performance*, p. 11.

36 See for example, Tanya Krzywinska, *A Skin for Dancing In: Possession, Witchcraft and Voodoo in Film* (Trowbridge: Flicks Books, 2000).

37 MacCabe: *Performance*, pp. 24–7 and 38–43.

38 Ibid., p. 51.

39 See Jon Savage, 'Performance: Interview with Donald Cammell' in Steve Chibnall and Robert Murphy (eds), *British Crime Cinema* (London: Routledge, 1999), pp. 110–16.

40 MacCabe: *Performance*, p. 53.

41 Ibid., p. 54.

42 Walker: *Hollywood, England*, p. 423.

43 Quoted in Savage: 'Performance: Interview with Donald Cammell', p. 112.

44 MacCabe: *Performance*, p. 53.

45 Philip Auslander, *From Acting to Performance* (London: Routledge, 1997), p. 8.

46 MacCabe: *Performance*, pp. 57–8.

47 Ibid., p. 58.

48 Ibid., p. 60.

49 Ibid., p. 61.

50   Quoted by Robert Gustafson, '"What's happening to our pix biz?": From Warner Bros. to Warner Communications Inc.' in Balio (ed.): *The American Film Industry*, p. 576.
51   Ibid.
52   Janet Wasko, *Movies and Money: Financing the American Film Industry* (Norwood, NJ: Ablex Publishing Corp., 1982), p. 181.
53   David Trotter, *Cooking with Mud: The Idea of Mess in Nineteenth Century Art and Fiction* (Oxford: OUP, 2000), pp. 5–6.
54   For a detailed description of the Borges-influenced iconography of the Powis Square set design see Christopher Gibbs's interview with Jon Savage, 'Tuning into Wonders', *Sight and Sound*, 5/9 (September 1995), pp. 24–5.
55   William Ian Miller, *The Anatomy of Disgust* (Cambridge, Mass.: Harvard University Press, 1997), p. 44.
56   Trotter: *Cooking with Mud*, pp. 20–1.
57   Donald Cammell, *Performance* (London: Faber and Faber, 2001), p. 98.
58   Ibid., p.106.
59   See Georges Bataille, *Eroticism*, trans. by Mary Dalwood (London: Marion Boyars, 1987).
60   Savage: 'Tuning into Wonders', p. 25.
61   Cammell: *Performance*, pp. 99–100.
62   MacCabe: *Performance*, p. 73.
63   See http://groups.yahoo.com/group/Performance_Movie1/. The group is moderated by one Pherber_Morphann86 who is 19. Significantly, perhaps, the membership is predominantly female.
64   Fredric Jameson, *The Political Unconscious* (Ithaca: Cornell University Press, 1981), pp. 17–103. I owe this interpretation, as I do much of the groundwork for this chapter, to MacCabe: *Performance*, p. 79.

Case Study 1: *Get Carter* (1971)

65   Steve Chibnall, *Get Carter*, The British Film Guide 6 (London: I.B.Tauris, 2003), p. 4.
66   See http://www.btinternet.com/~ms.dear and http://www.mbspecial. worldonline.co.uk/getcarter/.
67   See http://www.xlab.co.uk/photos/read/31 and http://www.getcarpark.org/.
68   Chibnall: *Get Carter*, p. 13.
69   Quoted by Robert Murphy, 'A Revenger's Tragedy – *Get Carter*', in Chibnall and Murphy (eds): *British Crime Cinema*, p. 130.
70   Ibid.

Chapter 3
A Clockwork Orange (1971)

1   Timothy Corrigan, 'Film and the Culture of the Cult' in Telotte (ed.): *The Cult Film Experience*, p. 126.
2   See http://fans.luminosus.net/clock/. Retrieved 23 June 2005.
3   Quoted in Gene D. Phillips and Rodney Hill, *The Encyclopaedia of Stanley Kubrick* (New York: Checkmark Books, 2002), p. 64.
4   Ibid.
5   Ibid., p. 65.

6 This critical assessment of the Warhol film is provided by J. Hoberman, op. cit.

7 Vincent LoBrutto, 'The Old Ultra-Violence', *American Cinematographer*, 80/10 (1999), p. 53.

8 Alexander Walker also links another prominent photographer, David Bailey, with *A Clockwork Orange* and the Rolling Stones (see Walker: *Hollywood, England*, p. 321).

9 Quoted in James C. Robertson, *The Hidden Cinema: British Film Censorship in Action, 1913–1972* (London: Routledge, 1989), p. 143.

10 Nick James, 'At Home with the Kubricks', *Sight and Sound*, 9/9 (September 1999), p. 15.

11 Robertson: *The Hidden Cinema*, p. 144.

12 Phillips and Hill: *The Encyclopaedia of Stanley Kubrick*, p. 51.

13 Arlene Schindler, 'A Clockwork Orange', *Creative Screenwriting*, 6/4 (1999), p. 40.

14 James: 'At Home with the Kubricks', p. 25.

15 The original published edition was designed in three parts each of seven chapters, which is the form of the classical concerto but also plays with numbers around Shakespeare's seven ages of man, and 21 (chapters) as the (then) legal age of majority.

16 Mario Falsetto, *Stanley Kubrick: A Narrative and Stylistic Analysis*, 2nd edn (London: Praeger, 2001), p. 53.

17 LoBrutto: 'The Old Ultra-Violence', p. 54.

18 Stephen Mamber, 'A Clockwork Orange' in Mario Falsetto (ed.), *Perspectives on Stanley Kubrick* (New York: G. K. Halt & Co., 1996), p. 174.

19 Philip Strick, 'Kubrick's Horrorshow', *Sight and Sound*, 41/1 (1971/2), p. 45.

20 Falsetto: *Stanley Kubrick: A Narrative and Stylistic Analysis*, p. 58.

21 Though it might be considered to *not* be a science-fiction film in the same way that *The Wicker Man* is *not* a horror film. See, for example, James Chapman, '"A bit of the old ultra-violence" – *A Clockwork Orange*' in Ian Q. Hunter (ed.), *British Science Fiction Cinema* (London: Routledge, 1999), pp. 128–37.

22 Kubrick quoted in Alexander Walker, *Stanley Kubrick Directs* (London: Davis-Poynter Ltd., 1972), p. 45.

23 Ibid., p. 46.

24 Christopher Isherwood, *The World in the Evening* (London: Methuen, 1954), p. 125.

25 Robert Hughes, 'The Décor of Tomorrow's Hell' in Falsetto (ed.): *Perspectives on Stanley Kubrick*, pp. 185–6.

26 Switzer, quoted in Falsetto: *Stanley Kubrick: A Narrative and Stylistic Analysis*, p. 56.

27 Ibid., p. 56.

28 Ibid., p. 118.

29 Philip French, 'A Clockwork Orange', *Sight and Sound*, 59/2 (February 1990), p. 84.

30 James: 'At home with the Kubricks', p. 26.

31 Strick: 'Kubrick's Horrorshow', p. 45.

32 McDowell in interview with Gordon Gow, 'Something More', *Films and Filming*, 22/1 (October 1975), p. 15.

33 Ibid.

34 Malcolm McDowell, *The Guardian*, Friday 3 September 2004. Retrieved from http://film.guardian.co.uk/features/featurepages/0,,1295915,00.html, on 15 June 2005.

35 McDowell in Gow: 'Something More', p. 16.

36 Ibid., p. 15.

37 Kubrick quoted in Phillips and Hill: *The Encyclopaedia of Stanley Kubrick*, p. 54.

38 Ibid.

39   Kubrick quoted in Philip Strick and Penelope Houston, 'Interview with Stanley Kubrick', *Sight and Sound*, 41/2 (February 1972), p. 65. *A Clockwork Orange* was the first feature film to employ Dolby systems on all aspects of the sound mixing according to LoBrutto: 'The Old Ultra-Violence', p. 60.
40   Robert Hughes in Falsetto (ed.): *Perspectives on Stanley Kubrick*, p. 186.
41   Blake Morrison, 'Introduction' to Anthony Burgess, *A Clockwork Orange* (London: Penguin, 1996), p. xiii.
42   Walter Evans and Vivian Sobchak, both quoted in Phillips and Hill: *The Encyclopaedia of Stanley Kubrick*, pp. 52–3.
43   Jackson Burgess, 'Review: A Clockwork Orange', *Film Quarterly*, 25/3 (1972), p. 33.
44   Ibid., pp. 34–5.
45   It is a thesis that has since been elaborated elsewhere, notably by Kenneth Moskowitz in 'The Vicarious Experience of *A Clockwork Orange*', *Velvet Light Trap*, 16 (autumn 1976), pp. 28–31.
46   Gordon Gow, 'Review: A Clockwork Orange', *Films and Filming*, 18/5 (1972), p. 49.
47   Strick: 'Kubrick's Horrorshow', p. 46.
48   Jan Dawson, 'Review: A Clockwork Orange', *Monthly Film Bulletin*, 39/457 (1972), p. 29.
49   Phillips and Hill: *The Encyclopaedia of Stanley Kubrick*, p. 55.
50   Ibid., p. 56.
51   Ibid.
52   See Tony Parsons, 'Sex Through the Looking Glass', *Empire*, 54 (December 1993), p. 71.
53   Robertson: *The Hidden Cinema*, p. 147.
54   See Walker: *National Heroes*, pp. 48–9.
55   Chapman: '"A bit of the old ultra-violence" – *A Clockwork Orange*', p. 135.
56   Michael E. Stein, 'The New Violence or Twenty Years of Violence in Films: An Appreciation', *Films in Review*, 46/1–2 (January/February 1995), p. 40.
57   Ibid., p. 42.
58   Falsetto: *Stanley Kubrick: A Narrative and Stylistic Analysis*, p. 149.
59   Ibid., p. 154.
60   French: 'A Clockwork Orange', pp. 86–7.
61   Kubrick quoted in Strick and Houston, 'Interview with Stanley Kubrick', p. 63.
62   Ibid.
63   Kubrick quoted in LoBrutto: 'The Old Ultra-Violence', p. 58.
64   Parsons: 'Sex Through the Looking Glass', pp. 66–70.
65   Nick James, 'Violence: A Comparison of A Clockwork Orange and American Psycho', *Sight and Sound*, 10/5 (October 2000), p. 24.
66   See http://groups.yahoo.com/group/clockworkorange2.
67   Anthony Burgess quoted by Morrison: 'Introduction' to *A Clockwork Orange*, p. xxiv.

Chapter 4
The Wicker Man (1973)

1   Theodore Roszak, 'Youth and the Great Refusal', *The Nation*, 25 March 1968, quoted in Marwick: *The Sixties*, p. 11.
2   Marwick: *The Sixties*, p. 11.
3   David Bartholomew, 'The Wicker Man', *Cinéfantastique*, 6/3 (winter 1977), pp. 4–18 and 32–46.

4   'The Wicker Man was the best film I've ever been in, the best part I've ever had', Christopher Lee, quoted in Allan Brown, Inside 'The Wicker Man': The Morbid Ingenuities (London: Sidgwick & Jackson, 2000), p. 39.

5   Christopher Lee quoted in a letter to Cinéfantastique, 6/3 (winter 1977), p. 60.

6   Leon Hunt, 'Necromancy in the UK: witchcraft and the occult in British horror', in Steve Chibnall and Julian Petley (eds), British Horror Cinema (London: Routledge, 2002), pp. 92–3.

7   Brown: Inside 'The Wicker Man', pp. 3 and 28. In fact, Michael Deeley claims that the National Film Finance Corporation's controlling share in British Lion Films ensured 'that the company preserved Shepperton Studios as a filmmaking centre and did not redevelop the land'. See Michael Deeley with Matthew Field, Blade Runners, Deer Hunters & Blowing the Bloody Doors Off: My life in cult movies (London: Faber and Faber, 2008), p. 132.

8   Ibid., p. 29.

9   'John Bentley . . . commissioned the film only to placate fermentation within the British film unions, with little thought for The Wicker Man's commercial or creative future', ibid., pp. 38–9.

10 Anthony Shaffer, op. cit., p. 14.

11 Ibid.

12 Ibid., pp. 15–18.

13 Ibid., p. 166.

14 Eco: 'Casablanca: Cult Movies and Intertextual Collage', p. 198.

15 Walker, National Heroes, pp. 120–2.

16 Brown: Inside 'The Wicker Man', p. 104.

17 Christopher Lee, op. cit., p. 104. For his part, Michael Deeley has recently gone on record as saying 'that, were it not for my actions, the picture would never have been released at all'. See Michael Deeley with Matthew Field, Blade Runners, Deer Hunters & Blowing the Bloody Doors Off: My life in cult movies, p. 98.

18 Ibid., p. 105.

19 Ibid., p. 106.

20 Ibid., p. 107.

21 Ibid., pp. 113–14.

22 Nigel Andrews, 'Holiday Fodder' (Film Review), Financial Times, 14 December 1973, p. 3.

23 Dilys Powell, 'Just Men' (Film Review), Sunday Times, 16 December 1973, p. 37.

24 Margaret Hinxman, 'Sting in the Tail of the Year' (Film Review), Sunday Telegraph, 23 December 1973, p. 10.

25 Alan Howard, 'The Wicker Man', The Hollywood Reporter, 231/18, 9 May 1974, p. 3.

26 The Wicker Man (British Lion Press Book, 1974), p. 3.

27 Letter from Stephen Murphy to R. M. D. Lee of Crawley, W. Sussex, 1 April 1974. BBFC files.

28 Brown: Inside 'The Wicker Man', p. 127.

29 Ibid., pp. 128–9.

30 Ibid., pp. 129–30.

31 Ibid., p. 131.

32 Ibid., p. 133.

33 Ibid., pp. 134–5.

34 Ibid., p. 145.

35 Ibid., pp. 146–7.

36 Ibid., pp. 133–4.

37   Ibid., pp. 134–5.
38   Ibid., p. 140.
39   Robin Hardy, op. cit., p. 143.
40   Ibid.
41   Ibid., p. 144.
42   Ibid., p. 151.
43   Ibid., pp. 24–6.
44   Ibid., p. 45.
45   Cited in Bartholomew: 'The Wicker Man', p. 36.
46   Edward Hall, 'A system for the notation of proxemic behaviour', *American Anthropologist*, 65/5 (1963), pp. 1018–19.
47   William Shakespeare, *Macbeth*, Act I, Scene iv.
48   Cited in Bartholomew: 'The Wicker Man', p. 16.
49   Eco: '*Casablanca*: Cult Movies and Intertextual Collage', p. 198.
50   Fred Kaplan, *Dickens and Mesmerism: The Hidden Springs of Fiction* (Princeton, NJ: Princeton Univ Press, 1975), p. 9.
51   Ibid., pp. 34–5.
52   Quoted in Chris Shilling, *The Body and Social Theory*, 2nd edn (London: Sage, 2003), p. 85.
53   Richard Dyer, *Stars* (London: BFI, 1998), p. 31.
54   Robin Theobald, *Charisma: some empirical problems considered*, Research Paper No. 5, 1975 (London: Polytechnic of Central London School of the Social Sciences and Business Studies), p. 6.
55   Ibid., p. 59.
56   Laura Mulvey, 'Visual Pleasure and Narrative Cinema', in Jessica Evans and Stuart Hall (eds), *Visual Culture: The Reader* (London: Sage, 1999), p. 389.
57   See Raymond Williams, *Marxism and Literature* (Oxford: OUP, 1977), pp. 121–7.
58   Mulvey: 'Visual Pleasure and Narrative Cinema', p. 388.
59   Ibid.
60   Erving Goffman, *The Presentation of Self in Everyday Life* (Harmondsworth: Penguin Books, 1959), pp. 59–60.
61   See Brown: *Inside 'The Wicker Man'*, pp. 169–71.
62   See for example, http://movies.groups.yahoo.com/group/wickerman/.
63   The original film soundtrack was issued on a limited-pressing CD in the summer of 1998 and sold out within three weeks; copies are now reported, according to Allan Brown, to change hands for anything up to £120. See Brown: *Inside 'The Wicker Man'*, pp. 170–1.
64   *The Sun*, 13 December 1998. Ibid., p. 166.
65   See http://www.sandrew.demon.co.uk/wickerman/.
66   Brown: *Inside 'The Wicker Man'*, pp. 168–9.
67   Indeed, a version of this chapter is to be found in the first of these volumes. See my 'Things that go Clunk in the Cult Film Text: Nodes and interstices in *The Wicker Man*', in Jonathan Murray, Lesley Stevenson, Stephen Harper and Benjamin Franks (eds), *Constructing 'The Wicker Man': Film and Cultural Studies Perspectives* (Dumfries: University of Glasgow Crichton Publications, 2005), pp. 123–38.
68   Williams: *Marxism and Literature*, p. 133.

Case Study 2: *Monty Python and the Holy Grail* (1975)

69   Produced by Michael White who had brought *The Rocky Horror Show* to the London stage.

70 Michael Palin, *Diaries 1969–1979: The Python Years* (London: Orion Books, 2007), pp. 163–4.
71 Terry Jones, *The Pythons' Autobiography by the Pythons* (London: Orion Books, 2003), p. 239.
72 Michael Palin, op. cit., p. 200.
73 Ibid., p. 212.
74 Eric Idle, *The Pythons' Autobiography by the Pythons*, p. 264.
75 Palin: *Diaries*, pp. 253 and 258.
76 For detailed information about medieval sources see Elizabeth Murrell, 'History Revenged: Monty Python translates Chrétien de Troyes' *Perceval, Or the story of the Grail* (again)', *Journal of Film and Video*, 50/1 (spring 1998), pp. 50–62.

Chapter 5
Tommy (1975)

1 Robin Bean, 'Tommy' (review), *Films and Filming*, 21/8 (May 1975), p. 35.
2 John H. Dorr, 'Tommy' (review), *The Hollywood Reporter*, 235/27, 12 March 1975, p. 14.
3 Pete Townshend interviewed by Matt Kent at Eel Pie Studios on 10 February 2004 for Odyssey Quest Productions (DVD).
4 See http://movies.groups.yahoo.com/group/tommytherockopera.
5 Walker: *National Heroes*, p. 71.
6 Pete Townshend, 'Who's Tommy', *Films and Filming*, 21/9 (June 1975), p. 21.
7 Richard Barnes and Pete Townshend, *The Story of Tommy* (Twickenham: Eel Pie Publishing, 1977), p. 30.
8 Sue Clarke, 'Tommy' (preview), *Photoplay*, 26/5 (May 1975), p. 16.
9 Ray Connolly, 'Tommy', *Time Out*, 265, 28 March 1975, p. 10.
10 '"Tommy" Opera Reverses Flow', *Variety*, 15 May 1974, np.
11 Walker, *The Once and Future Film*, p. 100.
12 *Variety*, 26 February 1975.
13 See David Castell, 'Daltry's Tommy', *Films Illustrated*, 4/44 (April 1975), p. 300, Bean: 'Tommy' and Clarke: 'Tommy'.
14 Pete Townshend interviewed by Matt Kent.
15 Ken Russell quoted in John Baxter, *An Appalling Talent: Ken Russell* (London: Joseph, 1973), p. 228.
16 Ibid.
17 Joseph A. Gomez, '*Tommy*' in Thomas R. Atkins (ed.), *Ken Russell* (New York: Simon & Schuster, 1976), p. 84.
18 Ibid., p. 87.
19 Gene D. Phillips, *Ken Russell* (Boston: Twayne, 1979), p. 158.
20 Ken Russell interviewed by Mark Kermode for Odyssey Quest (DVD), 2004.
21 Phillips: *Ken Russell*, p. 159.
22 Judith Sims, 'Townshend's Mixed Blessing', *Rolling Stone*, 24 April 1975, np.
23 Pete Townshend interviewed by Matt Kent.
24 Jon Landau, 'Tommy: Too Big, Too Late', *Rolling Stone*, 24 April 1975, np.
25 Ken Russell interviewed by Mark Kermode.
26 Wilson: 'Tommy', p. 193.
27 Ken Russell interviewed by Mark Kermode.
28 Quoted in Clarke: 'Tommy', p. 19.
29 *Tommy – Synopsis* (London: Helmdale International Films Ltd., 1974).

30   Pete Townshend interviewed by Matt Kent.
31   Ibid.
32   Ken Russell interviewed by Mark Kermode.
33   Pete Townshend interviewed by Matt Kent.
34   Ibid.

Chapter 6
The Man Who Fell to Earth (1976)

1   'Hawk', *Variety*, 24 March 1976, p. 20.
2   See Dyer: *Stars,* and Jackie Stacey, *Star Gazing: Hollywood cinema and female spectatorship* (London: Routledge, 1994).
3   Walker: *The Once and Future Film*, p. 97.
4   Don Buday, 'The Many Images of David Bowie', *The Hollywood Reporter*, 30 June 1976, p. 10.
5   Michael Watts, '1972: Oh You Pretty Thing' in Hanif Kureishi and Jon Savage (eds), *The Faber Book of Pop* (London: Faber and Faber, 1995), p. 393.
6   Paul Mayersberg, 'The Story So Far . . .', *Sight and Sound,* 44/3 (March 1975), p. 230.
7   David Gregory, dir., *Watching the Alien* (Blue Underground Inc./Anchor Bay Entertainment, 2002).
8   Fred and Judy Vermorel, '1976: Julie: He's Got a Lot to Answer for', in Kureishi and Savage: *The Faber Book of Pop*, p. 457.
9   Alexander Stuart, 'Review: The Man Who Fell To Earth', *Films and Filming*, 22/8 (May 1976), p. 28.
10   David Bartholomew, 'The Man Who Fell To Earth', *Film Heritage*, 12/1 (fall 1976), pp. 19–20.
11   Tom Milne, 'The Man Who Fell To Earth', *Sight and Sound*, 45/3 (summer 1976), pp. 145–6.
12   Interview in Gregory: *Watching the Alien.*
13   Nicolas Roeg quoted in Buday: 'The Many Images of David Bowie', p. 12.
14   David Bowie quoted in British Lion Press Pack for *The Man Who Fell to Earth*, 1976.
15   Si Litvinoff interviewed in Gregory: *Watching the Alien.*
16   Graeme Clifford interviewed in Gregory: *Watching the Alien.*
17   For this comparison see Salwolke: *Nicolas Roeg Film by Film*, p. 53.
18   Mayersberg: 'The Story So Far . . .', p. 226.
19   Nicolas Roeg interviewed in Gregory: *Watching the Alien.*
20   David Pirie and Chris Petit, 'After The Fall', *Time Out*, 313, 12 March 1976, p. 13.
21   Nicolas Roeg interviewed in Gregory: *Watching the Alien.*
22   Including Roeg regulars Tony Richmond (cinematography) and Graeme Clifford (editor) on *Walkabout, Don't Look Now* and *The Man Who Fell to Earth.* Brian Eatwell (production designer on the last) was joined by his wife, costume designer May Routh and Richmond's partner Linda DeVetta (make-up).
23   This telling anecdote is derived from Walker: *National Heroes*, pp. 135–43.
24   *Screen International*, 22 May 1976, quoted by Walker: *National Heroes*, p. 142.
25   Tony Richmond interviewed in Gregory: *Watching the Alien.*
26   James Leach, 'The Man Who Fell To Earth', *Literature/Film Quarterly*, 6/4 (fall 1978), pp. 371–9.

27   Mayersberg: 'The Story So Far . . .', p. 226.
28   Ibid., p. 230.
29   Ibid., p. 231.
30   Salwolke: *Nicolas Roeg Film by Film*, p. 54.
31   Nicolas Roeg interviewed in Gregory: *Watching the Alien*.
32   Mayersberg: 'The Story So Far . . .', p. 227.
33   Macnab: 'Loving the Alien', p. 151.
34   Leach: 'The Man Who Fell To Earth', p. 374.
35   See for example Bartholomew: 'The Man Who Fell To Earth'. 'Roeg follows a total alien into a well known milieu, thus blocking our necessary identification with the protagonist, confusing us and making us aloof from all the characters equally'. Rosenbaum is blunter in dubbing the whole 'an extremely photogenic mess'. See 'The Man Who Fell To Earth' (review), *Monthly Film Bulletin*, 43/507 (April 1976), p. 86.
36   Leach: 'The Man Who Fell To Earth', p. 376.
37   Pirie and Petit: 'After The Fall', p. 12.
38   Fred and Judy Vermorel: '1976: Julie: He's Got a Lot to Answer for', pp. 458–9.
39   John Bowlby, *Attachment and Loss, Vol. 2: Separation* (Harmondsworth: Penguin, 1975), p. 207.
40   Ibid.
41   Chris Weedon, Andrew Tolson and Frank Mort, 'Theories of Language and Subjectivity' in Stuart Hall (ed.), *Culture, Media, Language* (London: Routledge, 1980), p. 205.
42   Ibid., p. 206.
43   Kaja Silverman, 'The Subject', in Evans and Hall (eds): *Visual Culture: The Reader*, p. 343.
44   Ibid.
45   Valentin Volosinov, *Freudianism: a Marxist Critique,* trans. by Irwin R. Titunik (London: Academy Press, 1976), p. 39.
46   Nicolas Roeg, quoted in interview with Jason Wood, 'His Brilliant Career', *The Guardian*, Friday 3 June 2005, p. 10. See http://film.guardian.co.uk/hay2005/story/0,,1497877,00.html. Retrieved 15 September 2005.
47   Ibid.
48   See www.geocities.com/worldenterprises_rpg/. Retrieved 3 January 2006.

Case Study 3: *Quadrophenia* (1979)

49   Kevin J. Donnolly, *Pop Music In British Cinema: A Chronicle* (London: BFI, 2001), p. 59.
50   Dave Allen, 'Middle-Class Mods and Working-Class Sods: Quadrophenia and the construction of popular histories', unpublished paper presented at *British Culture in the 1970s Conference*, University of Portsmouth, July 2008, p. 4.
51   Franc Roddam interviewed by Colin Vaines, 'The Mods and the Movie', *Screen International*, 166, 25 November 1978, p. 26.
52   Roy Baird, who was executive producer on the Goodtimes Enterprises films *That'll Be the Day* (1973) and *Stardust* (1974), had an established track record in realising 'cross-over' product. Roddam was ably assisted by television cameraman Brian Tufano (later to work on *Shallow Grave* and *Trainspotting*), who was chosen for his ability to capture live action on location.
53   Alan Fletcher, quoted in Catterall and Wells: *Your Face Here*, p. 161.

54   See Jon Savage's informed critique on its re-release in 1997: 'I don't wanna be like everybody else', *Sight and Sound*, 7/2 (February 1997), pp. 16–17.

Chapter 7
Withnail & I (1986)

1   *Statistical Information relating to some aspects of the British Film Industry* (London: Film Education, 1993), p. 5.
2   Ibid., p. 2.
3   Ibid., p. 6.
4   See http://www.bbfc.org.uk/statistics/. Retrieved 13 June 2005.
5   Mark Jancovich and Lucy Faire with Sarah Stubbings, *The Place of the Audience: Cultural Geographies of Film Consumption* (London: BFI, 2003), p. 154.
6   Ian Macdonald, 'UK Television and the British Film Industry in the Seventies' in Linda Wood (ed.), *British Films 1971–1981* (London: BFI, 1983), p. 8.
7   Quoted by Louise Brealey, 'Withnail & I', *Premiere*, 4/1 (February 1996), p. 79.
8   Ibid., p. 80.
9   Quoted by Alan Hunter, 'Robinson's Country', *Films and Filming*, 401 (February 1988), p. 16.
10   Kevin Jackson, *Withnail & I*, BFI Modern Classics Series (London: BFI, 2004), p. 38.
11   Ibid., p. 72.
12   Ibid., p. 56.
13   Will Self, 'Play Things', *Sight and Sound*, 5/11 (November 1995), p. 35.
14   Alastair Owen, *Smoking in Bed: Conversations with Bruce Robinson* (London: Bloomsbury, 2000), p. 106.
15   Jackson: *Withnail & I*, p. 37.
16   Richard E. Grant, *With Nails: The Film Diaries of Richard E. Grant* (London: Picador, 1996), p. 41.
17   Ibid., p. 28.
18   Bruce Robinson, *Withnail & I* (London: Bloomsbury, 1995), p. 8.
19   Ibid., pp. 9–10.
20   Ibid.
21   Grant was required by Robinson to 'lose about a stone to look really wasted', for which he enlisted the help of a 'diet-agent'. Grant: *With Nails*, p. 17.
22   Interview with the author, 26 June 2003. A version of this chapter with a specific focus on the film's costume design is to be found in *Fashion Theory*, 9/3 (September 2005), pp. 305–22.
23   Grant: *With Nails*, p. 40.
24   Robinson: *Withnail & I*, p. 29.
25   Ibid., p. 8.
26   Ibid., p. 15.
27   Ibid., p. 22.
28   Ibid., p. 32.
29   Quoted by B. Dunn, *Gentleman's Quarterly*, retrieved from www.andreagaler.co.uk, 19 January 2004.
30   Quoted by David Cavanagh, 'You're my bessht friend (sic)' in *Empire*, 81 (March 1996), p. 79.
31   Robinson: *Withnail & I*, p. 104.
32   Ibid., p. 109.

33   Ibid., p. 119.
34   Quoted by Cavanagh: 'You're my bessht friend (sic)', p. 81.
35   Robinson: *Withnail & I*, p. 34.
36   Ibid., p. 97.
37   Ibid., p. 127.
38   Ibid., p. 128.
39   Jackson: *Withnail & I*, p. 65.
40   Trotter: *Cooking with Mud*, p. 5.
41   Donald W. Winnicott, *Playing and Reality* (London: Tavistock, 1971), p. 1.
42   Ibid., p. 14.
43   Matt Hills, *Fan Cultures* (London: Routledge, 2002), p. 106.
44   Ibid., p. 108.
45   Ibid., p. 106.
46   Quoted by Brealey: 'Withnail & I', p. 84.
47   http://www.reelprogress.com/atavistically/cult-movies/.
48   Cavanagh: 'You're my bessht friend (sic)', p. 78.
49   Ibid.
50   Joanne Entwistle, *The Fashioned Body: Fashion, Dress and Modern Social Theory* (Cambridge: Polity, 2000), p. 113.
51   For a full account of his career breakthrough see Grant: *With Nails*.

Case Study 4: *Trainspotting* (1996)

52   Behind *Four Weddings and a Funeral* (Newell, 1994), *Trainspotting* has grossed over $60 million worldwide.
53   Catterall and Wells: *Your Face Here*, p. 208.
54   Caroline Westbrook, 'Just the Ticket . . .', *Empire*, 83 (May 1996), p. 20.
55   Spencer Vignes, 'Station Spotting', *Empire*, 104 (February 1998), p. 16.
56   Danny Boyle, 'Geoffrey MacNab talks to the team that made *Trainspotting*', *Sight and Sound*, 6/2 (February 1996), p. 11.
57   Alison Powell, 'Train Tracks', *Interview*, 26/8 (August 1996), p. 106.

Conclusion

1   Hewison: *Too Much: Art and Society in the Sixties, 1960–75*, p. 276.
2   Yuri M. Lotman, *Universe of the Mind: A Semiotic Theory of Culture*, trans. by Ann Shukman (London: I.B.Tauris, 1990), p. 224.
3   Ibid., p. 226.
4   Michel Foucault, *The Order of Things: An Archaeology of the Human Sciences* (New York: Pantheon, 1971), pp. 379–80.
5   Lotman, *Universe of the Mind*, p. 226.
6   Ibid., pp. 233–4.
7   Kaja Silverman, *Male Subjectivity at the Margins* (London: Routledge, 1992), p. 46.
8   Ibid., p. 55.
9   See Sue Harper, *Picturing the Past: The Rise and Fall of the British Costume Film* (London: BFI, 1994).
10   Silverman: *Male Subjectivity*, p. 52.
11   Joli Jenson, 'Fandom as Pathology: The Consequences of Characterization' in Lisa A. Lewis (ed.), *The Adoring Audience: Fan Culture and Popular Media* (London: Routledge, 1992), p. 20.

12   Hills: *Fan Cultures*, p. 180.
13   Ibid.
14   See my chapter, '*The Wicker Man* Digest: A web ethnography of a cult fan community' in James Chapman, Mark Glancy and Sue Harper (eds), *The New Film History* (Basingstoke: Palgrave/Macmillan, 2007), pp. 229–44.
15   Paul Willis, *Common Culture* (Milton Keynes: Open University Press, 1990).
16   Ibid., p. 10.
17   See Althusser: 'Ideology and Ideological State Apparatuses', pp. 153–64.
18   John Patterson, 'On Film', *The Guardian 'Friday Review'*, 18 March 2005, p. 3.
19   The late 1990s – the so-called 'Cool Britannia' era, post-*Trainspotting* – also witnessed high-profile re-releases of *Withnail & I* (1996), *Quadrophenia* (1997), and *A Clockwork Orange* (1999), branded as 'cult' films.
20   Lotman: *Universe of the Mind*, p. 272.
21   www.oed.com. Retrieved 15 December 2005.
22   Christopher Shaw and Malcolm Chase (eds), *The Imagined Past: History and Nostalgia* (Manchester: Manchester University Press, 1989), p. 1.
23   Ibid.
24   Ibid., p. 3.
25   Ibid.
26   Ibid., p. 15.
27   Silverman: *Male Subjectivity*, p. 18.
28   Ibid., p. 20.

SELECT BIBLIOGRAPHY

Unpublished Material

British Board of Film Classification Files
Letter from Stephen Murphy to R. M. D. Lee of Crawley, W. Sussex, 1 April 1974.

British Film Institute Library (London)
Press Books on individual films discussed (where available).

Mass-Observation Archive (University of Sussex)
Spring Directive, No. C 283819 (April 1999).

Unpublished Conference Paper
Dave Allen, 'Middle-Class Mods and Working-Class Sods: *Quadrophenia* and the construction of popular histories', unpublished paper presented at *British Culture in the 1970s Conference*, University of Portsmouth, July 2008.

Books and Chapters in Edited Volumes

Abercrombie, Nick and Brian Longhurst, *Audiences: A Sociological Theory of Performance and Imagination* (London: Sage, 1998).
Aldgate, Anthony, James Chapman and Arthur Marwick (eds), *Windows on the Sixties: Exploring Key Texts of Media and Culture* (London: I.B.Tauris, 2000).
Argyle, Michael, *Bodily Communication*, 2nd edn (London: Routledge, 1988).
Argyle, Michael and Mark Cook, *Gaze and the Mutual Gaze* (Cambridge: Cambridge University Press, 1976).
Auslander, Philip, *From Acting to Performance* (London: Routledge, 1997).
Baillieu, Bill and John Goodchild, *The British Film Business* (Chichester: John Wiley & Sons Ltd., 2002).
Balio, Tino (ed.), *The American Film Industry,* 2nd edn (Madison: University of Wisconsin Press, 1985).

Barker, Martin and Kate Brooks, *Knowing Audiences: Judge Dredd, Its Friends, Fans and Foes* (Luton: University of Luton Press, 1998).

Barnes, Richard and Pete Townshend, *The Story of Tommy* (Twickenham: Eel Pie Publishing, 1977).

Barthes, Roland, *The Pleasure of the Text* (London: Jonathan Cape, 1975).

Barthes, Roland, *Image – Music – Text* (London: Fontana, 1977).

Bataille, Georges, *Eroticism*, trans. by Mary Dalwood (London: Marion Boyars, 1987).

Baxter, John, *An Appalling Talent: Ken Russell* (London: Joseph, 1973).

Bennett, Tony, et al. (eds), *Popular Culture – Block 5: Politics, Ideology and Popular Culture, Vol. 1* (Milton Keynes: The Open University, 1981).

Betts, Ernest, *The Film Business: A history of British cinema, 1896–1972* (London: Allen & Unwin, 1973).

Birdwhistell, Ray L., *Kinesics and Context: Essays on Body-Motion Communication* (Harmondsworth: Penguin Books, 1970).

Booker, Christopher, *The Seventies* (Harmondsworth: Penguin Books, 1980).

Bourdieu, Pierre, *Distinction: A Social Critique of the Judgement of Taste*, trans. by Richard Nice (London: Routledge & Kegan Paul, 1984).

Bowlby, John, *Attachment and Loss, Vol. 2: Separation* (Harmondsworth: Penguin, 1975).

Brecht, Bertolt, *Brecht on Theatre* (London: Hill and Wang, 1964).

Bromley, David G. and J. Gordon Melton (eds), *Cults, Religion and Violence* (Cambridge: Cambridge University Press, 2002).

Brown, Allan, *Inside 'The Wicker Man': The morbid ingenuities* (London: Sidgwick and Jackson, 2000).

Burgess, Anthony, *A Clockwork Orange* (London: Penguin Books, 1996).

Cammell, Donald, *Performance* (London: Faber and Faber, 2001).

Catterall, Ali and Simon Wells, *Your Face Here: British Cult Movies Since the Sixties* (London: Fourth Estate, 2001).

Certeau, Michel de, *The Practice of Everyday Life*, trans. by Steven F. Rendall (Berkeley: University of California Press, 1984).

Chapman, Graham, John Cleese, Terry Gilliam, Eric Idle, Terry Jones, Michael Palin, with Bob McCabe, *The Pythons' Autobiography by the Pythons* (London: Orion Books, 2003).

Chapman, James, Mark Glancy and Sue Harper (eds), *The New Film History* (Basingstoke: Palgrave/Macmillan, 2007).

Chibnall, Steve, *Making Mischief: the cult films of Pete Walker* (Godalming: FAB Press, 1998).

Chibnall, Steve, *Get Carter*, The British Film Guide 6 (London: I.B.Tauris, 2003).

Chibnall, Steve and Robert Murphy (eds), *British Crime Cinema* (London: Routledge, 1999).

Chibnall, Steve, and Julian Petley (eds), *British Horror Cinema* (London: Routledge, 2002).

Coe, Jonathan, *The Rotters' Club* (London: Viking, 2001).

Cohen, Stanley, *Folk Devils and Moral Panics* (St Albans: Palladin, 1973).

Conrich, Ian, '*The Wicker Man*: A View to Pleasure', in Andy Black (ed.), *Necronomicon: Book Three* (1999), pp. 161–71.

Darley, Andrew, *Visual Digital Culture* (London: Routledge, 2000).

Davies, Steven Paul, *The A–Z of Cult Films and Film-makers* (London: B.T. Batsford Ltd., 2001).

Deeley, Michael, with Matthew Field, *Blade Runners, Deer Hunters & Blowing the Bloody Doors Off: My life in cult movies* (London: Faber and Faber, 2008).

Dickinson, Roger, Ramaswami Harindranath and Olga Linné (eds), *Approaches to Audiences – A Reader* (London: Arnold, 1998).

Donnolly, Kevin J., *Pop Music In British Cinema: A Chronicle* (London: BFI, 2001).

Douglas, Mary, *Purity and Danger: An analysis of concepts of pollution and taboo* (London: Routledge, 1966).

Douglas, Mary (ed.), *Witchcraft Confessions and Accusations* (London: Tavistock, 1970).

Durkheim, Emile, *Elementary Forms of Religious Life*, trans. by Karen Fields (New York: Free Press, 1995).

Dyer, Richard, *Stars* (London: BFI, 1998).

Eco, Umberto, '*Casablanca*: Cult Movies and Intertextual Collage' in *Faith in Fakes: Essays*, trans. by William Weaver (London: Secker & Warburg, 1987), pp. 197–212.

Ellis, John (ed.), *British Film Institute Productions Catalogue, 1951–76* (London: BFI, 1977).

Entwistle, Joanne, *The Fashioned Body: Fashion, Dress and Modern Social Theory* (Cambridge: Polity, 2000).

Evans, Christopher, *Cults of Unreason* (London: Harrap, 1973).

Evans, Jessica and Stuart Hall (eds), *Visual Culture: The Reader* (London: Sage, 1999).

Falsetto, Mario, *Stanley Kubrick: A Narrative and Stylistic Analysis,* 2nd edn (London: Praeger, 2001).

Falsetto, Mario (ed.), *Perspectives on Stanley Kubrick* (New York: G. K. Halt & Co., 1996).

Fiske, John, *Reading the Popular* (Boston: Unwin Hyman, 1989).

Foucault, Michel, *The Order of Things: An Archaeology of the Human Sciences* (New York: Pantheon, 1971).

Foucault, Michel, *The Birth of the Clinic: An Archaeology of Medical Perception*, trans. by Alan M. Sheridan Smith (London: Routledge, 1990).

Foucault, Michel, *The History of Sexuality: Volume 1, The Will to Knowledge,* trans. by Robert Hurley (Harmondsworth: Penguin Books, 1990).

Franks, Benjamin, Stephen Harper, Jonathan Murray and Lesley Stevenson (eds), *The Quest for the Wicker Man: History, folklore and Pagan perspectives* (Edinburgh: Luath, 2006).

Frazer, Sir James G., *The Golden Bough: A Study of Magic and Religion*, 3rd edn, 12 vols (London: Macmillan, 1911–15).

French, Karl and Philip French, *Cult Movies* (London: Pavilion, 1999).

Goffman, Erving, *The Presentation of Self in Everyday Life* (Harmondsworth: Penguin Books, 1959).

Gomery, Douglas, *Shared Pleasures: a history of movie presentation in the United States* (Madison: University of Wisconsin Press, 1992).

Gomez, Joseph A., *Ken Russell: The Adaptor as Creator* (London: Frederick Muller Ltd., 1976).

Gomez, Joseph A., '*Tommy*', in Thomas R. Atkins (ed.), *Ken Russell* (New York: Simon & Schuster, 1976), pp. 82–95.

Grant, Richard E., *With Nails: The Film Diaries of Richard E. Grant* (London: Picador, 1996).

Hakken, David, *Cyborgs@Cyberspace: An Ethnographer Looks to the Future* (London: Routledge, 1999).

Hall, Stuart, 'The centrality of culture: notes on the cultural revolution of our times', in Kenneth Thompson (ed.), *Media and Cultural Regulation* (London: Sage/The Open University, 1997), pp. 207–38.

Hall, Stuart and Tony Jefferson (eds), *Resistance Through Rituals: Youth subcultures in post-war Britain* (London: Unwin/Hyman, 1989).

Harper, Sue, *Picturing the Past: The Rise and Fall of the British Costume Film* (London: BFI, 1994).

Harper, Sue, *Women in British Cinema: Mad, Bad and Dangerous to Know* (London: Continuum, 2000).

Harper, Sue and Vincent Porter, *The Decline of Deference: British Cinema of the 1950s* (Oxford: OUP, 2003).

Haslam, Dave, *Not Abba: The Real Story of the 1970s* (London: Fourth Estate, 2005).

Hay, James, Lawrence Grossberg and Ellen Wartella (eds), *The Audience and its Landscape* (Boulder, Colorado: Westview Press, 1996).

Hebdige, Dick, 'Subculture: The meaning of style', in Ken Gelder and Sarah Thornton (eds), *The Subcultures Reader* (London: Routledge, 1997), pp. 130–42.

Hewison, Robert, *Too Much: Art and Society in the Sixties, 1960–75* (London: Methuen, 1986).

Higson, Andrew, 'A Diversity of Film Practices: renewing British cinema in the 1970s', in Bart Moore-Gilbert (ed.), *The Arts in the 1970s: Cultural Closure?* (London: Routledge, 1994), pp. 216–39.

Hills, Matt, *Fan Cultures* (London: Routledge, 2002).

Hine, Christine, *Virtual Ethnography* (London: Sage, 2000).

Hoberman, Jay and Jonathan Rosenbaum, *Midnight Movies* (New York: Harper & Row, 1983).

Hollows, Joanne and Mark Jancovich (eds), *Approaches to Popular Film* (Manchester: Manchester University Press, 1995).

Hunt, Leon, *British Low Culture: From Safari Suits to Sexploitation* (London: Routledge, 1998).

Hunter, Ian Q. (ed.), *British Science Fiction Cinema* (London: Routledge, 1999).

Hutchings, Peter, *Hammer and Beyond: The British Horror Film* (Manchester: Manchester University Press, 1993).

Isherwood, Christopher, *The World in the Evening* (London: Methuen, 1954).

Izod, John, *The Films of Nicolas Roeg: Myth and Mind* (London: Macmillan, 1992).

Jackson, Kevin, *Withnail & I*, BFI Modern Classics Series (London: BFI, 2004).

Jameson, Fredric, *The Political Unconscious* (Ithaca: Cornell University Press, 1981).

Jancovich, Mark, '"A Real Shocker": Authenticity, genre and the struggle for distinction', in Graeme Turner (ed.), *The Film Cultures Reader* (London: Routledge, 2002), pp. 469–80.

Jancovich, Mark, Antonio Lázaro Reboll, Julian Stringer and Andy Willis (eds), *Defining Cult Movies: The cultural politics of oppositional taste* (Manchester and New York: University of Manchester Press, 2003).

Jancovich, Mark and Lucy Faire, with Sarah Stubbings, *The Place of the Audience: Cultural Geographies of Film Consumption* (London: BFI, 2003).

Jenkins, Henry, *Textual poachers: television fans and participatory culture* (London: Routledge, 1992).

Jones, Steve (ed.), *Doing Internet Research: Critical Issues and Methods for Examining the Net* (London: Sage, 1999).

Kaplan, Fred, *Dickens and Mesmerism: The Hidden Springs of Fiction* (Princeton, NJ: Princeton University Press, 1975).

Kelly, Terence, with Graham Norton and George Perry, *A Competitive Cinema* (London: The Institute of Economic Affairs, 1966).

Kitses, Jim, *Horizons West: studies of authorship within the western* (London: Thames and Hudson/BFI, 1969).

Krzywinska, Tanya, *A Skin for Dancing In: Possession, Witchcraft and Voodoo in Film* (Trowbridge: Flicks Books, 2000).

Kureishi, Hanif and Jon Savage (eds), *The Faber Book of Pop* (London: Faber and Faber, 1995).

Landy, Marcia, *Monty Python's Flying Circus*, TV Milestones Series (Detroit: Wayne State University Press, 2005).

Laplanche, Jean and Pontalis, Jean-Bertrand, 'Fantasy and the origins of sexuality', in Victor Burgin, James Donald and Cora Kaplan (eds), *Formations of Fantasy* (London: Methuen, 1986), pp. 5–34.

Lefebvre, Henri, *Introduction to Modernity*, trans. by John Moore (London: Verso, 1995).

Lefebvre, Henri, *Critique of Everyday Life*, trans. by John Moore (London: Verso, 2002).

Lent, Adam, *British Social Movements since 1945* (London: Palgrave, 2001).

Lewis, Gilbert, *Day of Shining Red: An essay on understanding ritual* (Cambridge: Cambridge University Press, 1988).

Lewis, Lisa A. (ed.), *The Adoring Audience: Fan Culture and Popular Media* (London: Routledge, 1992).

Lewis, Ted, *Jack's Return Home* (London: Michael Joseph Ltd, 1970).

Lindholm, Charles, *Charisma* (Oxford: Blackwell, 1990).

Lotman, Yuri, *Universe of the Mind: A Semiotic Theory of Culture*, trans. by Ann Shukman (London: I.B.Tauris, 1990).

MacCabe, Colin, *Performance*, BFI Modern Classics Series (London: BFI, 1998).

Marwick, Arthur, *The Sixties: Cultural Revolution in Britain, France, Italy and the United States, c.1958–1974* (Oxford: OUP, 1998).

Mathijs, Ernest and Xavier Mendik, (eds), *The Cult Film Reader* (Maidenhead: Open University Press/McGraw-Hill, 2008).

Mayne, Judith, *Cinema and Spectatorship* (London: Routledge, 1993).

Meehan, Eileen R., 'Leisure or Labour?: Fan ethnography and political economy' in Ingunn Hagen and Janet Wasko (eds), *Consuming Audiences? Production and Reception in Media Research* (Cresskill, New Jersey: Hampton Press Inc., 2000), pp. 71–92.

Mendik, Xavier and Graeme Harper (eds), *Unruly Pleasures: the cult film and its critics* (Godalming: FAB Press, 2000).

Mendik, Xavier and Steven J. Schneider (eds), *Underground USA: Filmmaking Beyond the Hollywood Canon* (London: Wallflower Press, 2002).

Mercer, Colin, 'Pleasure' in *Popular Culture*, U203, Block 4, Unit 17 (Milton Keynes: Open University Press, 1981), pp. 45–75.

Miller, Daniel and Don Slater, *The Internet: An Ethnographic Approach* (Oxford: Berg, 2000).

Miller, William Ian, *The Anatomy of Disgust* (Cambridge, Mass.: Harvard University Press, 1997).

Moores, Shaun, *Interpreting Audiences: the ethnography of media consumption* (London: Sage, 1993).

Morley, David, 'Changing paradigms in audience studies' in Ellen Seiter (ed.), *Remote Control: television, audiences and cultural power* (London: Routledge, 1989), pp. 16–43.

Morley, David, *Television, Audience and Cultural Studies* (London: Routledge, 1992).

Morley, David, 'Theories of Consumption in Media Studies' in Daniel Miller (ed.), *Acknowledging Consumption – a review of new studies* (London: Routledge, 1995), pp. 296–327.

Morrison, Blake, 'Introduction' to Anthony Burgess, *A Clockwork Orange* (London: Penguin, 1996).

Murphy, Robert, 'Under the Shadow of Hollywood', in Charles Barr (ed.), *All Our Yesterdays: 90 Years of British Cinema* (London: BFI, 1986), pp. 47–71.

Murphy, Robert, *Sixties British Cinema* (London: BFI, 1992).

Murphy, Robert (ed.), *The British Cinema Book*, 2nd edn (London: BFI, 2001).

Murray, Jonathan, Lesley Stevenson, Stephen Harper and Benjamin Franks (eds), *Constructing 'The Wicker Man': Film and Cultural Studies Perspectives* (Dumfries: University of Glasgow Crichton Publications, 2005).

Newman, Kim, *The BFI Companion to Horror* (London: BFI/Cassell, 1996).

Nixon, Sean, 'Exhibiting Masculinity' in Stuart Hall (ed.), *Representations: Cultural Representations and Signifying Practices* (London: Sage/The Open University, 1997), pp. 302–36.

Owen, Alastair, *Smoking in Bed: Conversations with Bruce Robinson* (London: Bloomsbury, 2000).

Palin, Michael, *Diaries 1969–1979: The Python Years* (London: Orion Books, 2007).

Palmer, William J., *Dickens and New Historicism* (New York: St Martin's Press, 1997).

Peary, Danny, *Cult Movies* (New York: Delta, 1981).

Peary, Danny, *Cult Movies: the classics, the sleepers, the weird, and the wonderful* (New York: Delacorte Press, 1981).

Peary, Danny, *Cult Movies: a hundred ways to find the reel thing* (London: Vermilion, 1982).

Peary, Danny, *Cult Movies 2* (London: Vermilion, 1984).

Peary, Danny, *Cult Movie Stars* (New York: London: Simon & Schuster, 1991).

Phillips, Gene D., *Ken Russell* (Boston: Twayne, 1979).

Phillips, Gene D. and Rodney Hill, *The Encyclopaedia of Stanley Kubrick* (New York: Checkmark Books, 2002).

Pirie, David, *A Heritage of Horror: The English Gothic Cinema 1946–72* (London: Gordon Fraser, 1973).

Rigby, Jonathan, *English Gothic: a century of horror cinema* (London: Reynolds and Hearn, 2000).

Riley, Denise, *War in the Nursery: Theories of the Child and Mother* (London: Virago, 1983).

Robertson, James C., *The Hidden Cinema: British Film Censorship in Action, 1913–1972* (London: Routledge, 1989).

Robinson, Bruce, *Withnail and I* (London: Bloomsbury, 1995).

Salwolke, Scott, *Nicolas Roeg Film by Film* (Jefferson, N. Carolina: McFarland & Co. Inc., 1993).

Sanjek, David, 'Twilight of the Monsters: The English Horror Film, 1968–1975', in Wheeler Winston Dixon (ed.), *Re-Viewing British Cinema, 1900–1992, Essays and Interviews* (Albany: University of New York Press, 1994), pp. 195–209.

Sarris, Andrew, *Confessions of a Cultist: On the Cinema, 1955–1969* (New York: Simon & Schuster, 1970).

Schechner, Richard, *The Future of Ritual: Writings on Culture and Performance* (London: Routledge, 1993).

Schwartz, Carol, *Videohound's Complete Guide to Cult Flicks and Trash Pics* (New York: Visible Ink Press, 1996).

Shail, Robert (ed.), *Seventies British Cinema* (London/Basingstoke: Palgrave/BFI, 2008).

Shaw, Christopher and Malcolm Chase (eds), *The Imagined Past: History and Nostalgia* (Manchester: Manchester University Press, 1989).

Shilling, Chris, *The Body and Social Theory*, 2nd edn (London: Sage, 2003).

Silverman, Kaja, *Male Subjectivity at the Margins* (London: Routledge, 1992).

Simpson, Paul (ed.), *The Rough Guide to Cult Movies: The Good, the Bad and the Very Weird Indeed* (London: Penguin, 2001).

Sinyard, Neil, *The Films of Nicolas Roeg* (London: Charles Letts & Co. Ltd., 1991).

Smith, Murray, *Trainspotting*, BFI Modern Classics (London: BFI, 2002).

Sontag, Susan, 'Notes on "Camp"', in *A Susan Sontag Reader* (Harmondsworth: Penguin Books, 1983), pp. 105–19.

Sounes, Howard, *Seventies: The Sights, Sounds and Ideas of a Brilliant Decade* (London: Simon & Schuster, 2006).

Spicer, Andrew, *Typical Men: The Representation of Masculinity in Popular British Cinema* (London: I.B.Tauris, 2003).

Stacey, Jackie, *Stargazing: Hollywood Cinema and Female Spectatorship* (London: Routledge, 1994).

Stevens, Anthony, *On Jung* (London: Penguin Books, 1991).

Stokes, Melvyn and Richard Maltby (eds), *Identifying Hollywood's Audiences – Cultural Identity and the Movies* (London: BFI, 1999).

Storey, John (ed.), *Cultural Theory and Popular Culture: A Reader*, 2nd edn (Hemel Hempstead: Prentice Hall/Harvester, 1998).

Street, Sarah, *Transatlantic Crossings: British Feature Films in the USA* (New York & London: Continuum, 2002).

Tasker, Yvonne, *Spectacular Bodies: gender, genre and the action cinema* (London: Comedia/Routledge, 1993).

Taylor, Greg, *Artists in the Audience: Cults, Camp, and American Film Criticism* (Princeton: Princeton University Press, 1999).

Telotte, J. P. (ed.), *The Cult Film Experience: Beyond All Reason* (Austin: University of Texas Press, 1991).

Tevis, Walter, *The Man Who Fell To Earth* (London: Bloomsbury/*Sight and Sound*, 2000).

Thornton, Sarah, *Club Cultures: Music, Media and Subcultural Capital* (Cambridge: Polity, 1995).

Tosh, John, *The Pursuit of History*, 3rd edn (Harlow: Pearson Education, 2000).

Trevelyan, John, *What the Censor Saw* (London: Joseph, 1973).

Trotter, David, *Cooking with Mud: The Idea of Mess in Nineteenth Century Art and Fiction* (Oxford: OUP, 2000).

Turner, Alwyn W., *Crisis? What Crisis?: Britain in the 1970s* (London: Aurum Press Ltd., 2008).

Tyler, Parker, *The Three Faces of the Film: the art, the dream, the cult* (South Brunswick, NJ: A. S. Barnes, 1967).

Van Ghent, Dorothy, *Keats: The Myth of the Hero* (Princeton, NJ: Princeton University Press, 1983).

Volosinov, Valentin, *Freudianism: a Marxist Critique*, trans. by Irwin R. Titunik (London: Academy Press, 1976).

Walker, Alexander, *Stanley Kubrick Directs* (London: Davis-Poynter Ltd., 1972).

Walker, Alexander, *National Heroes: British Cinema in the Seventies and Eighties* (London: Harrap, 1985).

Walker, Alexander, *Hollywood, England: The British Film Industry in the Sixties* (London: Harrap, 1986).

Walker, John, *The Once and Future Film: British Cinema in the Seventies and Eighties* (London: Methuen, 1985).

Wasko, Janet, *Movies and Money: Financing the American Film Industry* (Norwood, NJ: Ablex Publishing Corp., 1982).

Watson, Robert, *Film and Television in Education: An Aesthetic Approach to the Moving Image* (London: The Falmer Press, 1990).

Weedon, Chris, Andrew Tolson and Frank Mort, 'Theories of Language and Subjectivity', in Stuart Hall et al. (eds), *Culture, Media, Language* (London: Routledge, 1980), pp. 195–216.

Welsh, Irvine, *Trainspotting* (London: Minerva, 1993).

Williams, Linda, *Viewing Positions: Ways of Seeing Film* (New Brunswick, NJ: Rutgers University Press, 1994).

Williams, Raymond, *Marxism and Literature* (Oxford: OUP, 1977).

Willis, Paul, *Common Culture* (Milton Keynes: Open University Press, 1990).

Winnicott, Donald W., *Playing and Reality* (London: Tavistock, 1971).

Wollen, Tana, *Film & Audiences* (London: Film Education, 1988).

Wood, Linda (ed.), *British Films 1971–1981* (London: BFI, 1983).

Wright, Will, *Sixguns and Society* (Berkeley: University of California Press, 1975).

Articles in Journals, Periodicals, Newspaper Reviews and Other Papers

Where newspaper or magazine reviews are cited without page references, the sources are press cuttings on BFI microfiches.

Andrews, Nigel, 'Holiday Fodder' (film review), *Financial Times*, 14 December 1973, p. 3.

Anon., 'Britt . . . and the Fury of Provost Plunkett', *Daily Record*, 18 December 1972, p. 3.

Anon., '"Tommy" Opera Reverses Flow', *Variety*, 15 May 1974, np.

Anon., 'Market Study Maps Safeway Path To "Tommy"; Lure of Ann-Margret, Jack N., Reed?', *Variety*, 26 February 1975, np.

Anon., 'Tommy' (review), *Variety*, 12 March 1975, p. 18.

Anon., 'Tommy' (review), *CinemaTV Today*, 10129, 12 April 1975, p. 16.

Anon., *Variety*, 24 September 1975, p. 22.

Anon., *Screen International*, 353, 24 July 1982, p. 6.

Anon., *Statistical Information relating to some aspects of the British Film Industry* (London: Film Education, 1993).

Anon., *Film Review*, Classic Film Special, 16 (1996), pp. 31–5.

Anon., 'Just the ticket . . .', *Empire*, 83 (May 1996), p. 20.

Anon., 'A British success: making and selling *Trainspotting*', *Sight and Sound* supplement money (September 1996), pp. 10–11.

Arkin, Laurent, 'I was a regular Frankie fan: *The Rocky Horror Picture Show*'s mode d'emploi', *Vertigo*, 10 (1993), pp. 102–3.

Austin, Bruce A., 'Portrait of a Cult Film Audience: The Rocky Horror Picture Show', *Journal of Communications*, 31 (1981), pp. 450–6.

Austin, Greta, 'Were the peasants really so clean? The Middle Ages in film', *Film History*, 14 (2002), pp. 136–41.

Bartholomew, David, 'The Man Who Fell To Earth', *Film Heritage*, 12/1 (fall 1976), pp. 18–25.

Bartholomew, David, 'The Wicker Man', *Cinéfantastique*, 6/3 (winter 1977), pp. 4–18 & 32–46.

Bean, Robin, 'Tommy' (review), *Films and Filming*, 21/8 (May 1975), pp. 35–6.

Brealey, Louise, 'Withnail & I', *Premiere*, 4/1 (February 1996), pp. 79–84.

Brown, Geoff, 'Review: Monty Python and the Holy Grail', *Monthly Film Bulletin*, 42/495 (April 1975), pp. 84–5.

Buday, Don, 'The Many Images of David Bowie', *The Hollywood Reporter*, 30 June 1976, pp. 10 & 12.

Burgess, Jackson, 'Review: A Clockwork Orange', *Film Quarterly*, 25/3 (1972), pp. 33–6.

Cardullo, Bert, 'Fiction into Film, or Bringing Welsh to a Boyle', *Literature/Film Quarterly*, 25/3 (October 1997), pp. 158–62.

Castell, David, 'Tommy' (review), *Films Illustrated*, 4/44 (April 1975), p. 286.

Castell, David, 'Daltry's Tommy', *Films Illustrated*, 4/44 (April 1975), pp. 300–2.

Cavanagh, David, 'You're my bessht friend (sic)', *Empire*, 81 (March 1996), pp. 76–81.

Chute, David, 'Outlaw Cinema', *Film Comment*, 19/5 (September/October 1983), pp. 9–11, 13 & 15.

Clarke, Sue, 'Will Rocky Horror Turn You On (Or Off)?', *Photoplay*, 26/3 (March 1975), pp. 20–1 & 46.

Clarke, Sue, 'Tommy' (preview), *Photoplay*, 26/5 (May 1975), pp. 16 & 19.

Connolly, Ray, 'Tommy', *Time Out*, 265, 28 March 1975, pp. 10–11.

Dawson, Jan, 'Review: A Clockwork Orange', *Monthly Film Bulletin*, 39/457 (1972), pp. 28–9.

Day, Barry, 'The Cult Movies: *Casablanca*', *Films and Filming*, 20/11 (August 1974), pp. 20–4.

Dean, Peter, 'Cult-films and video release of *The Avengers*', *Sight and Sound* New Series, 3/11 (1993), p. 62.

Dinsmore-Tuli, Uma, 'The pleasures of "home cinema", or watching movies on telly: an audience study of cinephiliac VCR use', *Screen*, 41/3 (autumn 2000), pp. 315–27.

Dorr, John H., 'Tommy' (review), *Hollywood Reporter*, 235/27, 12 March 1975, p. 14.

Eimer, David and Mark Salisbury, 'Away Day', *Empire*, 88 (October 1996), p. 16.

French, Philip, 'A Clockwork Orange', *Sight and Sound*, 59/2 (February 1990), pp. 84–7.

Frumkes, Roy, 'Document of the dead – the 12-year saga of the remake of what has been called a lost cult classic', *Films in Review*, 41 (October 1990), pp. 470–6.

Gabbard, Krin and Glen O. Gabbard, 'Play it again, Sigmund – Psychoanalysis and the Classical Hollywood Text', *Journal of Popular Film and Television*, 18/1 (spring 1990), pp. 6–17.

Gill, Andy, 'One From The Heart', *Empire*, 8 (February 1980), pp. 52–61.

Gow, Gordon, 'Review: A Clockwork Orange', *Films and Filming*, 18/5 (February 1972), pp. 12 & 49.

Gow, Gordon, 'he said with incredible arrogance . . .', *Films and Filming*, 21/3 (December 1974), pp. 12–17.

Gow, Gordon, 'Review: Monty Python and the Holy Grail', *Films and Filming*, 21/8 (May 1975), p. 40.

Gow, Gordon, 'Something More', *Films and Filming*, 22/1 (October 1975), pp. 10–16.

Grant, Barry Keith, 'When Worlds Collide: The Cool World', *Literature Film Quarterly*, 18/3 (1990), pp. 179–88.

Grundy, Gareth, 'Hey! Hey! We're the junkies!', *Neon* (February 1998), pp. 100–5.

Halasz, Piri, 'You Can Walk Across It On The Grass', *Time*, 15 April 1966, pp. 30–4.

Hall, Edward, 'A system for the notation of proxemic behaviour', *American Anthropologist*, 65/5 (1963), pp. 1018–19.

'Hawk', 'The Man Who Fell To Earth', *Variety*, 24 March 1976, p. 20.

Hawkins, Joan, 'Sleaze mania, Euro-trash, and high art: the place of European art films in American low culture', *Film Quarterly*, 53/2 (winter 1999/2000), pp. 14–29.

Hentzi, Gary, 'Little cinema of horrors + b-movie cult films', *Film Quarterly*, 46/3 (1993), pp. 22–7.

Hind, John, 'The Holy Grail', *Hotdog*, 4 (October 2000), pp. 54–9.

Hinxman, Margaret, 'Sting in the Tail of the Year' (film review), *Sunday Telegraph*, 23 December 1973, p. 10.

Hoberman, Jay and Jonathan Rosenbaum, 'Curse of the cult people – a history of cult film subculture and its central figures', *Film Comment*, 27/1 (January/February 1991), pp. 18–21.

Hogan, David, 'Cult Movie Stars Review', *Filmfax*, 31 (February/March 1992), pp. 12–14.

Holben, Jay, 'Pedal to the metal', *American Cinematographer*, 81/6 (June 2000), pp. 34–50.

Howard, Alan, *The Hollywood Reporter*, 231/18, 9 May 1974, p. 3.

Hunt, Leon, '*Making mischief: The cult films of Pete Walker* by Steve Chibnall' (book review), *Cultural Studies*, 13/3 (1999), pp. 535–6.

Hunter, Alan, 'Robinson's Country', *Films and Filming*, 401 (February 1988), pp. 16–17.

Hunter, Allan, 'Marketing Focus: Trainspotting: Platform Release', *Screen International*, 1044, 9 February 1996, p. 40.

James, Nick, 'At Home with the Kubricks', *Sight and Sound* New Series, 9/9 (September 1999), pp. 12–18.

James, Nick, 'Violence: A Comparison of *A Clockwork Orange* and *American Psycho*', *Sight and Sound* New Series, 10/10 (October 2000), p. 64.

James, Richard, 'Into the Valley', *Films and Filming*, 425 (March 1990), pp. 36–7.

Jancovich, Mark, 'Cult fictions: Cult movies, subcultural capital and the production of cultural distinctions', *Cultural Studies*, 16/2 (2002), pp. 306–22.

Jones, Alan, 'The Rocky Horror Picture Show' (interview feature), *Starburst*, 36 (1981), pp. 46–9.

Jones, Alan, 'A Cult above the rest', *Radio Times*, 3–9 January 1998, p. 43.

Jones, Oliver, 'Shoot Me Up, Scotty', *Premiere*, 9/11 (July 1996), pp. 60–1.

Kennedy, Harlan, 'Kiltspotting: Highland Reels', *Film Comment*, 32/4 (July 1996), pp. 28–33.

Kinkade, Patrick and Michael Katovich, 'Toward a Sociology of Cult Films: Reading Rocky Horror', *Sociological Quarterly*, 33/2 (summer 1992), pp. 191–210.

Kolker, Robert Phillip, 'The Open Texts of Nicolas Roeg', *Sight and Sound*, 46/2 (spring 1977), pp. 82–4 & 113.

Kuzniar, Alice A., 'Zarah Leander and transgender specularity', *Film Criticism*, 23/2–3 (winter/spring 1999), pp. 74–93.

Landau, Jon, '*Tommy*: Too Big, Too Late', *Rolling Stone*, 24 April 1975, np.

Lawson, Chris, '"Melancholy Clowns": The Cult of *Hamlet* in *Withnail & I* and *In the Bleak Midwinter*', *Shakespeare Bulletin*, 15/4 (fall 1997), pp. 33–4.

Leach, James, 'The Man Who Fell To Earth', *Literature/Film Quarterly*, 6/4 (fall 1978), pp. 371–9.

LoBrutto, Vincent, 'The Old Ultra-Violence', *American Cinematographer*, 80/10 (1999), pp. 52–61.

McCarty, John, 'Tommy' (review), *Cinéfantastique*, 4/3 (autumn 1975), p. 33.

McCarthy, Todd, 'Highland Fling', *Premiere*, 9/12 (August 1996), pp. 18–19.

Macnab, Geoffrey, 'Geoffrey MacNab talks to the team that made *Trainspotting*', *Sight and Sound* New Series, 6/2 (February 1996), pp. 8–11.

Macnab, Geoffrey, 'Loving the Alien', *Time Out*, 30 August 2000, p. 151.

Mayersberg, Paul, 'The Story So Far . . .', *Sight and Sound*, 44/3 (autumn 1975), pp. 225–31.

Meuwese, Martine, 'The Animation of Marginal Decorations in *Monty Python and the Holy Grail*', *Arthuriana*, 14/4 (2004), pp. 45–58.

Milne, Tom, 'The Man Who Fell To Earth', *Sight and Sound*, 45/3 (summer 1976), pp. 145–7.

Monk, Claire, 'Heritage films and the British Cinema audience in the 1990s', *Journal of Popular British Cinema*, 2 (1999), pp. 22–38.

Morrison, Alan, 'The Making of Trainspotting', *Empire*, 169 (July 2003), pp. 115–21.

Moskowitz, Kenneth, 'The Vicarious Experience of *A Clockwork Orange*', *Velvet Light Trap*, 16 (autumn 1976), pp. 28–31.

Murrell, Elizabeth, 'History Revenged: Monty Python translates Chrétien de Troyes' *Perceval, Or the story of the Grail* (again)', *Journal of Film and Video*, 50/1 (spring 1998), pp. 50–62.

Naughton, John, 'Now wash you hands', *Empire*, 81 (March 1996), pp. 96–7.

O'Hagan, Andrew, 'The boys are back in town', *Sight and Sound* New Series, 6/2 (February 1996), pp. 6–8.

Parsons, Tony, 'Sex Through the Looking Glass', *Empire*, 54 (December 1993), pp. 64–71.

Patterson, John, 'On Film', *The Guardian 'Friday Review'*, 18 March 2005, p. 3.

Pennington, Ron, 'The Rocky Horror Picture Show' (film review), *The Hollywood Reporter*, 238/14, 24 September 1975, p. 15.

Petley, Julian, 'Review of Allan Brown, *Inside "The Wicker Man": The Morbid Ingenuities*' (London: Sidgwick and Jackson, 2000), *Journal of Popular British Cinema*, 5 (2002), pp. 166–70.

Pirie, David and Chris Petit, 'After The Fall', *Time Out*, 313, 12 March 1976, pp. 12–15.

Powell, Alison, 'Train Tracks', *Interview*, 26/8 (August 1996), p. 106.

Powell, Dilys, 'Just Men' (film review), *Sunday Times*, 16 December 1973, p. 37.

Rapping, Elayne, 'Hollywood's youth cult films', *Cineaste*, 16/1–2 (1988), pp. 14–19.

Rayns, Tony, 'The Rocky Horror Picture Show' (film review), *Monthly Film Bulletin*, 42/499 (August 1975), pp. 181–2.

Rosenbaum, Jonathan, 'Tommy' (review), *Monthly Film Bulletin*, 42/495 (April 1975), pp. 88–9.

Rosenbaum, Jonathan, 'The Man Who Fell To Earth' (review), *Monthly Film Bulletin*, 43/507 (April 1976), pp. 86–7.

Rosenbaum, Jonathan, 'The Rocky Horror Picture Cult', *Sight and Sound*, 49/2 (spring 1980), pp. 78–9.

Sanjek, David, 'Fans' notes: The Horror Film Fanzine', *Literature Film Quarterly*, 18/3 (1990), pp. 150–60.

Savage, Jon, 'Tuning into Wonders', *Sight and Sound* New Series, 5/9 (September 1995), pp. 24–5.

Savage, Jon, 'I don't wanna be like everybody else', *Sight and Sound* New Series, 7/2 (February 1997), pp. 16–17.

Schindler, Arlene, 'A Clockwork Orange', *Creative Screenwriting*, 6/4 (July/August 1999), pp. 38–41.

Sconce, Jeffrey, 'Trashing the Academy: taste, excess and an emerging politics of cinematic style', *Screen*, 36/4 (1995), pp. 371–93.

Self, Will, 'Play Things', *Sight and Sound* New Series, 5/11 (November 1995), pp. 34–5.

Sellers, Robert, 'The Pythons Hall of Fame – Kings of Comedy', *Empire*, 171 (September 2003), pp. 106–13.

Sims, Judith, 'Townshend's Mixed Blessing', *Rolling Stone*, 24 April 1975, np.

Smith, Adam, 'Altar'd States', *Empire*, 106 (April 1998), pp. 92–8.

Smith, Justin, 'Withnail's Coat: Andrea Galer's Cult Costumes', *Fashion Theory*, 9/3 (September 2005), pp. 305–22.

Steele, Barbara, 'Cult Memories', *The Perfect Vision*, 6/23 (October 1994), pp. 59–63.

Stein, Michael Eric, 'The New Violence or Twenty Years of Violence in Films: An Appreciation', *Films in Review*, 46/1–2 (January/February 1995), pp. 40–8.

Strick, Philip, 'Kubrick's Horrorshow', *Sight and Sound*, 41/1 (1971/2), pp. 45–6.

Strick, Philip and Penelope Houston, 'Interview with Stanley Kubrick', *Sight and Sound*, 41/2 (February 1972), pp. 62–6.

Stuart, Alexander, 'The Rocky Horror Picture Show' (film review), *Films and Filming*, 21/12 (September 1975), p. 31.

Stuart, Alexander, 'Review: The Man Who Fell To Earth', *Films and Filming*, 22/8 (May 1976), pp. 28–9.

Studlar, Gaylin, 'Midnight S/Excess: Cult configurations of "femininity" and the perverse', *Journal of Popular Film and Television*, 17/1 (spring 1989), pp. 2–14.

Theobald, Robin, *Charisma: some empirical problems considered*, Research Paper No. 5 (London: Polytechnic of Central London School of the Social Sciences and Business Studies), 1975.

Thompson, Andrew O., 'Trains, veins and heroin deals', *American Cinematographer*, 77/8 (August 1996), pp. 80–6.

Townshend, Pete, 'Who's Tommy', *Films and Filming*, 21/9 (June 1975), pp. 18–21.

Tudor, Andrew, 'Why horror? The peculiar pleasures of a popular genre', *Cultural Studies*, 11/3 (1997), pp. 443–63.

Vaines, Colin, 'The Mods and the Movie', *Screen International*, 166, 25 November 1978, pp. 25–6.

Vignes, Spencer, 'Station Spotting', *Empire*, 104 (February 1998), p. 16.

Von Gunden, Kenneth, 'The RH Factor', *Film Comment*, 15/5 (September/October 1979), pp. 54–6.

Walker, John, 'Ken Russell's New Enigma', *Observer Magazine*, 8 September 1974, pp. 51–7.

Walsh, Ben, 'It's a mod world', *Premiere*, 5/1 (February 1997), pp. 36–8.

Westbrook, Caroline, 'Just the Ticket . . .', *Empire*, 83 (May 1996), p. 20.

Westbrook, Caroline, 'Runaway Train', *Empire*, 91 (January 1997), pp. 108–9.

White, Armond, 'Kidpix + youth-cult movies, with particular consideration of kreines/demott 'seventeen', *Film Comment*, 21/4 (1985), pp. 9–15.

Wilson, David, 'Tommy' (review), *Sight and Sound*, 44/3 (autumn 1975), pp. 192–3.

Winnert, Derek, '*Moviedrome*'s back!', *Radio Times*, 14–20 May 1994, p. 43.

Wollen, Peter, 'Possession', *Sight and Sound* New Series, 5/9 (September 1995), pp. 20–3.

Wood, Jason, 'His Brilliant Career', *The Guardian*, '*Friday Review*', 3 June 2005, p. 10.

Woronov, Mary, 'Cult Films', *The Perfect Vision*, 6/23 (October 1994), pp. 64–5.

Zizek, Slavoj, 'Looking Awry', *October*, 50 (autumn 1989), pp. 30–55.

Audio-Visual Sources

Abbott, Andrew and Russell Leven (dirs), *Burnt Offering: The Cult of The Wicker Man* (TV documentary, UK, Nobles Gate Film and Television Productions, 2001). First broadcast, Channel 4 Television, 30 December 2001.

Anon., *Rocky Horror Double Feature Video Show* (DVD documentary feature, Twentieth Century Fox Home Entertainment, 2004).

Gordon, Yvonne (dir.), *Withnail & Us* (DVD documentary feature, UK, 1999).

Gregory, David (dir.), *Watching the Alien* (DVD documentary feature, UK, Blue Underground Inc./Anchor Bay Entertainment, 2002).

Joyce, Paul (dir.), *The Return of A Clockwork Orange* (TV documentary, UK, Lucida Productions, 2000). First broadcast, Channel 4 Television, 18 March 2000.

Kent, Matt, Interview with Pete Townshend at Eel Pie Studios on 10 February 2004 (DVD special feature, Odyssey Quest Productions, 2004).

Kermode, Mark, Interview with Ken Russell (DVD special feature, Odyssey Quest Productions, 2004).

Macdonald, Kevin and Chris Rodley (dirs), *Donald Cammell: The Ultimate Performance* (TV documentary, UK, Figment Films, 1998). First broadcast, BBC2, 17 May 1998.

Electronic Sources

http://beam.to/transylvania
http://browse.guardian.co.uk/search?search=cult+film
http://fans.luminosus.net/clock/
http://fii.chadwyck.co.uk/home
http://film.guardian.co.uk/
http://groups.yahoo.com/group/clockworkorange2
http://groups.yahoo.com/group/Performance_Movie1/
http://movies.dir.groups.yahoo.com/dir/Entertainment_Arts/Movies/Cult_and_Classic/Titles
http://movies.groups.yahoo.com/group/LipsDownOnDixieFans/
http://movies.groups.yahoo.com/group/tommytherockopera/
http://movies.groups.yahoo.com/group/wickerman/
http://rocky-horror-costume.co.uk/
http://tvtip.bufvc.ac.uk
http://www.andreagaler.co.uk/
http://www.bbc.co.uk/cult/
http://www.bbfc.org.uk/
http://www.bectu.org.uk/about/hisproj/hisproj.html
http://www.bfi.org.uk/
http://www.billdouglas.org/
http://www.brunel.ac.uk/about/acad/sa/artresearch/smrc/cultfilm/
http://www.bufvc.ac.uk/
http://www-cntv.usc.edu/resources/resources-wbarchive.cfm
http://www.cult-film.com/
http://www.cult-media.com/
http://www.cultmovies.info/
http://www.fabpress.com/system/index.html
http://www.filmsite.org/cultfilms.html
http://www.geocities.com/cultconfessor/
http://www.geocities.com/worldenterprises_rpg/home.html
http://www.imdb.com/
http://www.nuada98.fsnet.co.uk/nuada%203/
http://www.oed.com
http://www.phinnweb.com/roeg/films/themanwhofelltoearth/articles/cultmovies.html
http://www.reelprogress.com/atavistically/cult-movies/

http://www.stellascreen.co.uk/stellascreen/index.jsp

http://www.sw-scotland-screen.com/wickerman_trail/further_information.html

http://www.timewarp.org.uk

http://www.thespinningimage.co.uk/index.asp

http://www.thewickermanfestival.co.uk/

http://www.tv-ark.org.uk/itvlondon/thamesmain-new.html

http://www.ukfilmcouncil.org.uk/

http://www.wickerman.clara.co.uk/

McDowell, Malcolm, *The Guardian*, Friday 3 September 2004, http://film.guardian. co.uk/features/featurepages/0,,1295915,00.html

Select Filmography

Boyle, Danny (dir.), *Trainspotting* (UK, Channel Four Television Corporation/Figment Films/Noel Gay Motion Picture Company, 1996).

Cammell, Donald and Nicolas Roeg (dirs), *Performance* (UK, Warner Bros./Goodtimes Enterprises, 1970).

Gilliam, Terry and Terry Jones (dirs), *Monty Python and the Holy Grail* (UK, National Film Trustee Company Ltd./Python [Monty] Pictures/Michael White, 1975).

Hardy, Robin (dir.), *The Wicker Man* (UK, British Lion Film Corporation, 1973).

Hodges, Mike (dir.), *Get Carter* (UK, MGM, 1971).

Kubrick, Stanley (dir.), *A Clockwork Orange* (UK, Warner Bros./Polaris Productions/Hawk Films, 1971).

Robinson, Bruce (dir.), *Withnail & I* (UK, HandMade Films, 1986).

Roddam, Franc (dir.), *Quadrophenia* (UK, Who Films/Polytel Films, 1979).

Roeg, Nicolas (dir.), *The Man Who Fell To Earth* (UK, British Lion Film Corporation, 1976).

Russell, Ken (dir.), *Tommy* (UK, Robert Stigwood Organisation, 1975).

Sharman, Jim (dir.), *The Rocky Horror Picture Show* (UK, Houtsnede Maatschappij N.V./ Twentieth Century-Fox Film Corporation/Michael White Productions, 1975).

INDEX